THE POET AND THE HISTORIAN

HARVARD SEMITIC STUDIES

HARVARD SEMITIC MUSEUM

Frank Moore Cross, Editor

Syriac Manuscripts: A Catalogue — Moshe H. Goshen-Gottstein

Dictionary of Old South Arabic — Joan C. Biella

The Poet and the Historian: Essays in Literary and Historical Biblical Criticism — Richard Elliott Friedman, Editor

THE POET
AND THE HISTORIAN
Essays in Literary
and Historical Biblical Criticism

Richard Elliott Friedman, Editor

Scholars Press
Chico, California

THE POET AND THE HISTORIAN
Essays in Literary and Historical Biblical Criticism

Richard Elliott Friedman, Editor

Library of Congress Cataloging in Publication Data
Main entry under title:

The poet and the historian.

(Harvard Semitic Studies ; 26)
Includes bibliographical references and index.
Contents: The prophet and the historian / Richard Elliott Friedman—The epic traditions of early Israel / Frank Moore Cross—Doctrine by misadventure / Baruch Halpern—[etc.]
1. Bible. O.T.—Historiography—Addresses, essays, lectures. 2. Bible as literature—Addresses, essays, lectures. I. Friedman, Richard Elliott. II. Series.
BS1197.P64   1983   221.9'072   83-9035
ISBN 0-89130-629-3

Printed in the United States of America

Publication of this volume was supported by the Jerome and Miriam Katzin Publication Fund of the Judaic Studies endowment at the University of California, San Diego.

The typeset text was prepared by Carol Cross at the Department of Near Eastern Languages and Civilizations, Harvard University.

034717

CONTENTS

Chapter I

THE PROPHET AND THE HISTORIAN:
THE ACQUISITION OF HISTORICAL INFORMATION
FROM LITERARY SOURCES

Richard Elliott Friedman
University of California, San Diego

One of the characteristics of the Hebrew Bible which contributes to its unique character among books is its particular mixture of literature and history. Herodotos began his work by introducing himself and stating his purpose:

> This book is the result of the historical inquiries *(historiē)* of Herodotos of Halikarnassos. Its purpose is twofold: to preserve the memory of the past by putting on record the astonishing achievements both of our own and of the Asiatic peoples; and more particularly, to show how the two races came into conflict.

Hekataios likewise:

> Hekataios of Miletos writes this. I write the following things believing them to be true; for the things said among the Greeks seem to me numerous and absurd.

The opening of the Bible, composed not very much earlier, begins:

> When God began to create the heavens and the earth, the earth was chaos and void.

Though its narrative books depict a continuous account of events, through a linear progression of time from Genesis to Ezra and Daniel, it begins in the formal manner of myth. Its (usually anonymous) authors and editors merged historical and literary genres in complex juxtapositions and interdependence. They all but eliminated any distinction between *characters* and *persons*, so that the very different historical value of the figures Adam, Abraham, Moses, and David became equalized—at least for the great majority of the audience— and they were joined as participants in an ongoing story, as were prophets and poets. The final product did not have the character of Herodotos' work, but it looked even less like that of Homer. Its particular blend of the historical and the literary is occasionally compared to the historical plays of Shakespeare, but this can be done only if one ignores completely the effective differences between prose and dramatic portrayal intended for stage performance, and if one ignores the fact that the Shakespearean characters are conversing in iambic pentameter.

The study of the Bible, therefore, has involved a confrontation with a singular combination of the historical and the literary. For over a hundred years, historical study has dominated the field. Its nearest rival for queen science has been theology, and probably linguistics after that. Literary study, meanwhile, has played a secondary role. True, the school of Wellhausen in Germany and that of Kaufmann in Israel engaged in literary criticism, but their ends were still *Geschichte* or *tôlᵉdōt 'ĕmûnāh* respectively (history, or history of religion), and the literary aspect of their work was, after all, more literary archeology than anything resembling what is done in the fields of literary criticism generally;[1] and in the school of Albright in America, clearly, historical/archeological study took precedence over the literary. To be sure, literary criticism has gone on all along in Biblical studies. (Richard Moulton's *The Literary Study of the Bible* appeared in 1895.)[2] But, first, it has not been in the mainstream of biblical scholarship, and, second, it has often been done by non-specialists, by scholars and teachers of English literature, for example, who have no access to the original languages of the text. They have justified their activity with claims that the King James version is a great work of literature in its own right, somehow independent of the original, though it is difficult to see how they could possibly know this.

Examine the leading works in the field, and almost all will deal with history of religion, literary and textual history, history of tradition, archeology, and especially political history. The exceptions are the theologies, and even they usually contain as much history of religion as theology. Examine the commentaries, and they are largely theological, philological, and historical.

It is not inappropriate that history should have been queen science first, since the Bible contains probably the first history writing, and one of the child's first questions in Sunday school is, "Is it true?" Currently, however, literary study of the Bible is growing and is being taken up by scholars who possess both experience with literary criticism and the traditional skills of Biblical scholarship. Some old questions are raised with a new seriousness. Above all, is the book really literature? Who can read Psalm 23 and say that it is not literature? Who can read the Tabernacle description in Exodus 25-31 and say that it *is*? Is the book really history? Certainly not in the modern sense(s) of the word. Not really even in the classical sense. In Hekataios and Herodotos, the historians speak in first person, make statements of purpose, and make judgments about their material: social and ethical judgments, judgments of the historicity of their sources. The Biblical "historians," meanwhile, speak in third person; there is virtually no introduction of the self into the text, no identification of the narrative voice to remind the reader that this is a reporter of history at work. There are almost no explicit judgments

---

[1] Julius Wellhausen, *Prolegomena to the History of Israel* (Gloucester: Peter Smith, 1973), German edition 1883; Yehezkel Kaufmann, *The Religion of Israel*, trans. and ed., Moshe Greenberg (Chicago: University of Chicago Press, 1960), Hebrew edition 1937.

[2] Richard G. Moulton, *The Literary Study of the Bible* (London: Isbister, 1895).

at all. The historicity of everything reported is understood. Speaking as modern historians we can say that the Bible is not so much history as a *source* to be used in acquiring historical information. But then, at least in the case of *many* of the Biblical writers, we are really judging the quality of their final product. They seem to have been trying to write history, but we do not find their work to be very *good* history writing by our standards. To state it in terms of the comparison of the literary and the historical treatments of the Bible: When we do "Bible as Literature" we are investigating certain qualities of the book itself; when we do "Bible as History" we are trying to do what the Bible itself does, only better.

How then are we to categorize what the Bible does? Herbert Schneidau, in his *Sacred Discontent*, characterized Biblical narrative as "historicized fiction."[3] Robert Alter, in his essay titled "Sacred History and Prose Fiction," suggested that the phrase "fictionalized history" might be more accurate.[4] Jacob Licht, in his *Storytelling in the Bible*, favored the separation of the "historical" aspect from the "aesthetic" aspect of the text.[5] Alan Cooper, in his essay titled "The Act of Reading the Bible,"[6] expressed his sympathy for David Robertson's call for literary critics of the Bible to break cleanly and completely with historical criticism.[7] According to Cooper, "When we call for the literary study of the Bible, the context of that study ought not, in the first instance, to be history, religion, or society, but the realm of literature. We can define that realm as broadly or as narrowly as we wish, as long as its components are derived from the world of literature—from literary texts—and not from external non-literary dimensions of reality."[8] It is perhaps inappropriate to refer to Cooper's position in this context, because the others to whom I have referred were engaged in identification of the character of the text, while Cooper's concern is more with the approaches that modern scholars might choose to take toward the material.[9] Nonetheless, a response to the former has implications for Cooper's position.

---

[3] Herbert Schneidau, *Sacred Discontent* (Baton Rouge, 1977), 215.

[4] Robert Alter, "Sacred History and Prose Fiction," in *The Creation of Sacred Literature*, Near Eastern Studies 22 (Berkeley: University of California Press, 1981), R. E. Friedman, ed., 8. (This essay appears, in a somewhat modified form, in Alter, *The Art of Biblical Narrative* (Basic Books).

[5] Jacob Licht, *Storytelling in the Bible* (Jerusalem, 1978).

[6] Alan M. Cooper, "The Act of Reading the Bible," *Proceedings of the Eighth World Congress of Jewish Studies* (Jerusalem, 1981).

[7] David Robertson, "The Bible as Literature," *IDB Supplement* (Nashville: Abingdon, 1976) 547-551. "The new literary criticism may be described as inherently ahistorical." (548)

[8] Cooper is paraphrasing E. D. Hirsch, *Validity in Interpretation* (New Haven: Yale University Press, 1967), 146-147.

[9] See Cooper's discussion below, Chapter 5.

4

The problem, I suggest, is not to decide whether the biblical text is history or literature, or whether it is *primarily* history or primarily literature, or to identify which *portions* are history and which are literature. The problem is rather with the question. The contemporary analyst wants to categorize this corpus as history or literature; but it does not fit our categories, precisely because it is older than the formation of these categories. Its authors and editors wrote in a mixture which only centuries later was regarded as disciplinary *šatnēz*.

True, our inclination toward categories finds one of its earliest stages in the Bible itself, which opens with God's making a *distinction (wayyabdēl)* between light and darkness and thus ending a condition of chaos *(tōhû wābōhû)*. The priestly figure who set that text at the beginning of his Torah certainly cast his own priestly group as quintessentially in the divine image when he included the text which declared that the *function* of the priests is:

lhbdyl byn hqdš wbyn hḥl wbyn hṭm' wbyn hṭhr

To make a distinction between the holy and the profane and between the impure and the pure.

(Lev 10:10)

But we are not sitting only on *his* shoulders. He could hardly have guessed how refined the notion of categories could become in Aristotle; and Aristotle could hardly have foreseen what it would become in Mary Douglas. To whatever extent we are uncertain about identification of the particular character of the Bible, we are, in a sense, the victims of our own categorizing; and so is the Bible an ironic victim, having its own *wayyabdēl* turned back on itself. As the Bible is older than the categories, we, when we apply the categories back upon the Bible, do not enlighten. The literary scholar who ignores the history "behind" the text errs. What light does one shed on the Bible or on literature in general by treating David just as a character like Prince Mishkin? David lived. He did (or did not do) things which biblical prose and poetry ascribe to him. It requires different artistic sensitivities, and perhaps even different artistic skills, to compose the texts about him than to compose texts about a wholly fictional character. The Bible, as few other books, is a product of what is usually a balance—and often a tension—between the author's received data and his creativity.[10] Even if some of the units of these narratives and poetry are entirely fictional, there is still to be recognized the skill of combining one's own fictional material with one's portrayals which are based on historical sources—and the author's sense of history will have an

---

[10] Baruch Halpern treats this balance below, Chapter 3. See also my "From Egypt to Egypt: Dtr[1] and Dtr[2]," in *Traditions in Transformation: Turning-Points in Biblical Faith*, Essays Presented to Frank Moore Cross (Winona Lake: Eisenbrauns, 1981), J. Levenson and B. Halpern, eds., 167-192; and "Sacred History and Theology: The Redaction of Torah," in *The Creation of Sacred Literature*, 25-34.

impact even on the kind of fiction he conceives. To categorize away the history which is portrayed—and the literary history of the portrayal—can only set a barrier between the literary scholar and the integral character of the text.

If it is true that the literary scholar cannot make a "clean break" with history, one can say with at least as much certainty that the historian cannot move without literary skills, and literary concerns. One must deal with the matter of intention, with matters of narrative voice. One must be sensitive to ideological coloring of narrative. One must make judgments with regard to narrative reports: does the author report a fact in a certain manner because he believes that it happened that way, or because he seeks a certain artistic effect, e.g., a symmetry or paronomasia. Perhaps most important, and at the most basic level, one must have a sense of poetry. Compare the picture of the Red Sea event in the Song of the Sea (Exodus 15) with the prose depictions of the same event in the Yahwistic and Priestly narratives (Exodus 14)—as Frank Moore Cross has done[11]—and the point becomes clear enough. There we are fortunate to have complementary prose accounts, but more often we do not have such double witness. The book which is our primary source for a millennium of Israelite history is written *mostly* in poetry. The study of that material requires a particular combination of historical and literary skills.

Now one might respond that any first-rate historian of any culture and period knows these matters of treating literary sources. There is, however, a difference of degree in biblical history because we are so disproportionately dependent on the book for information. Our sole other channel is archeology, which only in a few instances has provided us with as *specific* information as we desire. Second, the fact is that our record in the literary avenues of biblical history-writing has not been very good. The leading histories of ancient Israel reflect more theological sensitivity than literary. Particularly in historical study of the prophets is this apparent. The historian and the prophet are engaged in what are probably antithetical professions to begin with, and the Biblical prophets' habit of speaking in poetry or in combinations of prose and poetry makes the derivation of historical data from their works a delicate task. This is particulary apparent in the case study which I have chosen as an example of the union of the literary and the historical in the Bible: Zechariah 7 and 8. It is a text which is half poetry and half prose, which is based on an intriguing weaving of received formulae which are known to us from Jeremiah and Ezekiel together with the author's own literary product, which employs a recurring *kh 'mr yhwh ṣb'wt* like a hammer on an anvil eleven times so that, read sensitively, its effect can be powerful.

In this text we have a depiction of an inquiry concerning the observance of a fast, and the prophet's response to the inquiry. The text is dated to the year of the completion of the Second Temple, the fourth year of Darius, 518

---

[11] Cross, "Song of the Sea and Canaanite Myth," in *Canaanite Myth and Hebrew Epic* (Cambridge: Harvard University Press, 1973), 112-144; and Chapter 2, below.

B.C. (Zech 7:1). The inquiring parties ask whether to continue observing the annual fast of the fifth month, the month of Ab, as they have done for years. Zechariah responds:

> When you fasted, mourning, in the fifth and the seventh for seventy years now, were you fasting for me? When you eat and when you drink, are you not the eaters and the drinkers?
>
> (Zech 7:5,6)

Following this remark, Zechariah traces the events of the preceding years; the failure of the people of Israel to fulfill their responsibilities to their covenant with Yhwh, the resulting destruction and exile, the return. He quotes Yhwh's intention to return to Zion, and he warns the people to act in a manner pleasing to Yhwh. He concludes with a declaration that a day of joy and peace will come and that the fast of the fifth month as well as three other fasts will become instead joyous holidays.

Modern interpretation has regularly identified this passage with the category of prophetic material which values the ethical above the ritual, drawing comparison especially with Isaiah 58, in which Isaiah attacks those who justify themselves by virtue of their fasting while ignoring matters of justice. Exegetes have viewed Zechariah's response to the question concerning the preservation of a fast to be a rebuke to the inquiring parties, directing them to revise their priorities and subordinate ritual concerns to ethical; Yhwh has no interest in fasts. Commentators conclude that Zechariah thus released the petitioners not only from the fast which was the subject of the inquiry (the fast of the fifth month), but from three other Temple-related fasts as well (the fasts of the fourth, seventh, and tenth months).[12] Medieval rabbinic commentators likewise understood that all of the fasts were cancelled following Zechariah's response.[13] Traditional Jews have observed fast days in the fourth, fifth, seventh, and tenth months from Talmudic times (at least) to this day, but the commentators attribute this to a resumption of the fasts following the Romans' destruction of the Second Temple. They thus regard the fasts as having been suspended from the time of the construction of the Second Temple in 518 B.C. to the destruction in 70 A.D. Major histories (Bright, Noth, Herrmann, de Vaux) do not refer to the event, even to evaluate its historicity positively or negatively.

---

[12] Peter Ackroyd, *Exile and Restoration* (London: SCM, 1968) 107n., 209; Otto Eissfeldt, *The Old Testament, An Introduction* (New York: Harper and Row, 1965) 74, 421; C. L. Feinberg, "Exegetical Studies in Zechariah," *BS* 99 (1942) 332-343 and *BS* 100 (1943) 256-262; Samuel Sandmel, *The Hebrew Scriptures* (New York: Random House, 1963) 204; H. G. Mitchell, "Zechariah," *ICC*, 199-215; D. Winton Thomas, "Zechariah," *The Interpreter's Bible*, 1081-1083; Paul Hanson, *The Dawn of Apocalyptic* (Philadelphia: Fortress, 1975) 104.

[13] See Rashi on B. Rosh Hashanah 18b.

The four fasts are first identified in the Gemara,[14] thus:

(1)   The fast of the fifth month is the fast of the ninth of Ab, commemorating the destruction of the First Temple. The date is designated in 2 Kgs 25:8ff. as the seventh of the month, in Jer 52:12ff. as the tenth of the month, and in Josephus as the first of the month. The Mishna speaks of the ninth and places the destruction of both the First and Second Temples on that date.

(2)   The fast of the fourth month is identified as the ninth of Tammuz, commemorating the initial breach in the city wall according to Jer 52:6f.

(3)   The fast of the seventh month is the fast of Gedaliah, observed on the third of Tishri (Jer 41:1ff.; 2 Kgs 25:25).

(4)   The fast of the tenth month is the fast of the tenth of Tebet, on which date the king of Babylon set his forces in siege against Jerusalem, according to Ezek 24:1f.

These dates and rationales of the fasts in the Gemara do not appear in scripture; and, to confuse the picture further, the fast of the fourth month, Tammuz, which the Gemara placed on the ninth of Tammuz had already been established in the Mishna as the seventeenth of Tammuz, traditionally regarded as the date of the breach in the city walls in the *second* destruction, in 70 A.D.

Did these fasts in fact exist? Did the prophet Zechariah release the nation from them on the occasion of the rebuilding of the Temple? Did the rabbis reinstitute them six hundred years later, after the destruction of the Second Temple? We must examine the sources at both ends of the period. The post-destruction sources do not support this. First, a Mishna states that, in six months of the lunar calendar, messengers were sent from Jerusalem to distant places to announce the day which had been appointed New Moon.[15] The six months were treated in this manner because a major holiday occurred in each of them; in order to make certain that the holidays were celebrated on the correct dates the messengers had to inform the communities whether the Beth Din had designated the new lunar month to begin on the thirtieth or the thirty-first day from the preceding New Moon. The fifth month, the month of Ab, is included, the Mishna states, "on account of the fast." The months of Tammuz and Tebet are not included. (The month of Tishri is included because the festival of Tabernacles falls in it.) Concerning this Mishna, the Gemara asks the following question:[16]

Why were they not sent out in Tammuz and Tebet? As R. Hana b. Bizna said in the name of R. Simon the Pious: "What is the meaning of the passage (Zech 8:19) 'Thus says the Lord of hosts, the fast of the fourth, and the fast of the fifth, and the fast of the seventh and the fast of the tenth shall become to the house of Judah joy and gladness.'? (It

---

[14] B. Rosh Hashanah 18b.
[15] Mishna Rosh Hashanah 1,3.
[16] B. Rosh Hashanah 18a.

means that only in) time of peace they shall be for joy and gladness, but when there is not peace they shall be fasts."

The response follows:

R. Papa answered: "It means this: in a time when there is peace, these days shall be for joy and gladness; in time of persecution they shall be fasts; in times when there is neither persecution nor peace, people may fast or not, as they see fit."

Neither of the Fourth Century Babylonian rabbis cited by the Gemara associated the passage from Zechariah with the existence or destruction of the Temples, but rather with the existence or absence of a condition of peace.

A second Talmudic passage records a disagreement among four rabbis of the Third Century in which two, Rav and R. Hanina, are said to hold that Zech 8:19 means that "in time of peace they are days of joy and gladness; but in time of persecution they are fast days . . . . " The others, R. Johanan and R. Joshua b. Levi, are said to hold that "Scripture makes them dependent on the rebuilding of the Temple . . . . "[17]

Certainly the usual cautions apply against assuming, because a rabbinic text says, "'āmar rāb PN," that that rabbi said what the text ascribes to him. But we can at least see in these texts that it was by no means a foregone conclusion or a clear tradition to the writers of the Talmud that the observances of the fasts had anything to do with the existence of the Temple. Perhaps even stronger is what the post-70 A.D. literature does *not* say. If formerly abandoned fasts had been reinstituted following the Second Temple's destruction, such reinstitution would have required a rabbinic decision, presumably requiring debate, interpretation of biblical texts (especially Zechariah 7 and 8), announcement. That such an event should have taken place and have not a single reference to it in all the literature is incredible. There is more than argument from silence at work here. The function and character of legal literature in general and rabbinic literature in particular would lead us to expect some report of the injunction.

There is, further, the extreme unlikelihood of the historical scenario which the commentators envision. Even if we allow for the re-establishment of the fast of Tammuz, perhaps owing to another coincidence of dates, it is difficult to picture the reinstitution of the fast of Tebet and the fast of Gedaliah after 70 A.D.

From this threshhold of skepticism, we turn back to the biblical end of the Second Temple period. Those who have seen in Zechariah's response an abolition of the four fasts have read that abolition in the statement of Zech 8:19,

Thus says Yhwh of hosts: the fast of the fourth and the fast of the fifth and the fast of the seventh and the fast of the tenth *will become*

---

[17]B. Rosh Hashanah 26b.

(yhyh l . . .) joy and gladness and holidays to the house of Judah; love truth and peace.

These commentators see a command here. It is at least as likely that the verse is a prediction. In context, the verses which immediately precede it are commands, and the verses which follow it are predictions. The question is whether it goes with that which precedes it or that which follows. In favor of the former, one can cite complementary wording. The preceding verses list the *debārîm 'ăšer ta'ăśû*, which conclude with שבעת שקר אל תאהבו (8:17). V. 19 concludes והאמת והשלום אהבו. The structural signs that v. 19 goes with the verses that follow, however, seem stronger. First, the *debārîm 'ăšer ta'ăśû* in vv. 16 and 17 are a recapitulation of the words of the early prophets with which Zechariah began his historical discourse (7:9,10). They are followed by a clause which seems to conclude the section, thus: כי את כל אלה אשר שנאתי, נאם ה'. V. 18 then begins with the formula: ויהי דבר ה' צבאות אלי לאמר plus the formula: כה אמר ה' צבאות. The two formulas together make a stronger break here than between any of the several units which precede this. Each of the other units has only the כא אמר ה' צבאות. The double formula, however, has not occurred since the opening of the chapter. Following these formulas the discourse changes from second to third person as well. It remains in third person through the predictions which follow to the end of the chapter with the exception of the והאמת והשלום אהבו which I mentioned above. Structurally, then, there is little justification for reading the key verse as an instruction. The wording of the verse itself, as well, does not justify this reading. That fast days will become joy and gladness is not the sort of thing that is accomplished by command in the Hebrew Bible. It is rather a figure which expresses a bright future. There is no more reason to take it literally than there is to take the verses which follow it literally: that the nations will come to seek Yhwh in Jerusalem. This is literature, not law.

Interpreters have judged Zech 8:19 to constitute an abolition of fasts under the influence of the opening words of the prophet's speech, 7:5,6.

> When you fasted, mourning, in the fifth and seventh for seventy years now, were you fasting for me? When you eat and when you drink, are you not the eaters and the drinkers?

It is also under the influence of this passage that interpreters have judged the whole of Zechariah 7 and 8 to be a rebuke to the enquiring parties and to the people as a whole for having placed a ritual matter in priority rather than ethical concerns.

A rebuke at that juncture in time was inappropriate generally, especially inappropriate in response to this particular inquiry, and out of character for the prophet Zechariah. References to Zechariah outside the book which bears his name, in Ezra and in Josephus, are all positive, portraying him (and Haggai) as a prophet of encouragement and support, urging the people of Israel on to return to Yhwh and to rebuild the Temple.[18] Further, the manner in which

---

[18]Ezra 5:1; 6:14; Josephus, *Jewish Antiquities* XI, 96, 106.

Zechariah speaks is the reverse of the manner of his fellow prophet of encouragement, Haggai. While Haggai urges the people on through reproach (Hag 1:1-11), Zechariah's words are positive and supportive, reproaching only the ancestors who had failed to heed the words of the early prophets, while urging his contemporaries to take advantage of the blessings of Yhwh's nearness. Whereas the tradition was established in the Exile that Yhwh had abandoned his people, Zechariah declares: Return to me, says Yhwh ṣebā'ōt, and I shall return to you (Zech 1:3). The visions of Zechariah likewise are visions of comfort and hope for Israel. In the first vision, the angel who speaks to Zechariah pleads with Yhwh for mercy upon Jerusalem and Judah, and Yhwh answers with "sweet words, comforting words," promising his return to Jerusalem with mercy, the rebuilding of his Temple, and prosperity (1:12-17). In the vision of the measuring line (Chapter 2) Yhwh again promises that he will dwell among his people (v. 10), a multitude will inhabit Jerusalem (vv. 4f.), and the spoiling nations will themselves become a spoil (vv. 8f.). The vision of the cleansing and charge of Joshua (Chapter 3) likewise concludes with a promise to erase the iniquity of the land, and with a prediction of brotherhood at each man's vine and fig tree (vv. 9f.). The vision of the candelabra and the olive trees (Chapter 5) predicts the success of Zerubbabel and the completion of the Temple. The vision of the flying scroll alone bears a negative communication (Chapter 5), yet even this vision bears no indictment or reproach, but rather predicts the destruction of evil. The final vision of the chariots (Chapter 6) promises the re-establishment of the priesthood and the Temple.

It is from this prophet of comfort and encouragement that the response to the inquiry comes. But suddenly he has turned into an angry, rebuking Isaiah, castigating the people for trusting in fasts instead of justice. Nowhere in the biblical narrative is there an indication that this generation was guilty of such shortcomings. Nowhere is there an indication that there was present an overbearing concern for law which excluded a concern for justice. Further, nothing in the inquiry of Zech 7:2f. indicates any misplaced sense of priorities. On the contrary, the question was manifestly appropriate to the moment. It was a question which had to be asked. The parties ask what impact the establishment of the new Temple is to have on the people's attitude toward their past. And who is more suited to respond to such an inquiry than the prophet whose encouragement had played a crucial role in the rebuilding of the Temple? When the inquiry is directed to the priests and the prophets, therefore, as to whether the building of the Second Temple means abandoning the acts of sorrow and remembrance of the First Temple, it is Zechariah who makes reply. His reply is no rebuke. His words in vv. 5f. are a serious and appropriate instruction based on a simple analogy. When one eats and drinks, one eats and drinks for oneself. When one abstains from eating and drinking, one does that for oneself as well, and not for God. The Jews themselves instituted the four fasts, not out of obedience to a divine ordinance, but rather as a result of events. Zechariah's recounting of that series of events follows. It is natural and properly placed and does not demand of us a suspicion of editorial addition. The people's ancestors had betrayed their covenant, disaster resulted, and they imposed fasts upon themselves out of their own feelings of sorrow and guilt. Establishment and repeal of such fasts are grounded in humans, not in Yhwh. Zechariah's response to the inquiring parties is neither abolition nor perpetuation of the fasts. It is a statement that Yhwh had not instituted the fasts and that Yhwh (and his prophets) would not cancel the fasts. A new commitment by the people of Israel to be loyal to Yhwh and to love his ways of justice, truth, and peace, however, would result in his return to their midst, and thus lead to a time of joy and gladness in which the fasts will disappear. The preconditions of the original institution of the fasts will no longer exist as justice and loyalty to Yhwh thrive and make sorrow and guilt groundless. In such an era, the fast days will become holidays. In Zechariah's response we have prediction and not prescription, explanation and not rebuke.

Neither the historical evidence nor the character of Zechariah's work, visions, and speeches as portrayed in the Bible (and Josephus) justifies the view that the prophetic response of Zechariah 7 and 8 constitutes a moral rebuke and an abolition of the observance of fasts. Nor does the text of Zechariah 7 and 8 itself justify such interpretation. This interpretation has been widespread, I believe, owing primarily to the formulation of the first verses of Zechariah's response (vv. 5f.). The words "When you eat and when you drink, are you not the eaters and the drinkers" have appeared to most modern commentators to be a criticism cast in the form of other prophetic reproaches. The fact that ethical issues are among those which the prophet mentions in the beginning portion of his historical recounting further has led commentators to associate this passage with a genre of ritual-versus-ethical prophetic speech. Association with Isaiah 58 as also relating to fasts clinched the impression. But direction of a nation is accomplished through encouragement and promise of reward as well as reproach and promise of calamity.

Neither the biblical nor the rabbinic evidence justifies the standard understanding of the events portrayed in Zechariah 7 and 8. Admittedly, we are still left in the dark. Such not insignificant questions remain as: did the scene depicted in Zechariah 7 and 8 actually happen? Did these petitioners ask this question? Did Zechariah give this answer? Did the petitioners—or anybody— listen?

The point is that, even if we do not reckon the rabbinic materials, the commonly held view of this scene has never been warranted by the text. And, more important, there will *be* no historical solution in this matter without sensitivity to the literary life of this passage: its beauty and its power.

I suggest that this applies to the treatment of biblical prophecy in general. It is precisely in prophecy that categories fuse. In prophecy an ostensibly divine message is contained in a human medium. A message of personal, national, or occasionally cosmic importance must be conveyed in language which is composed in an aesthetic construction. The message almost always plays the part of a pivot between past and present. One must confront the prophet with a sense of these tensions: between divine and human, between content and form, set at charged junctures in time—which all must be conveyed in language which is at the same time beautiful. One must have a sense of this literature as always casting itself, implicitly or occasionally explicitly, as a vessel which can barely continue to hold its contents. Then one can appreciate the extent of the need for caution in searching for historical information in such territory, and one can appreciate the beauty to be enjoyed along the way.

Chapter II

THE EPIC TRADITIONS OF EARLY ISRAEL: EPIC NARRATIVE
AND THE RECONSTRUCTION OF EARLY ISRAELITE INSTITUTIONS

Frank Moore Cross
Harvard University

1.   The early narrative traditions of Israel preserved in the most archaic
sources of the Tetrateuch in some respects resemble historical narrative,
in other respects a mythic cycle. They recount the past of Israel, notably
the events which brought Israel into being as a nation. To be sure the narrative is "fraught with meaning," composed to reveal the meaning of Israel's
past, and therewith to define the identity and destiny of the nation. Further,
while the actors and human beings for the most part, and the events and
setting appear on the surface to be accessible to the historian, the principal
hero is a Divine Warrior, Yahweh of Hosts by name, who called the nation
into being, led them to victory over their enemies with many marvels, and
revealed himself as their ruler. In both the structure of the great complex of
tradition and in individual poetic units embedded therein,[1] a familiar mythic
pattern may be discerned. The Divine Warrior marched forth in wrath to win
a crucial victory—at the sea, or in variant tradition by cleaving through Sea—
and then led a triumphal procession to his mountain, where he appeared in
glory, constructed his sanctuary, and established his kingdom. A similar if
not identical pattern of themes is found in the mythic cycle of Ba'l in Late
Bronze Age Canaan (Ugarit), and in the classic Akkadian cosmogony known
as *Enūma eliš*. In the former, Ba'l-Haddu the young storm god defeats Prince
Sea and gains kingship among the gods. He builds his temple on Mount Ṣapon,
his "mount of victory," and displays his glory before the gods in the storm
theophany. In the Mesopotamian cosmogony, *Enūma eliš*, the young warrior
of the gods, Marduk, defeats *Tiamāt*, whose name means "the Deep," and
fashions cosmic order from her split carcass. He returns to the assembly of
the gods, receives kingship over the gods, and constructs his temple. In both
the West and East Semitic myths, the actors are exclusively the gods, the ter-
rain cosmic (or sacral). The Divine Warrior through his victory over watery
chaos or the sea creates order, conceived as a divine state. Yet beneath the

---

[1] Above all in Exodus 15 in the Song of the Sea.

surface of these great mythic compositions, one perceives a counterpoint: the establishment of earthly kingship, even the empire of Babylon, and the inauguration of earthly temples and cults. A characteristic dualism exists here which fixes or strives to fix human institutions in the created and eternal orders. Thus two levels run through these mythic compositions, though it must be emphasized that in these major Near Eastern myths, the focus of the narrative is wholly on cosmic events, and the divine actors in the cosmogonic drama exclusively dominate action. In Israel's early orally-composed narratives, these two levels, which we may term "divine-cosmic" and "historic-political" are present also, but in a quite different balance. The narrative action takes place for the most part in ordinary space and time; major roles are played by human enemies and human heroes; however shaped by mythic themes, the narrative is presented in the form of remembered events. In view of such traits, despite the role played by Israel's divine hero, the category "myth" ill suits the Israelite narrative complex. Nor does it appear precise or useful simply to describe Israel's early traditions as "historical narrative" in view of its shaping in detail and in structure by mythic elements, notably the *magnalia dei*. Ideally the term "historical narrative" should be reserved for that literary genre, usually composed in writing, in which the events narrated are secular or "ordinary," if memorable, in which the protagonists are palpable, historic men or women, and in which the primary level of meaning is immanent in the sequence of narrated events. In "historical narrative," a relatively late and sophisticated genre in ancient literature, divine activity, if alluded to by the narrator, is not so directly perceived or presented as in myth.

If we eschew the designations "mythic narrative" and "historical narrative" as inappropriate or misleading in describing the constitutive genre of early Israelite oral narrative preserved in the Tetrateuch, we do find a third literary genre which fits snugly, namely *epea*, traditional epic. I propose to call Israel's early narrative traditions which originated in oral composition by the term "epic." Moreover, I wish to define this term rather narrowly, drawing upon studies of Homeric epic for delineating the traits of epic and for analogies to aid in understanding the nature of Hebrew epic lore.

The Homeric epics were composed by an oral technique which utilized a complex of traditional themes and a common repertoire of poetic formulae. The epic elements were carried by a continuous stream of bards, *aoidoi*, reaching back into Mycenaean times, Greece's heroic age.[2] Canaanite epics of contemporary times, the Late Bronze Age of Syria, have survived in dictated

---

[2] See Martin P. Nilsson's *The Mycenaean Origin of Greek Mythology*, with a new introduction and bibliography by Emily Vermeule (Berkeley: University of California Press, 1972), the pioneer study of the subject, and, more recently, Cedric H. Whitman, *Homer and the Heroic Tradition* (Cambridge: Harvard University Press, 1963).

copies recorded in alphabetic cuneiform.[3] Canaanite epic verse also reveals characteristic oral formulae and themes. It does not use, of course, epic hexameter verse. Its prosody is characterized by parallelism in bicola and tricola, parallelism on phonetic, morphological, and semantic levels. On the last-mentioned level (the *parallelismus membrorum*, classically described by Bishop Lowth) are to be found word and phrase pairs which, in light of recent studies, are newly recognized as belonging to special categories of oral formulae.[4] Israel's early poetry stands in this Canaanite tradition utilizing substantially the same repertoire of formulae and themes, to be sure modified by time, by dialectical and cultural differentiation.[5]

Homeric epic has the concreteness and concentration on memories of the past that give it the appearance of historical narrative. "Yet, wherever it is possible to compare events in epic with their actual history, one sees that what is preserved in poetry bears only a special, sometimes slight, relation to fact, while it is quite normal for the places, dates, and even the characters of a recorded event to be magniloquently confused and distorted."[6] Further, while epic recounts events in the nation's heroic or normative past, nevertheless the recollection of these great events are reshaped using the structures and patterns of traditional myth;[7] and epic action takes place in both the human and divine spheres. ". . . Everything in the Iliad takes place twice," notes Cedric Whitman, "once on earth, and once in the timeless world of deity."[8] Israel's epic traditions and narrative poetry bear these same epic

---

[3] A colophon records the dictation of a tablet of the Ba'l cycle; see F. M. Cross, "Prose and Poetry in the Mythic and Epic Texts from Ugarit," *HTR* 67 (1974): p. 1, n.1.

[4] See Roman Jakobson's programmatic essay "Grammatical Parallelism and its Russian Facet," *Language* 42 (1966): 399-429; William Whallon, *Formula, Character, and Context* (Cambridge: Center for Hellenic Studies and Harvard University Press, 1969), pp. 117-172; and Stephen A. Geller, *Parallelism in Early Hebrew Poetry*, Harvard Semitic Monographs 20 (Missoula, Montana: Scholars Press, 1979).

[5] See U. Cassuto's remarkable early studies, "Parallel Words in Hebrew and Ugaritic," and "The Israelite Epic," *Biblical and Oriental Studies* II (Jerusalem: Magnes, 1975): 60-109; and the monumental collection edited by Loren R. Fisher, *Ras Shamra Parallels*, Analecta Orientalia 49-50- (Rome: Pontifical Biblical Institute, 1972—).

[6] Whitman, *Homer and the Heroic Tradition*, p. 17.

[7] See Albert D. Lord, *The Singer of Tales* (Cambridge: Harvard University Press, 1964), esp. pp. 141-197; and his more recent papers, "Interlocking Mythic Patterns in Beowulf," *Old English Literature in Context*, ed. John D. Niles (Suffolk: D. S. Brewer, 1981): 137-178; and "The Mythic Component in Oral Traditional Epic: Its Origins and Significance," forthcoming.

[8] Whitman, *Homer and the Heroic Tradition*, p. 248.

characters. The search for the "historical nucleus" of early Hebrew tradition by historical critics has paralleled the efforts of Homeric critics in seeking actual historical events lurking behind the Iliad, with not dissimilar results. The role of the divine in Homer and in Israelite epic is comparable given the peculiarity of Israel's preoccupation with only one god. Theomachy so structurally essential to the Iliad is found in Israelite traditional literature very rarely. Further, Greek epic did not play the central cultic role that we should ascribe to the Israelite epic cycle.

Certain other features of Homeric epic will be useful to mention in anticipation of our turning to an examination of Hebrew epic sources. Martin Nilsson initiated a new phase in Homeric studies in demonstrating that the epic preserved—alongside later accretions—elements of Mycenaean culture, its mythology, including archaic divine epithets, its social and political structures and customs, its military practices and accoutrements, its topography.[9] His conclusion, that the roots of Greek epic tradition and Greek mythology were no younger in origin than Late-Bronze-Age Greece, has been nuanced and qualified in subsequent research, but can no longer be questioned.[10] Cedric Whitman, writing from the perspective of the Parry School, expresses himself as follows: "Bardic memory, embalmed in formulae, could keep the general outlines of a culture clear; and though factual details and history in a modern sense were never its chief concerns, whenever such were relevant to the pattern of spiritual reconstruction, they might survive with surprising accuracy . . . . For all its conflations, confusions, and montages, epic has given us a picture of Mycenaean reality, corroborated and refined, rather than denied, by increasing historical knowledge."[11]

Homeric epic did not arise as an "original" effort of a single bard. The work of Milman Parry renders both the analyst and unitarian positions obsolete. The epic poet did not create his master work by piecing together disparate lays and traditions—a hero from this city or tribe, an enemy from another people or place, a heroic episode from one time and local tradition, another exploit from another time, and place. Major epic cycles shaped in public performances took complex form early in the bardic tradition. The outline or plot of the epic was itself traditional. To be sure, various heroic songs, of which only a few survive, once circulated and were drawn upon, and later treatments of major epics by skillful minstrels added accretions and rich

---

[9] Nilsson, *The Mycenaean Origin of Greek Mythology*, cited above, n.2, and *Homer and Mycenae* (London: Methuen, 1933).

[10] For contrasting perspectives on the extent of Mycenaean survivals in Homer, see Whitman, *Homer and the Heroic Tradition*, pp. 17-45; and M. J. Finley, *The World of Odysseus*, rev. ed. (New York: Viking, 1978). A more cautious approach is found in G. Kirk, "The Homeric Poems as History," *Cambridge Ancient History* II.2 (Cambridge, 1975), pp. 820-850.

[11] Whitman, *Homer and the Heroic Tradition*, pp. 44f.

ornamentation to the epic core. One finds it difficult to believe that the Iliad is not the fullest and most artful performance of the Trojan epic—even in the absence of records of variant renderings. But Homer (or the Homeric school) did not compose the Iliad as one sews together a patchwork quilt. A coherent, complex tale drawn from long-formed epic tradition provided his framework and central plot. In Nilsson's words, ". . . it appears that the background of Greek epos, i.e., the Trojan cycle in its chief features, the power of Mycenae, and the kingship of Mycenae, cannot possibly have come into existence through the joining together of minor chants and myths, but that it existed beforehand, being the cycle from which the minstrels took their subjects. A cycle of events with certain chief personages invariably appears in all the epic poetry of which we have a more definite knowledge than we have of Greek epics as the background from which episodes are taken and to which episodes are joined; it is a premise of epics, not their ultimate result."[1 2]

The epics of Homer have been called ecumenical or pan-Hellenic in intent and content. In historical times, we know, they were recited by rhapsodists at the great festivals known as the *panegyreis*, notably the Panathenaea to which pilgrims gathered from far and wide. There is good reason to believe that the original setting of oral presentation of Greek epic was precisely in such festivals, prehistoric forerunners of the Panathenaea, the Delia, and the Panionia.[1 3]

In recent years objections have been raised to my use of the term "epic" in defining the genre of Israel's earliest traditional literature.[1 4] Some of these objections have substance and require discussion. My choice of the designation "epic" draws on studies of Homeric epic, as we have seen, for

---

[1 2]Nilsson, *The Mycenaean Origin of Greek Mythology*, pp. 24f.

[1 3]See M. P. Nilsson, *Geschichte der griechischen Religion* I (Munich: C. H. Beck, 1941), pp. 778-782. The religious and cultic aspects of the Greek festivals have often been underestimated by classical scholars who have stressed their social, commercial, and entertainment aspects. Nilsson takes pains to correct this "Protestant view" which fails to perceive their easy union of religious service and "secular" activities. The reverse is probably true of scholarly reconstructions of the activities of Israel's pilgrimage festivals; probably the feasts in Israel as in Greece also took on many of the activities of fairs.

[1 4]See especially Charles Conroy, "Hebrew Epic: Historical Notes and Critical Reflections," *Biblica* 61 (1980): 1-30. Cp. S. Talmon, "The 'Comparative Method' in Biblical Interpretation—Principles and Problems," *Congress Volume: Göttingen, 1977. Supplement to Vetus Testamentum* XXIX (Leiden: Brill, 1978), pp. 352-356; and R. Alter, "Sacred History and Prose Fiction," *The Creation of Sacred Literature: Composition and Redaction of the Biblical Text*, ed. R. E. Friedman (Berkeley: University of California Press, 1981), pp. 7-24.

aid in understanding the nature of early Israelite literature. There are, however, evident contrasts between Greek epic and early Israelite traditional literature.

In the comparative study of epic, particularly in the monumental work of the Chadwicks, epic has been defined as "heroic" narrative. That is, epic deals with heroes, princes and kings and their followers, ordinarily a military elite, and is preoccupied with the social conventions of a heroic age: courage, strength, loyalty, and vengeance.[15] It is true that the Homeric epics, and, indeed, Western epic literature generally, are "heroic." I should concede immediately that early Israel was not a "heroic society" in the Homeric pattern. There are occasional heroic traits attributed to Abraham or Moses. But Israelite epic had only one hero, Yahweh of Hosts. One sings of his wrath, his mighty arm, his vengeance. He alone is the dragon slayer, the glorious king, the man of war, doer of wondrous deeds. Early Israelite society was egalitarian, and, there is good reason to believe, arose in opposition to the feudal structures of Canaan. Israel's "olden times" were not an age of human heroes and kings, and her soldiers were militiamen.

At the same time I believe it is permissible to define epic as the traditional narrative cycle of an age conceived as "normative," the events of which give meaning, self-understanding to a people or nation. The Homeric epics shaped the Greek self-consciousness, and gave normative expression to Hellenic mythology.[16] The Hebrew epic recounted "crucial events" of developing nationhood and gave classical expression to Yahwistic religion.

The use of the term "epic" by biblical scholars and Orientalists has often been loose, making no distinction between a purely mythic cycle (like the Baʻl "epic" or *Enūma eliš*, the "creation epic," actually a narrative cosmogony without a human actor), and epic of the Homeric type, or of the type of Keret, with its preoccupation with traditional events in ordinary time and space. Thus Cassuto reconstructed what I should term a mythic cycle, and termed it the Israelite epic. I should agree with those who reject such a conception of the Israelite epic, as will be apparent in the following pages. The alternate, however, is not to term the early traditional cycle of Israel "historical narrative." Robert Alter has recognized the inadequacy of applying the unqualified term "historical" and, following the lead of Herbert Schneidau, speaks of the (early) biblical narrative as "historical prose fiction" or "fictionalized history." I find such terms both misleading and condescending.

---

[15] H. M. and N. K. Chadwick, *The Growth of Literature*, 3 vols. (Cambridge University Press, 1932-40). See also C. M. Bowra, *Heroic Poetry* (London: Macmillan, 1961). The notion that epic reflects a "heroic age" is much more questionable, even in the West. Bowra has argued, correctly, I think, that Spain had no heroic age, despite its creation of the magnificent *Cantar de mío Cid*.

[16] See M. Finley (above n.10), p. 15.

The term "fiction" is chosen to point to the non-historical features of the narrative, presumably, but it suggests that the composer of Israelite traditional narrative chose to "write" what would look like historiography, but composed fiction in such a guise. I do not believe his intent was to compose history, or to compose "fiction," or to compose one under the guise of the other. I believe he was seeking to sing of Israel's past using traditional themes, the common stuff of generations of singers and tellers of tales. His story, prose or poetry (see below), dealt with the interactions of Yahweh and Israel in the normative past. The historian, even one given to fictionalizing, does not make a deity of his main character. The creator of fiction who wishes "to move away from the world of myth" does not make free use of such mythic themes in shaping his "historicized fiction." The term "fiction" like the term "history" is anachronistic when applied to Israel's national story, and derives—to use Ivan Engnell's strong language—from an arrogant *interpretatio europaeica moderna*. Fiction is invention. Cedric Whitman observed that "there is no evidence at all that the poet of the Iliad invented a single character or episode in his whole poem."[17] A similar (if more restrained) assertion could be made of the narrator of Israel's national epic. He received a well-shaped and articulated complex of narrative traditions, and recast, elaborated, even transformed it. There was, as in the case of Homer, a powerful creative element in his artistry. However, fictional "invention" is the wrong expression to use in describing the essential activity of the traditional poet or story-teller.

We shall continue to use the term "epic," defining it to include the following elements which apply equally to Homeric epic and early Israelite traditional narrative:

1) oral composition in formulae and themes of a traditional literature,
2) narrative in which acts of god(s) and men form a double level of action,
3) a composition describing traditional events of an age conceived as normative or glorious,
4) a "national" composition, especially one recited at pilgrimage festivals.

2.   The partition of the sources of the Pentateuch according to the Documentary Hypothesis posited four major sources: the Yahwist (J), the Elohist (E), old traditional documents, Deuteronomic tradition (D) composed largely in the seventh century B.C., and the Priestly document (P) of Exilic date. Our interest here is primarily with the Tetrateuch (Genesis-Numbers), which seems to have escaped systematic editing or expansion by the Deuteronomistic school. The writer has argued at length that the Priestly materials of the Tetrateuch never existed in the form of an independent narrative source;

---

[17]Whitman (above n.2), p. 14.

rather the Priestly Work must be seen as a systematic reworking of the traditional sources, JE, framed and restructured, and, at points of special interest,
greatly expanded by Priestly lore of diverse date, completed in the course of
the Exile.[18]

The pre-Priestly sources, the Yahwist and Elohist, JE, are the focus of
our interest. They recount the events which brought old Israel into being.
The outline of this history is roughly the same in each source: the call of the
patriarchs, the entry into Egypt, the victory at the sea, and the formation of
the covenanted league at Sinai-Horeb, and the march to the land promised
to the fathers. Close analysis of variant forms of tradition as well as assess-
ment of independent elements in each source make clear that neither source
was derived from the other. Rather one must conclude that the two rest on
an older basic traditional cycle. Martin Noth has labeled this basis of the JE
sources the *Grundlage*; Otto Procksch early proposed a happier designation the
Ursage.[19] I prefer to speak of J and E as variant forms of an older, largely
poetic epic cycle, and hence to term JE "epic sources." In their present form,
that is, in the form revised and presented in the P Work, they consist of prose
narrative, interlarded with poetic fragments, and occasionally, independent
poetic units, especially at crucial points in the narrative. It is not impossible
that the epic cycle in Israel was composed in a style in which prose narrative
dominated but at climactic moments utilized poetic composition. It is a style
widely distributed in oral epic literatures, and indeed characterized the pre-
Islamic epic tales of the *Ayyām el-'arab*.[20] There are compelling reasons,
however, to postulate that the Hebrew epic continued in the tradition of the
older Canaanite epic singers. We have noted above that the oral formulae
and themes of Late Bronze Age epics persist in early Hebrew poetry, and
particularly in the archaic poetry of the Pentateuch. The same prosodic
styles, "impressionistic" parallelism, repetitive or climactic parallelism, and
fundamental verse types, mark old Canaanite and early Hebrew poetry.[21]
Further, as has been often observed, the subject matter of the Keret Epic—
the securing of an heir, a promise of seed given in a revelation of 'El, an older
son passed over in favor of a younger son—has vivid parallels in the patriarchal
cycle in Genesis.

---

[18] F. M. Cross, *Canaanite Myth and Hebrew Epic* (Cambridge: Harvard
University Press, 1973), pp. 293-325.

[19] See M. Noth, *A History of Pentateuchal Traditions*, tr. B. W. Anderson
(Englewood Cliffs, N.J.: Printice-Hall, 1972), pp. 38-41; and for a fuller history of the discussion, C. Conroy (cited above, n.14).

[20] See recently, Ilse Lichtenstadter, "History in Poetic Garb in Ancient
Arabic Literature," *Harvard Ukrainian Studies* 3-4 (1979-80): 559-568.

[21] See F. M. Cross and D. N. Freedman, *Studies in Ancient Yahwistic
Poetry*, SBL Dissertation Series 21 (Missoula, Montana: Scholars Press, 1975),
including bibliography (pp. 189-191).

Further, if, as we shall argue, the epic was a creation of the league, and had a special function in the cultus of its pilgrim shrines, we expect its form to have been poetic. There can be no question of early Israel eschewing poetry as somehow inappropriate as a vehicle for recounting the mighty acts of Yahweh or Israel's early times. We possess lyric poems with strong narrative content in the Song of the Sea (Exodus 15) and the Song of Deborah (Judges 5).[22] In both instances we possess side by side prose narrative accounts (Exodus 14 and Judges 4), and in both instances the poetry is earlier, the prose secondary and derivative. We see the process of prosaizing poetic composition before our eyes.[23] The language which describes the theophany at Sinai in the prose of JE and P obviously derives from the poetic images of the storm theophany, objectified and concretized (or hypostatized) and in part misunderstood, especially by the P tradent.[24]

Even more instructive perhaps is the parallelistic diction and glimpses of poetry which lie immediately beneath the surface of many passages of prose in the epic sources.[25] Let me illustrate with a single example—not ordinarily cited—of prose when stripped of a few prose particles become exquisite poetry in epic style: Exodus 19:3-6:

כה תאמר לבית יעקב
תגד לבני ישראל

ראיתם מעשי במצרים
ואשאכם על כנפי נשר
ואבאכם בהר אלי

---

[22] I should make clear that I am not claiming that these two songs are "epics in miniature." They are lyric pieces.

[23] See the paper of Baruch Halpern in the present volume.

[24] See my discussion in *Canaanite Myth and Hebrew Epic* (hereafter *CMHE*) cited above in n.18, pp. 147-177.

[25] U. Cassuto has collected examples of "epic style" in the study cited in n.5. Moshe Weinfeld has called my attention to formulaic poetry which occurs not only in narrative texts in Genesis, but also in Psalm 72:11,17 (the latter verse reconstructed in part on the basis of the Septuagint):

וישתחוו לו כל מלכים
כל גוים יעבדוהו

which may be compared with Genesis 27:29:

יעבדוך עמים
וישתחו לך לאמים

and:

ונברכו בך כל משפחת האדמה
כל גוים יאשרהו

which may be compared with Genesis 12:3:

ואברכה מברכיך ומקללך אאר
ויתברכו בו משפחות האדמה

אם תשמעו בקולי
ושמרתם בריתי

תהיו לי סגלה
אתם לי גוי קדש
וממלכת כהנים

Thus you shall say to the house of Jacob,
Make known to the children of Israel,

You have seen my acts against the Egyptians,
How I lifted you up on eagle's wings,
And brought you to myself in the mount.

If you hearken to my voice,
And keep my covenant:

You shall become my special possession;
You shall be my holy nation,
And a kingdom of priests.

Herman Gunkel, who knew nothing of the Canaanite epics and thought in terms of short traditional units, recognized that the older form of many of these "sages," as he called them, were composed in poetry, and commented that "the older and strictly rhythmical form, which we must suppose to have been sung, would differ from the later prose form, which was recited, as does the ancient German epic from the *Volksbuch* ...."[26]

The phenomenon of oral poetic epic being converted to oral prose epic, or to written "historical narrative" is easily illustrated in the history of epic literatures. We shall choose a single instance of each.

There exists in Russian oral literature a type of oral prose narrative called the pobyvalshchina derived from the byliny (i.e., Russian epic verse) of the Kiev Cycle. To quote N. K. Chadwick:

"Although the metre has disappeared for the most part, the pobyvalshchiny frequently falls into a form of rhythmic prose . . . and their poetical origin can even be traced, and occasionally reconstituted where the conservative phraseology has preserved whole lines intact from the poetic original to

---

[26]H. Gunkel, *The Legends of Genesis*, trans. W. H. Carrutti (New York: Schocken, 1964), pp. 38f. These comments are from the introduction to his *Genesis* of 1901. In his third edition (1910), he adds a harsh critique of Ed. Sievers' *Metrische Studien* II, an attempt to scan the whole of Genesis in anapaestic meter. Gunkel correctly rejects Sievers' *tour de force*, and properly insists that the present form of the bulk of the narrative is prose. He also adds, in excessive reaction to Sievers I believe, that those materials first cast into poetry, later given prose form, may have been limited to myths and possibly to sanctuary legends. See *Genesis* 7. ed. (Göttingen: Vandenhoeck and Ruprecht, 1966), pp. xxvii-xxx.

phrase lengths in the prose version corresponding to the line length of the byliny."[27]

A second example is found in Spanish epic literature. Menéndez Pidal and his followers were successful in reconstructing substantial portions of lost Spanish epics preserved in medieval chronicles. Merle E. Simmons has described the circumstances as follows:

"In some cases a chronicler, using traditional songs as source materials for the writing of serious history, and apparently working in some instances with a manuscript of an epic poem before him (probably like the manuscript we have of the *Cantar de mío Cid*), rendered long poetic passages into prose that not infrequently still has lines that scan like poetry, retains unsuppressed rhymes, and in general preserves a lively and dramatic style that makes such passages stand out from the less sprightly narrative that surrounds them."[28]

My argument is not that there is a natural evolution from poetic epic to prose epic. Rather I am observing that the recasting of poetic epic in prose narrative, and indeed its use as a source for the composition of historical narrative, is not an isolated occurrence in Israel, and the techniques used here to reconstruct Israel's epic have precise analogies in literary scholarship.

The history of Pentateuchal studies from DeWette to Wellhausen has striking parallels to the history of Homeric studies from Friedrich August Wolf to Wilamowitz. A similar rationalistic, literary-critical set of presuppositions informed analysis and dictated conclusions giving rise to disintegration of the traditional complex into fragments, and the dating of traditional elements by the latest discernible anachronisms in the written sources. I have often wondered if Julius Wellhausen's change of title of his great work from *Geschichte Israels I* (1878) to *Prolegomena zur Geschichte Israels* (1885) was owing less to a desire for accuracy than a subtle claim to parallel rank with Wolf's *Prolegomena ad Homerum* (1795).[29] Hermann Gunkel was to surpass even Wellhausen in his impact on Pentateuchal studies. Unlike Wellhausen, who judged Pentateuchal traditions to reflect more or less on events and lore contemporary with their final authors, J and E, Gunkel recognized that the "*sage* materials" had a long prehistory in oral transmission. Influenced strongly by the classical labors of Eduard Norden (*Die antike Kunstprosa* I [1889]), he introduced *Gattungsforschung* into the study of Pentateuchal narrative. He regarded the undeveloped field of "literary history,"

---

[27] *The Growth of Literature* II, p. 165.

[28] See his paper, "The Spanish Epic," in *Heroic Epic and Saga*, ed. Felix J. Oinas (Bloomington and London: University of Indiana Press, 1978), esp. p. 222 and references.

[29] One notes that his *Israelitische und jüdische Geschichte* (1894), the completion of his Prolegomena, was dedicated to his colleague Wilamowitz as a *Gegengabe*.

Literaturgeschichte to be above all the history of literary units and *genres*.[30]
His analysis of the oral prehistory of the patriarchal legends led him to conclude that the period of their formation closed by about 1200 B.C. On the other hand, Gunkel looked upon J and E as collectors of individual units of tradition, and his vision of the final form of these sources was not different from Wilamowitz's conviction that the Iliad in its received form was a "wretched patchwork."[31]

Gunkel in developing his form-critical methods was concerned above all in isolating primitive units of tradition. Owing to the intellectual currents of his time—compounded of Romanticism, evolutionism, and German academic idealism—he assumed that complexes of tradition and complicated individual traditions were late; the simpler the tradition or *sage*, the closer it was to the primitive unit. "Das älteste hebräische Volkslied umfasst nur eine oder etwa zwei Langzeilen; mehr vermochten die damaligen Menschen nicht zu übersehen."[32] And he quotes with approval Wellhausen's assertion that "die Überlieferung im Volksmund kennt nur einzelne Geschichten."[33] The absurdity of such methodological assumptions is sufficiently shown simply by counting the lines of the Ba'l Cycle, or of the Keret and Aqhat epics of Ugarit, not to mention the 15000 lines of the Iliad. Gunkel speaks of the build-up of cycles of *sage* but, in his view, each move toward complexity is taken in a cultural vacuum, one unit spliced to a second, the two to a third until, *mirabile dictu*, a complex, coherent narrative emerges like a magpie's nest built from bits and tatters brought from far and wide. There is in Gunkel's application of his method no reckoning with a long and continuous tradition of epic singers and epic cycles, mythic cycles and heirophants. In fact, epic plots and bundles of themes, mythic patterns, and indeed tales sung based on memorable events, throughout the age of epic composition, existed as a background for each new performance of an epic tale, and furnished materials for shaping emerging new cycles of epic tradition. Complex traditions and units of tradition always, in my view, existed side by side. Units of tradition may have existed in independence in some instances; equally often they came into being only as an element in a complex, a *Gestalt*; sometimes a "unit" was a loose fragment shifted from one bundle of themes to another, but, like a particle in modern physics, had no existence except in one complex relationship or another. Moreover, if one finds short and long forms of a given tradition or epic tale, it does not follow necessarily that the short is older, the long

---

[30]See, e.g., his "Die Grundprobleme der israelitische Literaturgeschichte," *Reden und Aufsätze* (Göttingen: Vandenhoeck and Ruprecht, 1913): 29-38.

[31]*Apud* Whitman, *Homer and the Heroic Tradition*, p. 2.

[32]H. Gunkel, "Die Grundprobleme der israelitische Literaturgeschichte," p. 34.

[33]H. Gunkel, *Genesis*, p. xxxii, n.1.

secondary. It may be that the epic nucleus has gained secondary accretions. But singers of epic poetry also could expand or contract their songs to fit circumstance and occasion. Brief prose summaries of Israelite epic have sometimes been described as archaic on the grounds that they are short and omit secondary elements. Such (for example, G. von Rad's "short historical credos") are highly suspect; to be preferred, if available, are orally-composed poetic materials recounting epic themes (e.g., the Song of the Sea). I should find it surprising, indeed, if Israel's old epic cycle in its oral presentations did not rival or even exceed in length the preserved Yahwistic source.[34]

The legacy of Gunkel survives in lively form in contemporary tradition-criticism. There has been no revolution in biblical criticism comparable to that in Homeric studies initiated by Milman Parry. A number of scholars have engaged in formula analysis (Robert Culley, William Whallon, Richard Whitaker, William Watters, Stephen Geller to name a few). But aside from reexamination of some of the early narrative poems, notably the Song of the Sea and the Song of Deborah, little has been done to analyze early epic narrative in the light of the new perspectives afforded by Homeric studies and comparative studies of orally-composed epic.

The new perspectives offer little aid in attacking the problem of the actual historical content of a given epic tradition or complex. The degree of shaping given to historical memories by traditional themes and mythic motifs varies widely in epic material, and the extent of distortion in a given instance is not easy to gauge. On the other hand, the extreme scepticism about the ability of the ancient memory to preserve ancient elements of tradition—a recent scholar still asserts that "folk memory" at most spans two generations—is now shown to be without warrant. Epic tradition in particular is able to preserve the color and substance of old social and institutional forms as well as early cultic and religious lore. Alt's instinct that certain epithets of deity embedded in Genesis were extremely archaic is now reinforced by an understanding of the mechanism which carries precisely such lore over centuries of time, and confirmed in several instances by their appearance in texts of the second millennium. In view of the atlas of Mycenaean Greece preserved in the so-called Catalogue of Ships cited in the Iliad, it is no longer surprising that the Patriarchal traditions of Genesis attach the fathers to authentic Canaanite cities of the Middle and Late Bronze Ages, and not to the newly-established Israelite towns founded in the hill country at the beginning of the Iron Age.[35]

---

[34] I should not assign the long Joseph story to the Yahwist, and indeed its relation to the Epic Sources is problematical.

[35] The list includes Shechem, Hebron, Jerusalem, Dothan, Gerar (Tell Abu Hureirah—to be taken as both a land and a city)—and Beth-el. Special problems exist, which need not occupy us here, with Beersheba and, of course, the Cities of the Plain. In certain instances a late name is applied to an old city.

An understanding of the mechanisms in the transmission of epic poetry also clarifies and complicates questions of the date of an epic cycle and its accretions. In the Tetrateuch this problem is further complicated by the literary reworking and expansion of epic traditions by the Priestly tradent in the sixth century. Older approaches, dating materials by their latest accretions or by anachronisms, yield monarchic or even Exilic dates for the epic sources, and an occasional scholar will still solemnly assert an Exilic date for the Yahwist. The Trojan cycle evidently began to assume complex epic form not long after the events of which it sings took place, sufficiently early that some authentic memories of the Mycenaean Age were preserved in bardic tradition. It acquired additional shaping and accretions in the course of the so-called Dark Age, and in the Geometric Age in which it reached written form. The problems of dating Israel's epic tradition are no simpler. Our use of Homeric analogies obviously is qualified by the long era of literary recasting of biblical epic traditions which has no real counterpart in later recensional activity in the transmission of the text of Homer. On the other hand, Palestine throughout the Late Bronze and Early Iron Ages was a literate society, with alphabetic writing and, in the Late Bronze Age, several systems of writing in use. Thus one must reckon always with the possibility in Israel, as in Ugarit, of written as well as oral transmission of epic texts. In any case, one must take into account the fact that in the nature of epic composition the archaic and the late are intertwined, and that the distance in time between the old and the new may vary from generations to centuries.[36]

Perhaps it will be useful to illustrate old and new approaches to oral narrative by examination of a central, climactic portion of the Israelite epic: the Exodus and the revelation at Sinai—the Victory at the Sea and the creation of the covenant cult at the mount. The epic sources present these events as sequent, indeed the victory of Israel's divine warrior at the sea is preceded by the revelation of his name at the mount, and his call for the deliverance of nascent Israel, and provides the condition for the formation of the nation and its covenant institutions—law and cult—at the mount of revelation. In the Song of the Sea, in my opinion the oldest of Israel's narrative poems, the episode at the Sea is recounted: Yahweh defeats the Egyptians by casting the Egyptians into the Sea by stirring up the sea with the blast of his nostrils—the storm wind; he leads them to his desert encampment; there follows then allusion to the conquest, the crossing of Jordan, and finally to the establishment of the people in Yahweh's mount, the building of his sanctuary and his eternal rule over the people he had "created." Here the establishment of the people and the cultus in the land terminates the sequence of events

---

[36]Jeffrey Tigay in his extraordinary study, *The Evolution of the Gilgamesh Epic* (Philadelphia: University of Pennsylvania Press, 1982), furnishes much material illustrating conservatism and innovation in the transmission of epic.

initiated at the sea. In the prose epitome of the epic themes in Joshua 24, these central events receive much the same treatment, victory at the sea, the march through the desert, the conquest of the land, and finally formation of a covenant cultus at Shechem, the occasion for the recitation.

Now how does one analyze these refractions of the epic of Israel. One approach, articulated most effectively by G. Von Rad and Martin Noth, seeks out units of tradition. One nucleus is the Exodus-Conquest (or Settlement), a second is the revelation at Sinai. Noth adds a problematic "Leading in the Wilderness." Each of these in origin is unrelated to the other, and stems from an independent cult. The "historical" theme, Exodus-Conquest arises in one festival at one tribal shrine, the revelation theme with its law and theophany arises in another festival and shrine. The "kerygmatic" events are contrasted with law and covenant—Gospel vs. Law imported into ancient Israel—and stitched together only by the Yahwist (von Rad) or by G (Noth). One observes that "theophany" must be attached to a single theme; theophanic elements in the battle of the Divine Warrior must be secondary, or the theophanic motif at the mountain holy place must be secondary. Why? because one is simpler than two, not to mention three, and hence prior.

An alternate, and, I believe, superior, approach is open, at least, to the possibility that both the Battle at the Sea and the covenant-making and establishment of Divine Rule belong to a sequence of events or bundle of themes narrated in the primitive epic cycle. That the pattern existed before the elaboration of units in the Israelite epic—and indeed shaped the selection of events to be narrated—can be argued on the basis of the myth of the Divine Warrior from Ugarit, as well as from Hebrew poetry early and late. There are two, paired movements in the drama: (1) The Divine Warrior goes forth to battle against his enemy (Yamm [Sea], Leviathan, Mot [Death]). At his appearance, brandishing his weapons, nature convulses and the heavens languish. He conquers. (2) The victorious god returns to take up kingship and is enthroned on his holy mountain. He utters his voice from his temple, and nature responds to his fructifying appearance in the storm. His guests feast at his sanctuary and kingship is established or confirmed in heaven and earth.

The pattern has integrity. Theophany in "judgment" is paired with theophany in "salvation." The cosmogonic battle is the ground of the establishment of the divine state, and on earth temple and kingship reflect the cosmic establishment. The cultic character of the pattern is manifest in its terminus: the festival. In this pattern is a unity of structure and meaning, grounded in the cult, which is destroyed if severed into units.

Epic also has a concrete social function; its oral performances were public, and more specifically in cultic or national festivals. As the Ba'l cycle served as a libretto to the New Year's festival, and as the Greek epic has the setting in the *panegyreis* in Greece, so the Israelite epic was a feature of league festivals. Always an aspect of these celebrations was the reconstitution of the nation, the rearticulation of the identity of the community, the reinforcement of the unity of the people. In the Canaanite feudal state there was renewal of kingship—not merely a song of creation recited to inform the young or titillate the aesthetic sensibilities of the audience present. In Israel the covenant was renewed or confirmed—not merely a song of Yahweh's old glories sung to evoke nostalgia. Indeed there is reason to believe that the epic events were reenacted in ritual procession preliminary to the covenant rites proper. Norman Gottwald, approaching from a very different philosophical framework, comes to similar conclusions: "What I simply cannot imagine," he writes, "is a cult in early Israel in which the people merely recited past actions of deity *without any present cultic-ideological rootage in theophany, covenant, and law* [italics in Gottwald's text]."[37]

3. In order to take first steps in the reconstruction of the Hebrew epic cycle, we must begin with the most palpable transformation of the tradition, the Yahwistic source.

The Yahwistic work is best described, I believe, as a propaganda work of the empire. In Genesis 15:7-12, 17-18 there is a central Yahwistic passage in which archaic material is reworked in a fashion which reveals the Yahwist's intent and anticipates—in epic fashion—the denouement of the narrative. In the older level of the passage is recorded a covenant ceremony of typical primitive type: animals are cut up and fire passes among them, the Yahwist's version of the covenant with Abraham. The content of this covenant is specified as follows: "In that day Yahweh made a covenant with Abram, saying, 'To your seed I have given this land from the river of Egypt to the great river, the River Euphrates.' "[38] In a sequence of Yahwistic passages, the promise to the patriarchs of seed and land gives structure to the patriarchal narrative. In Genesis 15, however, there is on the one hand old material presuming covenant forms, ordinarily not an interest of the Yahwist, and, on the other hand, a specification of the promise of the land conforming only to the boundaries of the Davidic and Solomonic empire. The Promised Land in late sources (P, Ezekiel) included only "Canaan," Cis-Jordan, and there is some evidence that older sources claimed the Egyptian province of Canaan which included the Phoenician littoral, but not Transjordan.[39] In other words, in the structure of the Yahwistic epic, the promise to the Fathers is fulfilled politically in the Empire. The typology is, in effect, Abraham—David, rather than Abraham—Moses (Priestly Work), or the older fulfillment in the conquest.

---

[37] See F. M. Cross, *Canaanite Myth and Hebrew Epic*, pp. 79-144; and N. Gottwald, *The Tribes of Yahweh* (Maryknoll, New York: Orbis, 1979), p. 99.

[38] On the Abrahamic covenant, see the writer, *Canaanite Myth and Hebrew Epic*, pp. 265-273.

[39] Cf. Y. Kaufmann, *The Religion of Israel* (Chicago: University of Chicago Press, 1960), pp. 201f.; *The Biblical Account of the Conquest of Palestine* (Jerusalem, 1953, *passim*).

The typology "Abraham-David" has long been noted in the Yahwistic source. The juxtaposition of the revelation and promise of Genesis 15 with Genesis 14, 18-24, the narrative of Abram's dealings with Jerusalem, is significant here. Abram is presented as acknowledging the succor of "El Creator of Earth,"[40] an archaic epithet of 'El known from Late Bronze Age sources, as well as later, including an ostracon from eighth-century Jerusalem. His priest, Melchizedek, bearing a good Canaanite name, is pictured as king of Salem-Jerusalem. He blessed Abraham by "El Creator of Earth," and received Abram's tithe. We need not concern ourselves with the origins of the story concerning the war with the eastern kings, in every way a unique element in patriarchal tradition. Rather we are interested in the legitimation of a cult in Jerusalem and its evident function in legitimizing the national cult of David and Solomon.[41]

Unlike the Elohistic source, the Yahwist does not read prophecy *(sensu stricto)* back into ancient times. His tradition stems from an age before the height of the prophetic movement in the ninth century. Moreover, the Yahwist does not engage in polemics against Ba'lism, the chief issue in ninth century prophetic circles.[42] His work is essentially pre-prophetic in content.

The Yahwist's work, unlike much of the lore he draws upon, is somewhat removed from direct cultic interest. He has transformed cultically formed tradition and poetry into "history" and prose—or this was his intent. G. von Rad has remarked perceptively, "The atmosphere which surrounds the Yahwistic declaration of faith is almost wholly devoid of cultic associations, a fact which must cause intense surprise to anyone who has followed our investigation from that extremely close association with the cultus which characterizes most of his materials, to the stage where they are fused together in the literary work of the Yahwist."[43] We must suppose that the Yahwist turns epic materials into his prose work at a time when Israel's cultic institutions, notably the covenant festivals of the league, in which the epic events were recited and enacted, had fallen into desuetude, and epic tradition thus loosened from its primary setting and function. The freeing of the epic form its cultic connection no doubt coincides with the establishment of the royal cultus of Solomon, and it is precisely in the age of Solomonic grandeur, coinciding with far-reaching changes in religious institutions, that we should expect the transformation of the old epic into a prose propaganda work of empire. Von Rad speaks of the Yahwist as "redolent of the untrammeled days of Solomon."

[40] On the epithet, see F. M. Cross, *CMHE*, pp. 15f., 50-52.

[41] Compare G. von Rad, *Genesis*, trans. J. Marks (Philadelphia: Westminster, 1961), p. 175f.

[42] Note the Elohistic lore in Exodus 32 which presumes a polemic against Bethel and its bull iconography.

[43] G. von Rad, *The Problem of the Hexateuch and Other Essays*, trans. E. W. T. Dickens (New York: McGraw-Hill, 1966), p. 68.

And we agree. Its expansive faith in Yahweh's direction of history, its lack of any sense of crisis or foreboding, its wide-ranging interests, its freedom from polemic, all breath the spirit of triumphant Israel in the days of Empire. There are, obviously, anachronisms arising in days later than the United Empire. But in a work transmitted and reworked in subsequent centuries, massively in the Exile, anachronisms and modernization are expected.

In remarking above on the dissolution of covenant forms and festivals, and its reflection in the form of the Yahwist's composition, a further word should be said. In the patriarchal materials preserved in the Yahwist, he speaks more of the call or the promise to the patriarch than of covenants entered into by the patriarch. In the Sinai narrative, the Yahwist to be sure includes the revelation at Sinai, and a torso of a Yahwistic decalogue survives.[44] The Elohist has been the primary source utilized in the P-Work for reconstruction of the covenant ritual. This diminution of covenant forms and language—if not their suppression—is a reflection of a specific royal ideology characteristic of the Solomonic establishment. I have argued elsewhere on the basis of quite different evidence that, with the transformation of David's kingdom into a full-fledged international power in the days of Solomon, kingship and cultus came under the influence of Canaanite monarchical institutions and ideology. The "Davidic covenant"—a dynastic codicil, so to speak, in Israel's covenant—became an unconditional, eternal decree of deity, the mount of Zion his eternal dwelling place. In Solomonic kingship the language of divine sonship became normative, covenantal language disused or reinterpreted. Covenant language and forms survived in the North, to judge from the Elohistic epic source. It is revived and reformed in the nostalgic Deuteronomistic Work, and in the archaizing Priestly Work.[45]

In sum, we should argue that the Yahwistic epic is a prosaizing, propaganda work of the United Monarchy, and specifically the program of Solomon to constitute an Oriental monarchy in the Canaanite pattern. The older epic, cut loose from the covenantal cultus of the tribal sanctuaries of the league, was shaped by the Yahwist for new institutions and new functions.[46]

---

[44]Ex. 34:10, 14, 17, 27 preserve a torso including the earliest form of two of the commandments. Intruded, however, is a ritual calendar (34:18-26), a variant of the prescriptions in 23:14-19, and the remaining portion of the decalogue or dodecalogue displaced.

[45]See Cross, *CMHE*, pp. 219-265 and 295-300.

[46]The P-Work ends effectively with the death of Moses. While there are bits of Priestly lore—or Temple documents—in Joshua, Joshua like Judges, Samuel and Kings was edited by Dtr_1 and in the Exile by Dtr_2. It is a part of the Deuteronomistic Work. Thus the Israelite epic is truncated in the P-Work, in the Tetrateuch. Presumably some of the material in Joshua stems from epic tradition, but it is a moot question whether or not the epic sources JE can be isolated. On the problem, see S. Mowinckel, *Tetrateuch-Pentateuch-Hexateuch* (Berlin: Töpelmann, 1964).

We have not referred to the primeval history, Genesis 1-11. This cycle of tradition is firmly imprinted by the Yahwist, and has no counterpart in extant Elohistic tradition.[47] J's traditions are old, and the Priestly tradent drew on primeval material which, on rare occasions, betray poetic origins.[48]

I am not inclined, however, to believe that the creation and primeval accounts belonged to the earlier Israelite epic. Its prefixing to the patriarchal cycle is reminiscent of the prefixing of theogonies to the cosmogonic myths in *Enūma eliš*, Hesiod, and the third theogony of Sakkunyaton.[49] In any case, the primeval lore provides a universal setting for the central epic narrative, and underscores the theme of Israel's universal destiny in the Yahwist's presentation of Israel's history. While such a theme may have been older, and creation stories obviously circulated in pre-monarchic Israel, its addition to the epic by the hand of the Yahwist, in imperial times, exquisitely fits the motivation and intent of his work.[50]

4. The epic cycle of old Israel in its mature form was a creation of the Israelite league. It cannot be later evidently than the epic sources of the early monarchy, the Yahwistic work from Solomonic times. At the core of the epic, as we have seen, is the Divine victory at the Sea and the formation of the league at Sinai: Exodus and Covenant. In archaic hymns, Yahweh marches from the southern mountains out to do battle, and leads his redeemed people back to his mountain sanctuary (e.g., in Hab. 3:3-15; Exodus 15:1-18; Dt. 33:2, 26-29). The movement is expressed in ultimate brevity in the archaic formula of holy war: "Arise Yahweh, let thy enemies be scattered, let thy adversaries flee before thee. Return Yahweh [with] the myriads, ['El with] the thousands of Israel" (Num. 10:25f.).[51] The Exodus-Sinai pattern, however, was shaped to conform to the cultic requirements of the festivals in the pilgrimage sanctuaries in the land. The victory at the sea is extended, so to speak, to include the conquest of the land. The crossing of the sea is typologically identified with the crossing of the Jordan, an equation rendered easy by the poetic formula which pairs sea and river (in myth: Prince Sea, Judge River). In Psalm 114 the parallelism of the Sea and Jordan is vividly

---

[47] For a contrary position, see S. Mowinckel, *The Two Sources of the Predeuteronomic History (JE) in Gen. 1-11* (Oslo: Norske Videnskaps-Akademi, 1937), and W. F. Albright, *JBL* 52 (1938): 230f., and *JBL* 53 (1939): 93-103.

[48] Notably Gen. 1:27; 7:11; cf. Cassuto, *Biblical and Oriental Studies* II, pp. 79f. and 103-109 on remains of "creation epic" traditions.

[49] See my discussion in *Magnalia dei*, G. Ernest Wright Volume, ed. F. M. Cross, W. E. Lemke, and P. D. Miller (New York: Doubleday, 1976), pp. 329-338, esp. pp. 333f.

[50] The case is eloquently argued by von Rad, *The Problem of the Hexateuch*, pp. 63-67.

[51] On the reconstruction of the verse, see the writer's comments, *CMHE*, p. 100.

expressed.[52] Cultic materials in Joshua 3-5 stemming from the shrine at Gilgal recapitulate the crossing of the sea, the setting up of twelve maṣṣebot at Sinai, in their spring festival. The "march to the sanctuary" symbolizes both the crossing of the sea and the march to the desert mount, the crossing of Jordan, and the March of the Conquest of the land.[53] The Song of the Sea, our earliest hymn describing the epic battle, had its original setting in this cultic context: the march of Yahweh, leading his people through the desert, bringing them across the river to his "mountain" sanctuary. Exodus and Conquest have thus become cultically fused themes. Similarly the mountain of God is identified with the shrines of the land where the covenant cultus was celebrated. This equation of covenant rites at Sinai with covenant rites in the land was recognized by Albrecht Alt and his school in their treatment of lore originating in the Shechem cult, notably Joshua 8:30-34; 24:2-28; and Deuteronomy 27:(11-)15-16. Indeed we may suppose that in the great pilgrimage festivals in the land, at Gilgal, Shechem, and though we have little data, presumably also at other pilgrimage shrines: Shiloh, Bethel, Hebron, the ritual processions reenacting the march of victory and its reenactment and confirmation in covenant rites, fused in cult the mount of God and the mount of the shrine in the land. Shrines, of course, were built on mountains, in fact, or in mythic identification of the shrine's platform with the cosmic mountain.[54] Finally, in transformations in later Israel, the "Holy Way" through the desert had as its goal and climax, the feast on Zion.

In the epic cycles sung in the shrines of the land, there is thus a displacement, so to speak, of the Sinai tradition. In the JE reformulation of the old epic, however, the Southern mountain of revelation was restored in its primitive place, and the covenant at Sinai intervenes between Exodus and Conquest. This reformulation, which involved combination of variant forms of the epic cycle, left "seams" in the narrative of the epic sources, exacerbated by the thorough reworking of the Sinai pericope by the Priestly tradent for whom it was the climax of history.[55]

The survival of variant streams of epic tradition from the major sanctuaries of the era of the league is significant evidence of the character of politics and religion in early Israel. We have noted special traditions traceable to Shechem and Gilgal. Special epic lore also is preserved which can be derived

---

[52] See also Psalm 74:12-15.

[53] See my detailed discussion, *CMHE*, pp. 103-105.

[54] See R. J. Clifford's excellent discussion, *The Cosmic Mountain in Canaan and the Old Testament, HSM* 4 (Cambridge: Harvard University Press, 1972).

[55] These "seams" have provided grounds for separating out the Sinai "theme" as alien to the epic events *(Heilsgeschichte)*, thus disintegrating the cultic and social integrity of the epic as well as its structural unity, leaving the *magnalia dei* suspended in air.

from the cult of Shiloh, Bethel, and the pilgrimage shrine in the southern mountains: Sinai-Teman-Se'ir. In each case the traditions are welded to the themes of Exodus and Covenant. At Shiloh we hear of the "Ark of the Covenant of Yahweh of Hosts who is enthroned on the cherubim," a cult name of the ark, peculiarly associated with Shiloh, as persuasively argued by Eissfeldt,[56] and its Mushite priesthood bears Egyptian names. At Bethel Jeroboam restored the bull iconography, by tradition (preserved in polemical attacks on the Bethel cult) created by Aaron himself at Sinai,[57] a tradition sufficiently archaic and established that it survived the handling of later Aaronid priests in the Priestly Work. Archaic poems—or poetic materials of early date reutilized in later hymns—preserve clear traditions of Yahweh of the Southern mountains: Sinai/Se'ir/Paran, parallel names in the Blessing of Moses, Teman/ Paran in Habakkuk 3, Se'ir/steppes of Edom, in the Song of Deborah. In the early sections of Habakkuk 3 the epic theme is sung in highly mythological dress. Yahweh marches forth from the Southern mountains to battle, appearing in blazing fire, accompanied by *Deber* and *Rešep*. Earth and nations shake, the ancient mountains shatter. The tents of Cushan and Midian tremble. His wrath is directed against Sea, against River, as he rides his chariots of victory. He smashes the head of his enemy (Sea), laying him bare tail to neck. His horses tread down Sea, as the mighty waters roil and foam. Thus he goes forth to save his people.[58] The sanctuary in the South persisted as a pilgrimage shrine at least into the ninth century as traditions in the Elijah cycle have long suggested, and as archaeological remains from Kuntillet 'Ajrud in Sinai on the road to Elat now confirm.[59] From the pilgrim station of 'Ajrud come references to "Yahweh of Teman" (*yhwh htmn*; cf. Zech. 6:6), alongside "Yahweh of Samaria," and preserved on plaster in a Phoenicianizing script, written in Hebrew, are fragments of a hymn echoing elements of Habakkuk 3.

The Midianite traditions found in both epic sources have led scholars to suspect that a pre-Israelite sanctuary of Yahweh lay in the mountains of the South in the lands on the east of the Gulf of Elath. The geographical terms Se'ir, Edom, Teman, as well as Cushan and Midian, point east of modern Sinai. Moreover, on the basis of both Egyptian records and surface exploration of

---

[56] O. Eissfeldt, "Jahwe Zebaoth," *Miscellanea Academia Berolinensia* (Berlin, 1950): 127-150 [*KS* III, 103-123].

[57] See my analysis of these traditions, *CMHE*, pp. 198-200.

[58] See U. Cassuto, *Biblical and Oriental Studies* II, pp. 3-15; W. F. Albright, "The Song of Habakkuk," *Studies in Old Testament Prophecy*, ed. H. H. Rowley (Edinburgh: Clark, 1950), pp. 1-18.

[59] See provisionally, Z. Meshel, *Kuntillet 'Ajrūd. A Religious Center from the Time of the Judaean Monarchy on the Border of Sinai* (Jerusalem: Israel Museum, 1978). See also M. Noth, *Der Wallfahrtsweg zum Sinai*, Palästinajahrbuch 36 (1940): 5-28 on the pilgrimage route to Sinai preserved in Numbers 33:2-49.

such sites as Qurayyeh southeast of Elath in Midian, we know that there was a substantial civilization in this area at the end of the Late Bronze Age and the beginning of the Iron Age.[60] On the other hand, the evidence for extensive occupation in the same period in modern Sinai is virtually nil despite intensive investigation.

At all events early Israel's epic cycle seems to have been at home in a number of sanctuaries in the land, and in addition in an old sanctuary in the South. The Ark of Yahweh moved from shrine to shrine, especially in times of Holy War. The league which celebrated the epic events and confirmed its bonds in the pilgrim festivals had no single, central sanctuary. This, of course, is the plain testimony of the tradition which informs the first of Nathan's oracles in 2 Samuel 7 (vv. 5-7): "I [Yahweh] have never dwelt in a temple from the day I brought the children of Israel from Egypt until this day, but I was moving about in a tent and in a tabernacle. Wherever among the children of Israel I moved to and fro, did I ever command any judge of Israel . . . saying why do you not build me a temple of cedar? " The force of this league tradition represented by Nathan effectively prevented David from building a permanent national shrine. Practice in early Israel ran counter to the so-called amphictyonic institutions of Greece with their focus on a central sanctuary. In Israel in the days of the league there was no single, fixed league sanctuary. Looked at from another perspective, many shrines served as league sanctuaries in the time of great pilgrim festivals. It may have been that the Ark of the Covenant moved about in its impermanent tent from season to season, and by its presence designated a given cultus as the focus of the league. Certainly this was the case in time of war.

The patriarchal traditions were an integral element in Israel's early epic (although it must be said that the history of the Patriarchs has been vastly expanded by later accretions before achieving its present agglutinative mass). Much of the Patriarchal lore is very old, some of it reaching back, perhaps, into the Middle Bronze Age. As an epic cycle it evidently existed prior to the epic materials recounting Exodus, Covenant, and Conquest. There is, on the other hand, no reason to believe that the bundle of Exodus, Sinai, and Conquest themes ever existed detached from or separated from Patriarchal epic tradition—save in its purely mythic prototype. The epic tradition was continuous, new elements expanding and replacing old, a dynamic process with changing times and institutions. The patriarchal narratives carry certain elements which perform a crucial function in league epic and cultus. The patriarchs legitimize the league sanctuaries of the land: Bethel, Shechem,

---

[60] See P. J. Parr, et al., "Preliminary Survey in N.W. Arabia, 1968," *Bulletin of the Institute of Archaeology* 8-9, 1968-69 (1970): 193-242; 10, 1970 (1972): 23-61; W. F. Albright, "The Oracles of Balaam," *JBL* 63 (1944): 227-230; and M. Weippert, "Semitische Nomader der zweiten Jahrtausend: über die šзsw der ägyptischer Quellen," *Biblica* 55 (1974): 265-280, 427-433.

Hebron, Beersheba. Cult aetiologies of each are narrated in the patriarchal lore. The archaic epithets of deity often associated with these sanctuaries, *'ēl 'ôlām* to Beersheba, *'ēl ĕlōhê yiśrā'ēl* at Shechem, *'ēl bêt-'ēl* at Bethel, together with *'ēl qōnê 'ereṣ* and *('ēl) šadday* are not randomly preserved. They all appear to be epithets of the patriarch of the gods, 'El. 'El, identified with Yahweh in league tradition, dominates the religious lore of the Fathers. Evidently the choice of patriarchal stories, shrine aetiologies, and divine epithets was a highly controlled process in the formation of the epic of the league. Canaan in pre-Israelite times was plentifully supplied with gods of a rich pantheon and their temples. Most are passed over in Israelite tradition. Save in the intrusive materials of Genesis 14, one detects little shaping by the interests of the Davidids and the Priestly school to promote a royal cultus and shrine.

One structure of the epic, the journey of the patriarch from land granted his fathers, and the return to the ancestral land, of course, legitimizes the land claims of the league and needs no elaboration on our part. Another structure does warrant some development here: the covenant of the fathers and the covenant of the league.

Characteristic of patriarchal religion is the "personal god," the god who revealed himself to the patriarch, blessed him with seed, led his clan in war and in migration, in short became "his god." The patriarch in turn, faithful to his special relationship, kept the god's cult, built his altars, paid his tithes and offerings, followed his directive. This special relationship is vivid in the onomasticon of patriarchal folk, and warrants comparison with Amorite names, names compounded with kinship terms or extended-kinship terms, in which the theophorous element is the (Divine) father, brother, uncle, or father-in-law, brother-in-law, etc. Society was structured by obligations of kinship and extended kinship, by marriage or by covenant. In the early form of the patriarchal tradition—better reflected in the archaizing lore of P than in the epic sources—the patriarchal narratives provided a sequence of covenants with the patriarchs—the covenant of Abraham, Isaac, and Jacob, leading to the covenant of the league.

Much writing has been done on the analogies of the Israelite covenant with the Hittite suzerainty treaties and the West-Semitic, especially Aramaic, treaty forms, refracted in Neo-Assyrian treaties.[61] These analogies are most useful, but have tended to obscure the actual covenant forms of tribal leagues, which develop out of the social and religious forms of a patriarchal society. The god of the father becomes the god of clans and tribes, and thereby the tribes are linked in obligation to their god and to each other by the "substitute" kinship relation afforded by covenant. Such covenants ordinarily bring with them the reordering of genealogies, and the "fiction" of actual kinship relations between the tribes, though the rites of covenant or covenant renewal perennially reaffirm their unity.[62]

---

[61] On the West-Semitic origins of Neo-Assyrian treaties, see H. Tadmor, "Treaty and Oath in the Ancient Near East," forthcoming in the volume of centennial lectures of the Society of Biblical Literature.

[62] On the function of genealogies, see R. R. Wilson, *Genealogy and History in the Biblical World* (New Haven: Yale University Press, 1977).

Confederations of tribes appear to have flourished in southern Palestine and in Northern Arabia before their evolution into "nation states" headed by kings: Edom, Moab, and Ammon on Israel's south and east, Midian, Ishmael, and Qedar further south.[63] In some cases there is evidence of groupings of twelve, in the pattern of Israel's twelve tribes, and characteristically there is reference to tribal leaders as neśi'im in Israel and in the southern confederations.

It should be noted in passing that Martin Noth's attempt to find the origin of the number twelve in the rota of the care of a central sanctuary is without solid basis either in Israel or in the Greek sacral leagues.[64] We can say no more than that the number twelve was traditional and held onto both in Israel and Greece, even when it did not reflect reality. In the instances we can control, these leagues rallied to the cult of a particular god, the god of the confederation. Israel may be called the 'am yahweh, Moab the 'am kĕmōš (Num. 21:29), and Arab league, the 'ahl 'attar. The national gods of Edom (Qōs), Moab (Chemosh), Ammon (Milcom), and Israel (Yahweh) play a role typologically distinct from the gods of the city states. In the Phoenician and Aramaean city states there are city gods, triads of city gods, patron gods of the king who often differ from the chief city gods, but in both documentary evidence and in the onomastica, we find multiple state deities and personal deities. On the contrary, the onomastica of Israel, Ammon, Moab, and Edom are dominated to a remarkable degree by the name or epithet of the national deity: in Israel by Yahweh or 'El (of which Yahweh is the characteristic league epithet), Moab by Chemōš, an epithet of 'Attar, Edom by Qôs, probably an

---

[63] The annals of Assurbanipal record confrontations with what appear to be Arab leagues, notably the "league" of Attarsamayn ('Attar of the Heavens') and Qedar. The text reads LÚ a'/i'-lu ša ᵈAtarsamain who are listed with the Qedarites, Nabayataeans, and Išamme' (Ishmaelites?). Akkadian a'lu/i'lu has been connected with Akk. e'ēlu/ā'alu "to bind to an agreement" and derivatives or, with Old South Arabic 'hl, Lihyanite 'l "people," "cultic association," Hebrew 'ālā 'oath' (< 'hl), ultimately related to Akk ālu, "city," and Heb 'ōhel, "tent." In any case, the term in the Akkadian annals applies best to a large group of Arabs who call themselves after the name of a god. From context, "league," "sacral confederation" fits best. See CAD I.1. 374; M. Weippert, Die Kämpfe des assyrischen Königs Assurbanipal gegen die Araben, WO 7 (1973): 39-85, esp. 66-69.

[64] See most recently, Fritz R. Wüst, "Amphiktyonie, Eidgenossenshaft, Symmachie," Historia III (1954-55): 129-153; and N. K. Gottwald, The Tribes of Yahweh, pp. 887-889. For a review of Noth's "Amphictyony hypothesis," see C. H. J. DeGeus, The Tribes of Israel (Amsterdam: Van Garcum, 1976); R. Smend, "Zur Frage der altisraelitische Amphiktyonie," Evangelische Theologie 31 (1971): 623-630; and Gottwald, pp. 345-386.

epithet of Hadad, and Ammon by 'El (almost exclusively, although his epithet Milcom is well known).[65]

Fundamental to league institutions is Holy War. The *ḥerem* is known outside Israel, notably in Moab, and it probably was a central feature of the southern leagues. The leader in holy war is the Divine Warrior, and the *'am yiśrā'ēl* fights the wars of Yahweh.

The central cult object is the battle palladium, the Ark of the Covenant. The epic sings of the victory of the Divine Warrior in the Exodus and Conquest, and the festivals of the league recite and reenact these epic events preparatory to reaffirming covenant bonds. The tribal league functions in the first instance as a mechanism for a creation of a militia. The parts of animals distributed to call up the militia recall the cutting into pieces of the animals in the rite of cutting a covenant, and with it the implied threat that the unfaithful will be dismembered or maimed.[66]

Israel's covenant forms root in the institution of sacral leagues of the South. They are not a theological construct or a literary borrowing based on the model of international suzerainty treaties. The suzerainty treaty used in West Semitic societies is not without use in providing analogies to league covenants; both stem from social institutions rooted in a common West Semitic ethos. The covenant forms of the league constitute an extended kinship group, provide means for group action in war by the creation of a militia in times of crisis, provide a limited judicial system for mediation of intertribal disputes. Unity and order arise in the cult of the Divine Warrior and Judge, in the rituals of Holy War and in the pilgrim festivals, rituals and festivals which are only variants of one another, and in the judicial decisions of the deity, or his inspired surrogate.[67] The system is marked by patriarchal and egalitarian

---

[65]One may compare early Israelite usage in which El names dominate, later replaced by Yahweh names.

[66]See *CMHE*, p. 266 and references; and R. Polzin, "HWQY' and Covenant Institutions in Israel," *HTR* 62 (1969): 227-240; and Cross, "The Ammonite Oppression of the Tribes of God and Reuben," *The Hebrew and Greek Texts of Samuel*, ed. E. Tov (Jerusalem: Academon, 1980), p. 118, n.23.

[67]R. Smend, *Yahweh War and Tribal Confederacy*, trans. M. G. Rogers (Nashville: Abingdon, 1970) attempts to find separate origins of the Institution of Holy War and of sacral league. I find this further atomization of complex tradition unconvincing. On the tribal sayings in Judges 5, see *CMHE*, p. 235, n.74, where it is pointed out that *lm(h)* here as in Ugaritic can mean "verily" as well as "why." There is no reason to suppose that the tribes whose "blessings," that is, characteristic descriptions, are listed were absent from battle. The cycles of blessings in Genesis 49, Deuteronomy 33, of which Judges 5:14-18 is also an example, probably were fitted into many contexts (not as units but as a set), in review of the tribes. One may compare the Catalogue of Ships in the Iliad. What is intriguing in the review in the Song of Deborah is the omission of Judah.

features quite distinct from the feudal forms of kingship. However, it does not arise *de novo* in Israel's revolt against feudal overlords. Both sets of institutions are found, already mixed, in the myths of 'El at Ugarit.

5. Israel's ancient epic is not a historical narrative. On the other hand it is not a collection of fragments. Its essential shaping came not from the Yahwist, but from the singers of the early Israelite league. An understanding of the mode of epic composition, most developed in Homeric studies, gives new perspectives on the mechanics of oral composition and the transmission of epic traditions over long periods of time.[68]

There is no reason to doubt that Israelite epic traditions preserve accurate reflections of the social institutions, and especially the religious lore of the old time of which it sings. Divine epithets and patriarchal covenants in epic tradition go back to pre-Israelite times. The twelve-tribe league is the presumption of the epic, and must have existed from the early days of the Israelite settlement of the land. The institutions of holy war and covenant law are integral to the functioning of the confederation.

Traditions which link epic events to the Southland, especially to Sinai, rest ultimately on historical memory. Proto-Israel or the "Mosaic group" came into the land from the South. With them came social, religious, and military customs and institutions imported, so to speak, into feudal Canaan. The twelve-tribe league took classical form in the land in the twelfth century, but its roots were in the customs and experiences of those elements of Israel who came from the Southern mountains. Models of peasant revolt, or infiltration into the hill country from urban centers in Canaan, currently popular in explaining Israel's settlement in the land and which are not without merit in explaining aspects of the archaeological record, should not be permitted to obscure evidence, preserved in epic, of Israelite connections with the peoples of the South who moved between Se'ir, Midian, and Egypt at the end of the Late Bronze Age and the beginning of the Iron Age. There is every reason to contend that there was an attack from the South through Transjordan by the

---

[68]We have not had opportunity to discuss certain problems of detail in light of the technique of epic composition. Epic formulae cherish multiple names and epithets, no less in parallelistic formulae than in quantitative formulae. The alternate names Jacob/Israel, Esau/Edom, Sinai/Horeb and Se'ir/ Teman arise inevitably in epic verse. The Achaeans, Argives, and Danaeans in the Iliad are merely alternate names. The attempt to see Jacob and Israel as unrelated names linked only late in tradition is wrong-headed I believe, and care must be taken in partitioning documents according to choice of one name in a name pair. To be sure, in turning poetry to prose, there was a tendency in a source to prefer a single name or epithet. I do not propose to scrap the partition of the Pentateuchal sources based in part on different preferences in usage. Neither do I propose to look in one place for Sinai, in another for Horeb. There is difficulty enough in locating one "mountain of god."

"*am* Yahweh," and that they formed the nucleus around which the early Israelite league took shape and from whom "All-Israel" took their identity and institutions. This is the testimony of the archaic hymns and the historical basis of the early epic. Traditions of the fathers linked in kinship bonds all elements of Israel. The 'El of cults and sanctuaries of the land was identified with 'El of the South, Yahweh the Divine Warrior. Israel's epic drew on older epic cycles in dynamic change, molding an epic which was forged into its main lines shortly after the establishment of the league in Canaan: covenants with the Fathers in the land of Canaan, and their migration to Egypt, Exodus and creation of the nation at Sinai, the return to the land and its conquest.

In its life in the cultus of the league the epic acquired accretions and variants in its recompositions by bards and heirophants, and developed multiforms in the festivals of the pilgrimage shrines. With the transition to monarchy, and the breakdown of league institutions, the epic went through further transformations to fit new settings and perform new functions, gaining further accretions and losing its close cultic connections. The final deposit was the great, conflate amalgam of many ages we call the Pentateuch.

Chapter III

DOCTRINE BY MISADVENTURE
BETWEEN THE ISRAELITE SOURCE AND THE BIBLICAL HISTORIAN *

Baruch Halpern
York University

(The lengthened shadow of a man
Is history, said Emerson
Who had not seen the silhouette
Of Sweeney straddled in the sun.)
T. S. Eliot

Of Roman history, great Niebuhr's shown
'Tis nine-tenths lying. Faith, I wish 'twere known,
Ere we accept great Niebuhr as a guide,
Wherein he blundered and how much he lied.
Salder Bupp
Ambrose Bierce

Few of us would admit to being historical determinists. Many of us are, however, in that we are physical determinists. We know not where, but our arrows fall to earth. And if we knew the nature, dimensions, position, direction, velocity and acceleration of every particle and non-particle in the universe, and all the characteristics of their interactions, we would be able fully to apprehend reality; we would be able to diagnose the past, to understand the present, to predict the future—touch wood. If we could tame the irrational—the scientifically undomesticated—the resultant sealed scientific system would be the eschaton of human understanding.

The empirical scientist works toward this positivistic end. He isolates determinants and determinands and generalizes the results. The generality is then hypostatized into a particularity falsely or provisionally supposed to exist independently, in itself. The abstraction, in turn, is applied to other transactions in different contexts. This, in application, is science's glory. Our

---

*I should like to thank Professors P. Swarney, K. S. Sacks, T. N. D. Mettinger and J. Kaufman for their encouragement and various suggestions relating to this study.

41

automobiles limp along trusting in Internal Combustion. But because they are limited, and isolated from the total context of all physical interactions, scientific theories are really bad approximations, reductions to mathematical formulae of a fuller, less mathematical reality. In short, the true deficiency of the scientific method is the scientist's inability—and due to the burgeoning of scientific disciplines it is a burgeoning inability[1]—to know, quantify and enter into calculation all the factors in the universe in their relation to one another. In a vacuum, force equals mass times acceleration, in theory. But what good is theory in a vacuum when we live concretely in a context? No one whose life was on the line would want the engineer of his vehicle calculating Force as mass times acceleration, at least in our universe. If one lives on the edge of application—if one sails for India across a flat world—precision in the quantification of all impinging factors is of the most central importance.

This is plainest in the successive failure of all prescriptive social science to cope with any contemporary problem. When economists, for example, prescribe rational remedies for rational economies, they treat patients that do not exist for badly misdiagnosed illnesses. Like his natural scientific counterpart, the economist neglects important factors in areas outside his sphere of competence—factors such as special pleading, gross incompetence and sunspots. A statistician might argue that these factors are irrelevant, or can be accounted for in gross "fudge factor" terms. They are, in fact, as relevant as anything the economist does take into account, given only the interdependence of all particular matter. Thus, in order to grasp reality in generalities, economics and the schematic social sciences reduce reality: This is science as seance, science at its most immoral. Only when the social sciences have become natural sciences, only when people are understood as the intermediaries of photons, quarks and neutrinos—as they really are—will the social scientists be able to quantify and yet particularize this world.[2]

---

[1] See G. Steiner, *Language and Silence. Essays on Language, Literature and the Inhuman* (New York: Atheneum, 1976) 14-21, 34-35.

[2] See N. Wiener, *The Human Use of Human Beings. Cybernetics and Society* (2nd ed.; Garden City: Doubleday, 1956) 10-11 on the effect such considerations have had on physics. Contrast the following remarks of Milton Friedman:

> A hypothesis is important if it "explains much by little," that is, if it abstracts the common and crucial elements from the mass of complex and detailed circumstances surrounding the phenomena to be explained and permits valid predictions on the basis of them alone. To be important, therefore, a hypothesis must be descriptively false in its assumptions; it takes account of and accounts for, none of the many other attendant circumstances, since its very success shows them to be irrelevant to the phenomena to be explained.
>
> (from "The Methodology of Positive Economics," in *Essays in*

But nothing could be less satisfying than such a set of chemical and physical formulae interplexed and iteratively sorted by computer. Once typed in, and with JRSTs and JUMPs to govern them, these can satisfy the compulsion of those who need to know, really Need to Know. But they cannot help people in their daily interactions with other people, in their continual confrontations with supra-particular reality. Ironically, science as a success can mean nothing to the living individual. Only as a failure, as unfinished business, can scientific theory contribute to social skills. It is because we are so far from the scientific nirvana, and because that nirvana would be so meaningless to us as people, that so few of us can be historical determinists.[3]

Until chemical formulae can capture complex reality, and until some modern-day Edward Fitzgerald or genetic engineer of the quantitative idiom can render chemical formulae useful, humanists are stuck with another mode of apprehension and impartment (Bernard Malamud's nagging reminders in *A New Life* indicate how far this medium carries a critical message). Metaphor, as Ernst Cassirer observed, is the essence both of our expression and of our thought.[4] Metaphor is to science what mysticism is to pragmatism: gapping

---

Positive Economics [Chicago: University of Chicago, 1953], reprinted in *Readings in the Philosophy of the Social Sciences*, ed. R. Brodbeck [New York: Macmillan, 1967] 508-527).
Friedman rides a lame horse when speaking of "success"; it would improve his case if a single macroeconomic theory could be singled out for this distinction. And if "success" is one's criterion (as it is Friedman's), then one should bet on red at roulette: if this play wins, one should keep betting on red; only when the play loses can a shortcoming in the theory be detected. Friedman sells verisimilitude too short here. For example, is election in a year whose last digit is zero really the "common and crucial" element in the deaths in office of American presidents? To make such a claim (as Friedman does) is to err on the side of alchemy (can one get the gold of reductionist insight from the dross of reality?) or mysticism or metaphor while claiming to champion the colors of science. See also S. Freud, *The Psychogenesis of a Case of Homosexuality in a Woman* (1920), in *The Complete Psychological Works of Sigmund Freud, Standard Edition* (v. 18; London: Hogarth, 1958) 167-168. Freud denies the predictive value of psychoanalytical method and characterizes it as purely descriptive. This is precisely the point. Social "sciences" are basically categories and terminologies without either experimental or experiential basis. They are valid taxonymically, not empirically, in their present state.

[3] Cf. R. G. Collingwood, *An Autobiography* (Oxford: Oxford University, 1970) 115. Collingwood's view of history as a field contributing to human knowledge of human nature, and as distinct in this respect as "the science of human affairs," is well founded and most congenial.

[4] E. Cassirer, *An Essay on Man* (New Haven: Yale University, 1944) 109-110.

our ignorance and inarticulation, it transposes reality not into a schematic bed of Sodom, but into an equally complex, layered and plumbable world. While deterministic theory inevitably reduces and castrates reality, metaphor can capture it whole. Metaphor does not define; it rather conveys an intuitive impression calculated to cut to the generative heart of a question, without excluding or even ignoring the rest. In just this sense, one learns more of language from Joyce, more of humanity from Freud, than B. F. Skinner or Noam Chomsky could hope to teach. No social scientific number cruncher holds a candle to Balzac.

But metaphor presents us with the same problem as does reality. Interpreters reduce it, often to one dimension. Successful metaphor must predispose its hearer to reject literal interpretation, to seek behind the words themselves the meaning being expressed. To grasp metaphor, one must inflate it, use it as a medium—and nothing more than a medium—to grasp an underlying, equally profound reality. This, too, is the job of the historian, the potential value of the social sciences, the merit of the Annales approach and the point of archaeology. One must locate the sources against a real context in order to inflate their verbal remains.

In biblical studies, we sometimes forget that the historians who produced our sources struggled with the same problems. On rare occasions, scholars produce studies of how historians adjudicated *conflicts* among their informants. Common wisdom has it that most authors would, like the rabbis selecting the text types that compose the canon, reject one version in favor of another; they did not, as the modern historian must, create a more likely, deduced but unattested reconstruction.[5] This is not, strictly speaking, accurate. Some of the succeeding examples will indicate that harmonization, rather than selection, was a dominant method of reconstruction from written sources (it most probably underlies the phenomenon of the Pentateuch's assembly as well). Harmonization does involve a rudimentary hypothetical-deductive procedure. But the greatest Israelite historian whose work has survived was explicitly conscious of the difficulty of dealing with conflicting testimony. The author of the Davidic biography, a circumstantial character history that makes Suetorius' *Tiberius* look like a comic book, takes his reader through David's development from shepherd to therapon to exiled mercenary to statesman to leader to victor to ruler. He traces the growth of a personal lust, an independence of the law, that results in murder and adultery; he imputes to it David's Lear-like status, and the tragedy of the old man unable to hold his own either politically or in bed.

---

[5] This is almost always the response to inquiries on the subject among the scholars of my acquaintance. However, I cannot find any instances in the field literature of a scholar arguing this (or any other) position on the issue. Presumably, my sources' unanimity derives from some hoary folk tradition.

This historian twice raises the issue of contradictory testimony in his account. In the first instance, after Absalom has murdered his half-brother, Amnon, the report reaches David that "Absalom has smitten all the king's sons; not one of them is left." David panics. But Jonadab ben-Shima, the king's cousin, dismisses the rumor, noting that Absalom had had it in for Amnon, and for Amnon alone, ever since Amnon raped Absalom's full-sister, Tamar. Shortly thereafter, Jonadab's deduction is corroborated by the sight of David's other sons fleeing toward the capital (2 Sam 13:28-36). Here, special knowledge (Jonadab's and David's) leads to a critical stance toward an exaggerated claim. The evidence in currency is tested against the background of the parties involved.

The second instance is more complex. A retainer accuses Jonathan's son, Meribbaal (Mephibosheth), of complicity in Absalom's revolt. David examines Meribbaal, whose lameness, dishevelment and counteraccusation all stand him in good stead. The historian, thus, implies but does not stand on Meribbaal's innocence. David then divides the baby of Meribbaal's estate between the master and the servant (2 Sam 16:1-4; 19:18,25-31). Here, the testimony of one witness is counterbalanced both by Meribbaal's denial and by the circumstantial evidence of Meribbaal's handicap and appearance. The case is inconclusive, and David must seek by his compromise to do the least injustice rather than justice itself. The incident would provide a piquing starting-point for inquiry into Israelite juridical procedures and ideals; its primary value is as testimony to a penetrating historiographic consciousness.

To this pair of cases, it would be marvellous to be able to add the famous act of Solomon with regard to the two harlots in 1 Kgs 3:16-27. In this pericope, without special knowledge, and with evidence that seems even more impenetrable than that confronted by David in Meribbaal's case, Solomon generates his own, compelling critical method. In just the way that Hume insisted the natural scientist must put "nature" to the torture, in just the way that the critical historian must, Solomon racks his sources. He thereby extorts the conclusive circumstantial evidence that eluded his father in other instances. Were this tale the work of the historian in 2 Samuel, that author would have proceeded from a case of judgment based on external knowledge to one of judgment based on criteria internal to the evidence (and generating a result much like harmonization) to one of judgment based on an active, critical stance by which the evidence is put to proof. Unfortunately, the last account probably stems from an author other than that of the first two.

These are not the only texts in which Israelite authors address, even if indirectly, the question of evidence (e.g., Deut 18:21-22 and any text involving the certification of divine intent). Yet the Israelite historian's approach to evidence has rarely, if ever, been addressed. And how the Israelite historian resolved differences between sources has never been studied in any systematic fashion. Scholars have, of course, dealt with the dependence of given texts on other given texts. P, for example, and the authors of Deuteronomy 1-11 are widely supposed to have had J and E before them. Unfortunately, only rarely do we learn from these instances about the mechanics of Israelite historical reconstruction. The issue is clouded by notions of variant traditions, theological reforms, and so forth. Historically, the biblical critic has thought most often in terms either of fabrication or of "inner-biblical exegesis."[6] Because we think in terms of editors, not historians—for reasons that have historically been sufficient—even the most basic historiographic questions rarely come into issue.

No question could be more basic for understanding the ancient historian's practices than that of how he approached his sources—not only with what skepticism he regarded them, but how he read or heard them in the first place. Because we must assume the good faith of our informants—these days even Herodotus is less the father of lies than a middleman of them—it is central to examine the nature and the frequency of our ancient colleagues' misprisions. This is the more true of biblical historigraphy because of the complex source- and redaction-critical problems, cross-references and rehearsals that lace the canon. The problem is worth addressing through an impressionistic (and so metaphorical) selection of cases in biblical literature.

*   *   *   *   *   *   *   *

For this purpose, one of the most fertile texts in the Bible is Judges 5, the song of Deborah, and Judges 4, its prose companion-piece. There are a few discrepancies between these chapters. The key one is that Judges 5 has at least six, and probably ten, Israelite tribes in array for the fight against Sisera;[7] Judges 4 claims that only Zebulun and Naphtali fought. In biblical studies, this problem has evoked the response it would have among the ancients: some scholars side with the prose, on the Viconian ground that it claims less for Israel (though one may argue that having fewer tribes defeat the same number of Canaanites would actually represent the greater claim for an ancient Israelite); other scholars side with the poem, because it is older (despite Vico's stricture that antiquity is less a guarantee of accuracy than is good, critical reading).[8] One scholar only—Arthur Weiser—has attempted to harmonize the

---

[6]This term carries varied implications. For a historically important study, see N. Sarna, "Psalm 89: A Study in Inner Biblical Exegesis," in *Biblical and Other Studies*, ed. A. Altmann (Cambridge: Harvard University, 1963) 29-46. Note also H. H. Hertzberg, "Die Nachgeschichte alttestamentlicher Texte innerhalb des Alten Testaments" BZAW 66 (1936) 110-121.

[7]Judg 5:11-18. See F. M. Cross, *Canaanite Myth and Hebrew Epic* (Cambridge: Harvard University, 1973) 235 n. 74 for MT *lmh* in vv 16,17 as the asseverative with *ma* enclitic. Cf. P. D. Miller, *The Divine Warrior in Early Israel* (*HSM* 5; Camridge: Harvard University, 1973) 96. My own view is that it is better to take the word as negative with enclitic.

[8]E.g., in favor of the poem, J. Wellhausen, *Israelitische und Jüdische Geschichte* (Berlin: G. Reimer, 1894) 20-22; R. de Vaux, *The Early History*

versions. He suggests that the tribes in Judges 5 are actually at a sanctuary, to the gates of which Judg 5:11 refers, celebrating the victory recorded in 5:18-22.[9] Unfortunately, Weiser's effort violates the plain sense of 5:13-15 at least. In harmonizing, Weiser has tried to make the poetry conform with the less tractable prose.

In short, there are three schools of thought on this issue: that the prose is right, that the poem is right, and that both are right. Instructive is the case of the Air Canada airliner which screeched to a dead halt seconds after touching down at Toronto International Airport. Coffee cups, drinks, hand-luggage, stewardesses—the whole cabin went flying toward the cockpit. When everything had crashed back down, the co-pilot turned to the pilot. "Gosh!" he said, "That's the shortest runway we've *ever* been on." "Yeah," rejoined the pilot, "But look how *wide* it is!" Perhaps, like the pilot, we would do better to adopt a different line of approach.

In his commentary on Judges, R. Boling observes that the prose account of Sisera's murder (Judg 4:18-21) turns on a misprision of its poetic parallel. Judg 5:26 ("She sent her hand to the peg, her right hand to the workers' club") describes Yael grabbing a blunt instrument with which to cosh the Canaanite; the poem includes one implement, one hand, and a parallel (or repetitive) structure. The prose historian erred by reifying the parallelism. He concluded that Yael had used two implements and both her hands.[10] He takes Judg 5:26 literally (see Figure B).

The historian's problem, as I have argued elsewhere (see n. 15), was probably that the term "peg" *(yātēd)* in standard Hebrew usage nearly always refers to some sort of nail (so in 13 of 15 occurrences in HB).[11] Taking it to denote a (tent-)peg, the historian of Judges 4 naturally looked for and found a mallet in the succeeding stich ("the workers' club" [i.e., the "peg"]). Though commentators convinced that goat's milk is a soporific (there is no evidence whatsoever that the ancient Israelite or Canaanite thought so) persistently deny it, the same relationship probably obtains between the poetic and prose versions of Sisera's drink (again, Figure B). The poem states that Sisera asked for and was given a beverage: the author of the prose has taken the triple parallelism (water//milk//ghee) in Judg 5:27 literally.

The prose historian found some support for his reconstruction of the murder in Judg 5:26, "she splintered, she pierced his spitter *(rqh)*":[12] the

of Israel (Philadelphia: Westminster, 1978) 729-730; for the prose, M. Noth, *The History of Israel* (2nd ed.; New York: Harper, 1960) 150-151.

[9] "Das Debora-Lied" *ZAW* 71 (1959) 67-97.

[10] Boling, *Judges* (*AB* 6A; Garden City: Doubleday, 1975) 98.

[11] The other exception is Deut 23:14, where it appears as a staff (throwing-stick?) that could be used for digging (cf. Num 21:18). The meaning probably became specialized when the implement ceased to be a standard part of the Israelite's battle-kit.

[12] For *rqh* as "spitter," cf. *rqq*, "to expectorate," *yrq*, "green, yellow,"

spike penetrated the *rqh*, and the prose records the fact duly (4:21). The "piercing," after all, confirmed the inference that a hammer and nail were the murder weapons (though the poet meant only that the club broke through to the *rqh*). But this led to a problem. Why, one may imagine the historian wondering, did Sisera stand still while Yael held a peg to his head and reared back with the cudgel? In the poetic narrative, Yael bludgeons Sisera as he drinks; Sisera falls to his knees and collapses. But with the more complex prose assassination came difficulties in staging to which the historian needed to respond. His initial recourse was indicated both by logic and by physics: Sisera was lying down (to absorb the blow); furthermore, he was under a cover, asleep, and neither saw nor felt Yael lurking sinister with the lethal tent-peg. Yet this solution produced a second problem: why did Judg 5:27 seem to describe Sisera falling if *(ex hypothesi)* he was already lying down asleep? Only when he comes to this last verse in the Yael sequence (5:27), at the end of his own account (4:21d) does the prose author confront the problem. He interprets the verbal sequence in 5:27 to refer to Sisera's having collapsed earlier in exhaustion (see Figure B). Boling, who caught the essence of the enigma when dealing with the peg and hammer, actually follows the prose as a guide to the poetry on this point, even though that reading violates the poetic sequence.[13] In the poetry, Sisera collapses not from exhaustion, but from Yael's blow (cf., incidentally, CTA 2.4:18-30 with *šbyn* as "our captive," on which see in turn Judg 5:12).

In short, the whole of the prose rendition of the murder can be traced from the single misapprehension in 4:21a-c. Given that one reification of the ode's metaphor, the rest of the reconstruction follows from successive questions and responses. Alternate explanations (such as independent traditions, and common sources) are not to be excluded on a rigorously logical basis. But the fact that the entire murder sequence can be educed from the reification of a metaphor and the problems it entailed is strong argument on grounds both of economy and of realism. Proceeding from his literalization of one couplet (this motivated by a semantic problem and shored up by a nearby verb), the author of Judges 4 misconstrued his source-text wholly.

What would be the result were we to apply the same principle to the question of which tribes fought? What if the prose historian read the poetry in the same slavish fashion that produced his idiosyncratic account of Sisera's killing? The evidence is reasonably clear: Except for Zebulun and Naphtali, the tribes are said to have come only to the gates, or "down with warriors"; though the poet plainly means to say that others did join the muster, at

---

yrqrq, "(?greenish) yellow glitter." Certainly, "temple" is not a translation consonant with the instances in Cant 4:3; 6:7.

[13] Boling, *Judges* 98. His rejection of MT "he was tired" is in my view unwarranted, therefore. Cf. Wellhausen, *Prolegomena to the History of Israel* (Cleveland: Meridian, 1957) 240-241.

least,[14] only verse 18 claims that any tribes risked death. The prose historian reports the involvement only of Zebulun and Naphtali because these are the only tribes whose presence in battle is explicitly mentioned in Judges 5. He read the song of Deborah in much the way that Weiser did. Thus, using the prose as a guide, Weiser uncovered not the thought of the poet, but that of the prose historian in interpreting the poetry. This is of course exactly what one would expect.

One other problem in these chapters merits brief attention and further indicates the dependence of the prose on the poetry. Judges 5 identifies Sisera as the leader of the army of the kings of Canaan (vv 19-20). The prose historian, were he looking for a head of the kings of Canaan, could have found one in Israel's tradition only in Joshua 11 (esp. v 10), where Yabin, king of Hazor, appears as the leader of the only other coalition of all Canaanite kings in biblical literature. What is more, Baraq fought, according to Judg 5:18-19, *'al mê megiddô* and *'al merômê šādeh*. Joshua's battle with Yabin occurs *'al mê mērôm*, which reads like a conflation of the two (and probably is). How does the prose historian identify Sisera? As the leader of the armies of Yabin, king of Hazor. As in Judg 4:5 (Deborah's Palm; cf. Gen 35:8), the historian supplies background data by rather a haphazard form of association. In this instance, however, he may not be so far from the mark. Many of his modern successors have mooted the identity of the two battles he here seems to telescope. Probably, the Joshua pericope had already take some of its shape from the song of Deborah by the time the prose historian came to it as a reference.

Judges 4 presents an instance of an Israelite historian wrestling with a source. The evidence, which considerably exceeds the limited sample presented above, and which I have explored elsewhere,[15] indicates that he was almost exclusively dependent on Judges 5 for particulars of the Deborah story. And his intentions were nothing short of the best. But his tendency here and there was to seize on a given problem, on a certain question that cropped up, and to solve it by the most agonizingly literal attention to his source-text. He did not invent; he merely reified the text, treated it as though it were some legal deposit intended to be read as it was written.

There is one other biblical narrative poem accompanied by a parallel prose account—the song of the sea. Exodus 15 celebrates the casting of the Egyptians into a sea at least four times (vv 1c, 4-5, 8-10, 12; the disposition of vv 6-7 is uncertain). Verses 8-10 read:

> At the wind of your nostrils the waters were heaped up;
> The currents stood like a *nēd*;
> The depths churned in the heart of the sea.

---

[14] This does not necessarily mean that they fought—see Judges 20. Still, the implication is that they appeared on the field for the battle.

[15] I have assembled the evidence and the argument in greater depth and detail in "The Resourceful Israelite Historian. The Song of Deborah and Israelite Historiography," forthcoming in *HTR*.

The enemy said, "I will pursue . . . . "

You blew with your wind; sea covered them;
They plummeted like lead in the mighty waters.

As F. M. Cross has argued, this may reflect a capsizing at sea. The song does not record Israel's crossing of a sea or any division of waters. In this respect, and in its style, syntax and morphology, it antedates the prose versions.[16] And the language of the prose versions indicates their heavy dependence on the poem.[17]

Still, the prose versions differ considerably from the poem and from each other; and while Cross's interest was absorbed predominantly by the song, ours now lies with the prose hermeneutic. J, in Exodus 14, camps the Egyptians on the seashore for the night, and the Israelites nearby. YHWH drives the sea back all night long with an east wind, and, in the morning, lets loose, drenching the Egyptians fleeing toward the sea from their camp.[18] How did J arrive at this reconstruction? His Israel, we may take it, fled on foot, with the song's armored cavalry in pursuit (15:1,3,9). He found the waters heaped up in verse 8, along with a wind to heap them; he found the sea covering the Egyptians after a wind-blast in verse 10 (and verse 5); and, since the "earth" swallowed the Egyptians in verse 12, it was a matter of elementary deduction to propose clogged chariot wheels delaying the Egyptians while a sea driven back by the night breeze returned to full strength at dawn. In fact, the J reconstruction, physics alone excepted, is of the highest quality; it would be strong were it not for the implication of 15:10 that the wind had immediate effect. J is farfetched but tries hard to do his sources justice.

The P reconstruction of the "Reed Sea Event" is the one familiar in every home and the stuff of screen spectaculars. Cross observes that P plays on mythic and ritual divisions of waters.[19] For P, the crossing was a new creation, filled no doubt with reverberations of cosmogonic conflict in Near

---

[16] Cross, CMHE, 121-138.

[17] The argument to this point is an extensive one. As a result, I must ask the indulgence of referring the reader to a forthcoming monograph, The Emergence of Israel in Canaan (chap. 1).

[18] J in Exod 14:5-7,8bc,10bc,11-14,19-20,21bc,24-25,27bcd,30; P in Exod 14:1-4,8a,9,10ad,15-18,21ad,22-23,26,27a,28-29,31. The division is particularly uncertain in vv 8-10 (though it is marked in part by the fact that P portrays Israel as encamped at that point, while J has Israel on the march). But any remaining E text (see B. S. Childs, The Book of Exodus. A Critical, Exegetical Commentary [OTL; Philadelphia: Westminster, 1974] 218-221 for a reasonable set of suggestions [the grounds, though, for assigning v 7 to E are not so compelling as the other considerations Childs injects into the discussion) is at least well hidden. There is no real call to find E here at all. Simple variants may now be riddling the text.

[19] Cross, CMHE, 112-120, 132-144.

Eastern and Israelite myth (but sanitized in P's theology). But P, like J, was also a historian. What conditioned the transition from historical lyric in Exodus 15 to mythic narrative in Exodus 14? The interpretation of the term, *nēd*, to which Cross points as a possible catalyst for P's innovations, is not quite enough to explain P's dissent from J. More likely, the answer lies in a misprision of Exod 15:13-17, the end of the song of the sea.

After at least four rehearsals of YHWH's victory at the sea, the author of Exodus 15 turns to describe Israel's migration and conquest:

> You guided in your fidelity the people you redeemed;
> You conducted them in your might to your holy pasturage.
> The peoples heard; they shook;
> Writhing seized the inhabitants of Philistia.
> Then the commanders of Edom were discomfited.
> The leaders of Moab—trembling seized them.
> All the inhabitants of Canaan melted away.
> There fell upon them dread and fear;
> At the size of your arm they were dumb as a stone,
> So that your people crossed over, YHWH,
> So that the people you acquired/created crossed over.
> You brought them and planted them in the mount of your posses-
> sion, etc.

(vv 13-17)

Rabbinic commentators and modern agree that the reference is to the conquest. The dispute is whether the "mount of your possession" is Jerusalem. In Ps 78:52-55, the answer is unequivocally negative:

> He moved his people like sheep,
> And piloted them like a flock in the steppe.
> He guided them securely, and they did not fear;
> And their enemies, the sea covered.
> He brought them to his holy territory,
> The mount that his right hand acquired/created.
> He expelled from before them peoples . . . ,

and settled the Israelites in. Shortly after, the poet says, YHWH set up shop in Shiloh (v 60). So, in a pre-exilic Jerusalemite text,[20] which here repeatedly echoes Exodus 15,[21] vv 13-17 are read as an account of the conquest, with no reference to Jerusalem.

---

[20]On Psalm 78, see now R. J. Clifford, "In Zion and David a New Beginning: An Interpretation of Psalm 78," in *Traditions in Transformation: Turning-Points in Biblical Faith. Essays presented to Frank Moore Cross on the occasion of his sixtieth birthday*, eds. B. Halpern and J. D. Levenson (Winona Lake: Eisenbrauns, 1981) 121-141.

[21]E.g., the use of *nḥḥ*; 78:53b reflects Exod 15:10ab with the direct antecedent "enemy" in 15:9a. Ps 78:52-53a = 15:13 in content and 78:55 =

But if we assume that P took Exod 15:13-17 mistakenly, but not unnaturally, as a fifth recital—after four clear recitals—of the victory at the Reed Sea, and read, as we might reasonably think he would be inclined to do, the terms "mountain of possession" and "sanctuary of my lord" as references to *Sinai*; and, in fact, thus attenuated the anachronism of having Moses describing the conquest and foundation not of Jerusalem, but of Shiloh—then the rest of P's scenario in Exodus 14 follows logically. Having inherited a drying-up of part of the sea from J and misreading Exod 15:16 to imply that Israel crossed the Reed Sea instead of the Jordan, P suddenly needed two heaps, two walls of water, to allow his crossing. He provided them, took 15:12 ("you stretched forth your right hand; earth swallowed them") and instantiated it in Moses' acting as YHWH's medium (14:27a,28), and so forth (generalizing Moses' action for water-work, e.g.). He reasoned further that the sea divided because it was the only alley of escape (14:2-3), exhibiting a sense of drama rarely ascribed to him. P's reconstruction follows from Exodus 15 and J, literally read, and from a grasp of spectacle, as well as from mythopoeic thought.

Ironically, Psalm 78 provides confirmation. The psalmist, who later construes Exod 15:13-17 correctly, twice alludes to these verses (with the verbs *nḥh, 'br*) while rehearsing P's account of the Reed Sea event in 78:13-14; a third allusion, Ps 78:13b, is the most direct quotation of Exod 15:8b in biblical literature.[22] Like Judges 4, which conflates Baraq's victory with its displacement upward to Joshua, Psalm 78 conflates the source-text (Exodus 15) with derivative, and in part incorrect, interpretations of it. It is worth mentioning that the psalm's account establishes that the P reconstruction was already current in pre-exilic Jerusalem. Isa 11:15-16 reflects the same fact (cf. Am 8:8-9, for J).

*   *   *   *   *   *   *   *   *

15:14-16 in content; note also the use of "territory," and *z* with *qnh* (these are the only instances of the juxtaposition in HB); and *gbwl qdšw* (78:54) and *nwh qdšk* (15:13). See further points of contact in Clifford, "In Zion and David" 134 n. 25.

[22] *nṣbw kmw nd nzlym* (Exod 15:8b); *wyṣb mym kmw nd* (Ps 78:13b). Only here does the verb *nṣb* appear with this simile. See further the relatively unusual lexemes *thwmwt* and *nwzlym* in Ps 78:15,16. There, they are applied to the "water from the rock" tradition. Both appear, however, in Exod 15:8, the verse the psalmist has just cited. Presumably, the psalmist has kept them in mind as he moved to the next item on his agenda. This is about as strong an argument for dependence (the verbs are not elsewhere applied to the "water from the rock" stories) as one can imagine. Inverse dependence remains a formal possibility. But since neither *thwmwt*, which refers to ocean depths or primeval depths most often, nor *nwzlym* ("flowers, currents") really exhibits any organic connection with the "water from the rock" notion, it would require either a very fresh interpretation or a formidable disregard for probability to defend that position.

In Exodus 14 and Judges 4, we have looked in on three historians at work. Their constructions seem to have been motivated by a genuine historical concern. Their reconstructions were compelled by their understandings of the evidence and the world. Their interpolations—Sisera, for example, in Judges 4, adds to his request for beverage the words, "for I thirst"—their interpolations into the evidence are not fanciful, not arbitrary, just as the modern historian's must not be. They also pose problems to themselves: who is Sisera? How did Yael manage that awkward assault with tent-peg and hammer? What does Exodus 15 mean when it refers to YHWH's wind-blasts? How did Israel manage to cross the sea? This *is* history. But the biblical historians do stumble, as do we, on occasional problems in semantics or literary modality, or on deficiencies in historical imagination.

Our awareness of these conditions can serve the modern historical enterprise in various ways. For example, in Judg 9:2, Abimelek pleads that he is the Shechemites' bone and flesh. This is a statement of candidacy for kingship, most probably in conformity with the "law of the king" in Deut 17:14-20, which crops up three times with respect to David's campaigns for the throne (2 Sam 5:1-3 = 1 Chr 11:1-3; 1 Chr 12:23-41; and 2 Sam 19:11-13; elsewhere Gen 29:4; cf. Gen 2:22); it is repudiated in the slogan, "We have no part in David nor possession in the son of Jesse" (2 Sam 20:1; 1 Kgs 12:16; 2 Chr 10:16).[23] Further, in Judges 9:18, a character derogates Abimelek as "the son of [Jerubbaal's] maidservant." This expression is sometimes used figuratively (as Ps 86:16; 116:16). It is entirely possible that the author in Judg 9:3 and in Judg 8:31 has made Abimelek the son of Gideon's Shechemite concubine because he took these texts literally.[24] Similarly, one cannot help but wonder whether Aaron was in early materials regarded as Moses' brother. The blood-brotherhood of P could easily derive by interpretation from Aaron's status as a "brother Levite" in J (Exod 4:14). Certainly, it is by metaphorical brotherhood (and theoretical equality at some level) in Israel that the "tribes" become sons of Jacob, or "clans" sons of a tribe; ultimately the ethnic brotherhood of the Israelites (as in Deuteronomy) became the physical brotherhood of the tribal eponyms. Routinely in Israelite prosopography, geographic and political kinship metaphor is reified by interpreters.[25] It should be noted that the same applies to names and epithets in transmission: Gual ben-Ebed ("the despised son of a slave," vocalized with Josephus) and Zabul ("prince, commissioner") in Judges 9, Shemebed ("his name is lost"), along with others in

[23] See my "The Uneasy Compromise: Israel between League and Monarchy," in *Traditions in Transformation* 82.

[24] I first suggested this in "The Rise of Abimelek ben-Jerubbaal" *HAR* 2 (1978) 90 n. 28.

[25] For other instances, see "Israelite Historian." A prime case, explored there, is Jephthah in Judg 11:1-3: Jephthah has assumed a genealogy by virtue of his location and profession.

Genesis 14:2, and the corrupt liturgy in 1 Chr 25:4 (from $\underline{h}^a n \bar{a} n \hat{\imath}$ forward), which has produced at least five and perhaps as many as nine sons of Heman, are some examples.[26]

Further reaching are the implications of Israelite reification for tradition-history. Take the city Salem in Genesis 14. AV and the Samaritans misread Gen 33:18 ("Jacob came intact [$\check{s}lm$] to the city of Shechem," their "Jacob came to Salem, the city of Shechem") to prove that Shechem is in point. But Ps 76:3 and most other commentators take the town to be Jerusalem. Now, the author of Genesis 14 is an antiquarian, fascinated by names to a degree unequalled except among the compilers of commercial mailing-lists; he understands Salem to be the antique name of whatever town he has in mind, probably Jerusalem (cf. 14:2,3,8,17). But outside of the derivative in Psalm 76, Jerusalem is never elsewhere called Salem. I suspect that this antiquarian made an error: in perusing cuneiform documents, he or one of his sources found the name Jerusalem, $\acute{u}$-ru-sa-li-mu, characteristically prefaced with the logogram uru, "city." He read this in one text (probably lacking the logogram) not as (uru) $urusalimu$, "the city, Jerusalem," but as uru, $salimu$, "the city, Salem." There is a graphic problem involved in this reconstruction; but it is far from insuperable.[27] The solution would clarify not just an onomastic question, but also the scholastic character of Genesis 14.[28]

---

[26] It is possible that the last are real names arranged for mnemonic purposes. Still, the phenomenon is widespread enough in genealogies and tales (Nabal in 1 Samuel 25; Benay in 1 Chr 24:23) that one need not stand on any single instance.

[27] See EA 287:46 for URU $\acute{u}$-ru-sa-lim^{ki}, EA 287:61; 290:15 for KUR $\acute{u}$-ru-sa-lim^{ki} ("the land/territory/district of [the city of] Jerusalem"). As the Amarna evidence illustrates, scribes sometimes sounded the logograms, so that the historian or one of his sources may have heard $\acute{u}$-ru as URU. Cf., for example, Rib-Addi's A.ŠÀ-ia $a\check{s}\check{s}ata$ $\check{s}a$ la $muta$ $ma\check{s}il$ $a\check{s}\check{s}im$ $bali$ $eri\check{s}im$ (EA 74:17; 75:15; 81:37; 90:42). There are other cases; but the principle remains the same. In the case of the pun in EA 85:19 ($yuballit$ ÌR-$\check{s}u$ $\grave{u}$ URU-$\check{s}u$), the URU sign may be meant to be sounded as '$\hat{\imath}r$, however.

[28] Note the names in v 2: $br^{\prime}$ and $br\check{s}^{\prime}$ could be construed as "in evil," the latter perhaps as a playful parallel for the former, which occurs as a real name. $\check{s}m^{\prime}bd$ is, as noted above, "the name is lost." $\check{s}n^{\prime}b$ could be "hated by his father." Moreover, the detail, particularly geographic, is overwhelming, esp. in its supposedly antique character (but v 14 Dan, not Laish, is a slip). Note that in vv 5-6 the Rephaim appear also in Deut 2:11,20; the Zuzim (if Qimhi is correct, and his instinct is unerring, in identifying them with the Zamzummim) appear in Deut 2:20; the Emim appear in Deut 2:10-11; and the Horites appear in Deut 2:12,22. Genesis 14 does not depend directly on Deuteronomy 2 (nor does Deuteronomy 2 depend on Genesis 14—Zuzim and Zamzummim). But both chapters are archaizing.

There are numerous candidates for similar treatment in the history of traditions, some of which will be relatively familiar to the reader. For example, the Davidic covenant tradition has been cited for years as an instance of "inner-biblical exegesis."[29] I have argued that the various lines of thought on this issue exhibited in biblical texts could conceivably derive by interpretation from some such formulation as that of Psalm 132.[30] The early formulations of the covenant spawned later partisan reinterpretations, each of which appealed to the earlier texts for proof. Similarly, the development of the centralization legislation in Deuteronomy and the cult of centralization must have based itself on appeals not just to the king's orders but also to sacred texts (and not a sudden, pious fraud): a whole exegetical movement must have accompanied the innovation, which may itself have been nurtured by just such exegeses.[31] These traditions grew by feeding on themselves. But insofar as the exegesis produced developments unforeseen by earlier authors, it represented misinterpretation of the sources.

Such major issues have attracted more than their share of attention. The less prominent passages also exhibit these problems and responses. John Holladay long ago observed that the historian in Josh 10:10-14 misconstrued a source-text from the "Book of Yashar." The poem, situated "in the day when YHWH gave the Amorites over before the children of Israel," reports a request for a favorable omen—that the sun should be visible in the east while the moon remained visible in the west—and the granting of that omen (Josh 10:12-13). The prose interprets the poetry not unreasonably to mean that the sun stood still.[32] This is a phenomenon quite like that observed above with reference to the song of Deborah and the song of the sea. Less of the narrative in Joshua, however, has been shaped by the poetic source.

Gen 14:4,9-11 contain imitation poetry (or poetic prose) in which Kudurlaomer is chief among the foreign kings. But the kings are listed alphabetically in v 1. In v 9, the list breaks to place K. first (and so assumes the order c, d, a, b): the alphabetical list is the basis for the order in v 9. How K. became the chief is unclear. But the names of the kings stem from some list conceivably derived from a selection of cuneiform texts (so Amraphel could conceal gutturals; cf. the loss of gutturals in P's Genesis 5 parallel to J's antediluvian list in Genesis 4; there, too, cuneiform mediation could be in point).

Finally, *miggēn* in v 20 is probably an interpretation of *māgēn* in 15:2, where the succeeding stich ("your reward . . . ") indicates it means "benefactor," and has been interpreted correctly here. Cf. O. Eissfeldt, *The Old Testament: An Introduction* (New York: Harper and Row, 1965) 211-212.

[29] See Sarna, "Psalm 89" for an original and weighty treatment.

[30] *The Constitution of the Monarchy in Israel* (HSM 25; Chico: Scholars, 1981) 47-49.

[31] "The Centralization Formula in Deuteronomy" *VT* 31 (1981) 20-38.

[32] J. S. Holladay, "The Day(s) the *Moon* Stood Still" *JBL* 87 (1968) 166-178.

Minor cases of this sort could be multiplied almost without limit.[33] Ordinarily, they would be classified under the rubric of "inner-biblical exegesis." In fact, they are simply instances of Israelite exegesis, or literary allusion, or reconstruction, or, better, historiography.[34] The ancient historian did not measure his repertoire of sources against the standard of our canon. Thus, "inner-biblical exegesis" is "inner-biblical" only by the accidents of history. There are exceptions, primarily where the exegete in question is conscious of dealing with sacred text, or, one might argue, sacred history. 1 Chr 22:7-9, for example, explain that YHWH disqualified David from building the temple because David had shed blood and waged wars. This is a stricture on temple-building that does not seem to have occurred to anyone elsewhere in the ancient world, including Israel. But 1 Kgs 5:17-18 recount that Solomon wrote to Hiram of Tyre, "David, my father . . . was not able to build a house for YHWH's, his god's name because of the war that surrounded him . . . . " This flatly contradicts 2 Sam 7:1b (which in all fairness must be regarded as a late addition to the text; cf. also 1 Chr 17:1); and the notion that human wars could have distracted YHWH from the fulfilment of his purposes would have rankled with the Chronicler in any case. In consequence, or perhaps simply coincidentally, the author of the passage in Chronicles has simply taken what Kings regarded as a distraction or temporary obstacle and interpreted it to be some sort of profanation, a disqualification. He may also have been influenced by Solomon's name (1 Chr 22:9) and by Exod 20:22 (reinterpreted in Deut 27:5; Josh 8:31; 1 Kgs 6:7 to be specific to iron), so that the ground for his interpretation was already friable. The excuse of 1 Kings 5 (David hadn't the time) has assumed a theological reality (war soiled him: it has been reified). In the sense that the author of 1 Chr 22:7-9 took 1 Kgs 5:17-18 as canon, as inviolable truth, this is inner-biblical exegesis. In the sense that other texts unknown to us may also have influenced that author, this is simply Israelite historiography.

Another instance will help to clarify the point. In Gen 18:12, J explains Isaac's name. Sarah laughed; so Isaac is called "he laughed." In Gen 17:17, P provides an alternate version. *Abraham* laughed; so Isaac is called "he laughed." P did not necessarily need to provide his own etymology of Isaac's name (he does not do so for Israel, Moses, or any other prominent character outside of Genesis 17). But there was a problem in the J account: if Sarah was the one who laughed, Isaac should be called "she laughed *(tiṣḥaq)*." The result is the P account—the result at least in part of this consideration. This is inner-biblical exegesis insofar as the texts involved are in the canon. But if P

---

[33] See, e.g., my *Constitution* 88 on Joshua 3-4; "Rise of Abimelek" 92-95 and also 96 n. 47; and "Israelite Historian" for one or two others.

[34] Cf. Childs, "Midrash and the Old Testament," in *Understanding the Sacred Text*, ed. J. Reumann (Valley Forge: Valley Forge, 1972) 47-59. See below, n. 60.

was promulgated as a doctrinal and confessional alternative to J,[35] it was nothing more than official revision of rejected documents.

There are, of course, other instances of misinterpretation in biblical literature. Probably, Ezra 3:11-13 report a cultic act that has now been taken to reflect some social or personal reality. Exod 21:15 *(mkh 'byw w'mw . . .)*, 17 *(mqll 'byw w'mw . . .)* may, with the relationship between them not quite clarified, have produced Deut 27:16 *('rwr mqlh 'byw w'mw)* and Exod 20:12 ("honor your father and mother"). None of this is any more surprising than the common misapplication of the English idiom, "the exception that proves the rule." The essence of the problem remains that reification, the semantic depletion of metaphor (or even, in the case of the English example, of verbiage), or the willful or ignorant appeal to texts that do not mean what the interpreter means to have meant. When literature is suddenly authoritative, it becomes a matter of manipulation to read one's own agenda into it: this is in fact the real test of canonicity (see below, n. 60). Matters are more interesting when the reconstruction is less germane to current dogma, but still affected by an inability to see what one's sources intend.

A case in point, and another broad area of application, is the plagues problem. Scholars have long agreed that the account of the ten plagues has grown in the telling. But this growth differs from that of the Davidic covenant tradition or the centralization legislation in Deuteronomy in that interpreters are unlikely to have had any *a priori* political interest at stake in the developments that resulted. Why, then, has the litany of plagues expanded? One possibility is this: in any list of the plagues, such as that of Ps 78:44-51, a poet will place discrete plagues in parallel with one another and, at the same time, synonyms for the same plague in parallel with one another. In Psalm 78, for example, "flies" appears in parallel to "frogs" while "locusts" appears in parallel to "locusts" (cf. Ps 105:28-36, where plagues are not so lightly mixed). If the hearer did not have a fixed plagues tradition, he might tend to infer the existence of distinct plagues wherever the semantic parallelism was sloppiest. Ritual and iconographic representations of the plagues were no doubt susceptible to the same sort of misinterpretation. Metaphoric expressions of the story have probably led the historians in Exodus to pad their accounts.

These cases are for the most part and in varying degrees speculative. They are intended to sketch out some areas in which an awareness of the process of reification might bear on our view of the history of traditions. Some, such as the last instance, are worse than others in that they infer the existence of literature we do not have. This raises an issue of method that can claim our attention as much for its general as for its specific implications: had we only the prose version of the Deborah story, would we be justified in reconstructing the poetic source? Had we only the sun standing still in Gibeon,

---

[35] As R. E. Friedman, *The Exile and Biblical Narrative* (*HSM* 22; Chico: Scholars, 1981) 44-119.

would it be reasonable to posit a metaphorical text misprised? The reality from which this hypothetical question diverts us provides an unequivocal answer. Yet how many of us would dream, imagining Yael with her mallet and peg, that the tableau arose from a misconstrued parallel couplet? And suppose that the instance were seemingly incontrovertible. Suppose that there were no Zech 9:9 to explain why in Matt 21:1-10 Jesus rides into Jerusalem on two mounts. How many editors would print the argument to a poetic source? How many readers would believe it?

I do not have any profound answers to this problem, although I do subscribe to Norman O. Brown's notion that a healthy, or "non-morbid" science is characterized by what he calls "erotic exuberance" rather than by (anal) sadism.[36] But when biblical scholars speak of tradition-history and the growth of traditions, they deny the identity of received texts with some posited originals of these texts. This is all to the good: if we ask, what did such and such a passage mean, or what did Isaiah mean in such and such a passage, we are also asking the more particular questions, "How did Isaiah come to mean this?" and "What does it mean that we have this passage preserved for us?" To ask what Isaiah meant is to ask what issues he grappled with, in what context, and what went through his mind when he responded to them.[37] The last is incomprehensible except on the basis of all the questions that preceded.

Biblical studies, like many others, is a profession in which standards are erected and theoretically enforced as though they were as pragmatic as municipal fire-codes, and in which the less rigorous practitioner sometimes evokes the sort of response appropriate to a slum-landlord. In a relatively moderate instance, a prominent archaeologist recently charged in print that William Foxwell Albright made it difficult to understand what he thought because he so often reversed himself.[38] The factual charge is accurate; but it necessitates these comments. Albright's conclusions are not the issue: how he arrived at them is. How we might arrive at the same or at different conclusions is even more central an issue. In other words, to understand the transmitted tradition meaningfully, we must understand some of the history of that tradition—some of the reasoning and other background to the choices made there. This, in the absence of overwhelming evidence, entails speculation, reconstruction, latent or consciously avowed.

---

[36] *Life Against Death. The Psychoanalytical Meaning of History* (London: Sphere, 1968) 210.

[37] See Collingwood, *Autobiography* 110-111. This is as clear a refutation of the fads of New Criticism and deconstructionism and the hollow-log-beating of the "intentional fallacy" as one can come by. For another approach, less compelling, see E. D. Hirsch, *Validity in Interpretation* (New Haven: Yale University, 1978).

[38] This is no isolated instance; the fact that the charge reached print is evidence that it is widespread, and at the least did not alarm the editors of the journal.

The historian deals with sources on the basis of unconscious and conscious understandings of circumstances in the past (largely the former). That is to say that he deals in scenarios rather than in compelled reconstructions. History, even if it hopes to be, is not rigorous, in that the understanding that produced the source—the sherd, the text, the town—can rarely, if ever, be recovered on any positivistic basis. Moreover, since that physical determination posited at the start of this treatment is susceptible to approximations (reductions?) of various kinds—psychological, sociological, economic, and so forth—a variety of causes, a variety of "processes" can and often do constitute the historian's legitimate concern in an attack on his problem. If Albright reversed himself on historical matters—problems of human action and reaction as distinct from questions of physical fact—and was not fatuous about it, he thereby enriched so much more the scholarly discussion. If, in our quest for Isaiah's meaning and how he came to mean it, we concentrated on Isaiah and not on what this or that scholar thought of Isaiah, we should be a great deal more open not only to two opinions stemming from the same author, but also to controlled speculation, dependent on the contextual realities of the text under analysis. Historians profess to reconstruct the past. But routinely, they claim to restrict themselves to the possibilities allowed by the evidence on the basis of certain regulations. The result is a castrated past, and usually rather a colorless one. One hypothesis, even if it tests the limits of the evidence (and so long as it does not test those of reality), that gets at the historical event itself is worth ten theories that get only at the historical evidence of that event. The overly literal, overly positivistic paradigm that pervades much of humanistic scholarship would not admit of it; but a proposal, in the absence of Judges 5, that Judges 4 based itself heavily, and occasionally mistakenly, on a poetic source, would by its sweep put most scissors-and-paste historical reconstructions to shame. The deficiency lies not in the evidence, which can only be what it is, but in the paradigms of philological history.[39] Our interest should rivet not on the rules of some artificial game, but on the question of what actually occurred. Thus, if we do not test the limits of insufficient or sparse or random evidence, we are not reconstructing history; we are advocating a case, just as in a court of law.

It is worthwhile invoking one example of a more creative and more productive process. The "discovery" of the enclitic *mem* led to an explosion of these markers in biblical literature, at least as it was treated in the field journals. Scholars suddenly penetrated problematic passages, explained away

---

[39]Most particularly in its refusal to admit inductive inference into argument, whatever its limitations. It is ironic that while physicists have learned to deal not in truth deduced but in probability educed from scenarios (as Wiener, *Human Use* 15-27), this historical field remains cemented to the dogmatic positivism of the 19th c. Note further A. Momigliano, *Essays in Ancient and Modern Historiography* (Middletown: Wesleyan, 1977) 99-100, 104-105.

troublesome plural forms, revised standard or long-accepted translations, argued new positions by positing an enclitic here or there, or simply pointed out new *mems* for the record and for the fun of recording them. The vast majority of these suggestions were doubtless inaccurate. But the exercise was in all quite a healthy one. Possibilities presented themselves; they were and are being adjudicated. New configurations opened up, and were dealt with.

The joy of that *mem*-hunt was Norman O. Brown's "erotic exuberance." And there is no reason that the process of sifting for the real enclitics should not engage the same spirit. Those who grumble about a lack of methodological control predominate; but they miss the point, and rather an obvious point. It is productive to raise the possibilities in the hope that new methods will arise for appraising them. It is a healthy development when the historian explores fresh scenarios precisely because that exercise can and sometimes does lead to the development of new methods in research. And the doctrine of falsifiability can generate epicycles, but not paradigmatic advances. Conservatism does not produce progress in method. New approaches to the evidence can.

To some readers, this confession will seem nothing short of outright apostasy; to others, it will be motherhood and apple pie. One can extend it, at any rate, one step further. Even when they are speculations, it seems to me that the historian's explorations of fresh possibilities can be worthwhile. To illustrate, it is necessary to move from passages in which reification may have affected the historical texts to the phenomenon of reification as a whole. Concrete instances will provide a serviceable jumping-off point for the discussion.

Most readers will already be familiar with the ensuing, rather classical case of harmonization. Deuteronomy 27, along with its reflexes in Josh 8:30-35; 24, is one of the most celebrated problem-children in all of biblical study. These texts indicate that immediately on crossing the Jordan River from the east, Israel were to erect pillars not on the western shore of that river, but on Mount Ebal, at Shechem. The difficulty arises from the fact that the narratives in Joshua 1-6 bring the Israelites across in the vicinity of Gilgal (or Jericho) and have them encamp there.[40] Without attempting to resolve the tension involved here, it is legitimate to turn to Deut 11:29-30. These verses locate Mount Ebal, and its sister peak, Mount Gerizim, "opposite Gilgal, by the oak(s) of teaching" in the wilderness. The Oak of Teaching (or Moreh) is located elsewhere near Shechem (as Gen 12:6). But the verses otherwise conflate the Joshua 1-6 with the later Deuteronomy and Joshua traditions. Harmonizing, the historian in Deut 11:29-30 has invented an Ebal and Gerizim neighboring Gilgal.

A substantially different instance with similar implications crops up in the biography of David. 2 Sam 5:21 reports that David carried off as spoil

---

[40]Cf. Eissfeldt, "Gilgal or Shechem?" in *Proclamation and Presence*, ed. J. Durham and J. R. Porter (Fs. Henton-Davies; Richmond: Knox, 1970) 90-101; von Rad, *Deuteronomy* (*OTL*; Philadelphia: Westminster, 1966) 86.

a set of abandoned Philistine idols—*way-yiśśā'ēm*, reads the text. 1 Chr 14:12 relates instead that the gods were burned—*way-yiśśārepû bā'ēš*. In varying ways, commentators since David Qimhi have argued that, if one assumes that the Chronicler had before him the text of Samuel, then the Chronicler deliberately rejected the obvious construction of that text. He repointed the received letters, *wyś'm*, from *way-yiśśā'ēm* ("he bore them off") to *way-yaśśî'ēm* (derivative from *maś'ēt*, "signal fire, bonfire," "he set them alight").[41] Thus he effected a semantic shift. Here, the evidence will stretch just a bit further: the Chronicler reasoned that David had no use for Philistine idols. David, after all, was a saint, faultless, an ideal. He scoured his own historiographic conscience and came up with the repointing of the letters in Samuel—of the literal truth. He then advanced another step by changing the text (which is unusual practice for the Chronicler) so that his own readers would not fall prey to thinking David an idolater. In this case, the process of literalization is plainly a conscious one. One might even say that the Chronicler read his source-text and his seemingly religious commitment to David in the same way that the author of Deut 11:29-30 read his two source-texts.

What has happened here? One might respond that the Israelite, like anyone else, made mistakes; that although divine inspiration left him precious little license to do so, he sometimes misinterpreted difficult texts or reinterpreted and re-edited troubling texts. This is all true. But it is not all. In these cases, the author's vision or meaning is no longer the object of interest, let alone of reverence. The words no longer convey a sacred truth. Now, the words—even the letters—*are* a sacred truth. They generate *ad hoc* meanings, new, fresh truths, that are taken to be as valid as the ideas their authors meant to express. The Chronicler misconstrues Samuel willfully, but abides by the letter of the truth. The same principle applies, without the element of personal willfulness (the willfulness, with the principle, had by then been generalized), to Matthew's use of biblical prophecy to vindicate Jewish messianism. But already in the pre-exilic period in the texts discussed above, and certainly no later than the Chronicler's time, the phenomenon of scripturalization, or of the institutional literalization of text, is in evidence. Certain texts are routinely deprived of their metaphoric interstices, converted into hollow verbal shells to be filled at the interpreter's pleasure. They are depleted semantically, reduced to a sequence of letters; their replenishment depends not on a system of internal relationships, nor indeed on contextual bearings, but on the reader's whimsy.

*   *   *   *   *   *   *

Any nation saddled with a legal establishment is necessarily prey to literalism. Strict constructionism and literalism rear their head at some point

---

[41] See M. Cogan, *Imperialism and Religion: Assyria, Judah and Israel in the Eighth and Seventh Centuries B.C.E.* (*SBLMS* 19; Missoula: Scholars, 1974) 116.

in every court, to some degree at least. But it does not follow that the legal tradition is the fount of Israelite literalism, even where the law itself is sacred scripture. Indeed, the phenomenon of doctrinnaire reification does not occur unaccompanied by a certain—at least crepuscular—consciousness of the conflict between literally possible and intended meanings. Many of the instances cited above fall into the category of unintentional misinterpretation or the naive reification of metaphor. But the instances located in P, Chronicles, and Deut 11:29-30 represent deliberate distortions of puzzling or unacceptable texts. The identical urge is found in Genesis 20, a variant, commonly ascribed to E, of a picaresque episode in Gen 12:10-20; 26:6-11.[42] Here, God is acquitted of savaging Abraham's innocent dupe (20:4-6; cf. 12:17; but note 20:17-18). But more important, Abraham is defended against the charge that he lied— and defended by appeal to literal, or what we might call technical grounds (20:12); the moral justification offered in all three versions (12:11-13; 20:11; 26:7) is now regarded as insufficient to bear the weight of Abraham's lie. The author of Genesis 20 has consciously reworked his materials to expunge the potential blot from Abraham's character. In this instance, as has long been observed, a hagiographic bent not dissimilar from the Chronicler's determines the manner in which the author supplements his source. This is neither the only nor the earliest example of such a phenomenon.[43] But it is early enough and clear enough to dispel the thought that Israelite literalism arose only late and stemmed from the experience of some central legal establishment.

Had we no further evidence, therefore, I should suggest that the preceding texts imply the end of a guild-centered religion, and the development of institutions, of bureaucracy, or of some other forum in which words were taken at face value. I should maintain that some loss of the ability to interpret religious metaphor had occurred, perhaps by virtue of the assimilation of differing factions, perhaps simply by bureaucratization; that ecstasy, mystical experience, visionary religion had given way to the demands of administration;

---

[42] Both are commonly imputed to J. The oral transmission and tradition-historical problems here are vexing. The E variant exhibits the same apologetic concerns as have reshaped the J account in Gen 16:4-14 in E's Gen 21:9-21 (esp. v 11). On E, see A. Jenks, *The Elohist and North Israelite Traditions* (*SBLMS* 22; Missoula: Scholars, 1977).

[43] Cf. Gen 25:29-34 against chap. 27; 1 Sam 21:11-16 against chap. 27; 1 Sam 29:1-30:24; 2 Sam 1 against 1 Chr 12:20 (and omit from v 20 *wl' 'zrm* to v 21 *nplw 'lyw* as an insertion marked by the epanalepsis *wmmnšh nplw 'l dwyd bb'w 'm plštym 'l s'wl, blktw 'l ṣqlg nplw 'lyw mmnšh*). Cf. 1 Samuel 24 after 1 Samuel 26. This is a particularly complex instance stemming from 2 Sam 23:15-17. In Greece, Homer's acquittal of Odysseus of the charge of being the liar Sisyphus' bastard son (as Polyaenus 6.52) is probably a similar instance.

that the religion of the rural "high places *(bāmôt)*" had been conquered by the ideologues of centralization. That would, I think, be a terrible misrepresentation, as one final instance, quite possibly the most speculative of the lot, will illustrate.

Commentators are in the habit of regarding the Priestly source in the Pentateuch as the incarnation of late Israelite religion. For apologetic reasons, some religious, some derived from Enlightenment optimism, P is regarded commensurately as more sophisticated than earlier materials. In fact, his seeming sophistication is the main ground for assigning to P a late date. Some critics distort or deplore the sophistication, arguing along the lines laid out in the preceding paragraph;[44] but sophistication it remains. P's god is more transcendent than J's, presiding from a loftier heaven over somewhat diminished mortals. And P attenuates the anthropomorphic language characteristic of other Israelite texts. This, most scholars agree, is a conscious penchant, conscientiously prosecuted.[45] P is not altogether free of anthropomorphism—after all, mankind is created in God's image (Gen 1:26,27) in the same way that children are begot in their parents' image (Gen 5:1-3). But he does seem to avoid wherever possible references, however metaphorical, to God's limbs, features or bodily functions. Confronted with anthropomorphism in P, the reader is not at all disposed to take it literally.

Except to a raving teleologist, there is nothing in this to indicate P's sophistication over against J. P's god may or may not be more transcendent than J's; all we can say with certainty is that P is more explicit than J about his god's transcendence. J, conversely, seems to emphasize his god's immanence. That is, P's concerns were not the same as J's: P was intent on taking a stand against anthropomorphism. What could have motivated his aversion? Let me admit from the start that I have only an alternate view, not proof. Perhaps P thought his audience were taking J literally.

Concerns of this sort are not infrequently found in antiquity. The Clementine homilies (2.52; 3.55-57) deplore precisely the anthropomorphism of the Pentateuch as being harmful to the reader and misleading to the worshipper. Plato's attacks on the Athenian poets and tragedians (particularly in the *Republic*) are similar, though not directed so much toward the portrayal of the gods as toward the casting of models for human behavior. Much earlier—in fact as early as the 6th century B.C.E.—the philosopher Xenophanes seems to have made the same point. Xenophanes understood the true god to be a transcendent one, omniscient, and in some other respects similar to P's

---

[44] See Wellhausen, *Prolegomena* 410, 412 and throughout. This tendency is now diminishing. See Levenson, "Theology of Commandment in Biblical Israel" *HTR* 73 (1980) 17-33 for discussion.

[45] See S. R. Driver, *Introduction to the Literature of the Old Testament* (8th ed.; New York: Scribner's, 1898) 140-141; Friedman, *Exile* 77.

god.[46]   He understood, further, that human beings would inevitably conceive of their god as human: had animals gods, those gods would be portrayed as animals:

> . . . mortals believe the gods to be created by birth, and to have their own *(mortals')* raiment, voice and body.

> But if oxen (and horses) and lions had hands or could draw with hands and create works of art like those made by men, horses would draw pictures of gods like horses, and oxen of gods like oxen, and they would make the bodies (of their gods) in accordance with the form that each species itself possesses.

> Aethiopians have gods with snub noses and black hair, Thracians have gods with grey eyes and red hair.[47]

But Xenophanes fretted over Homer's and Hesiod's presentations of the gods: the gods' whimsicality, their wantonness, their immorality in the works of those classical authors filled him with concern.[48]   Here is an interpreter who understands that anthropomorphism is, so to speak, an accident of chromosomes. He further notes that human inquiry into theology—and into other domains—amounts to nothing more than speculation.[49] Xenophanes' concern was not for Homer or Hesiod, still less for himself. He fretted primarily for the reader, who might take or perhaps did take quite seriously the shameful anthropomorphic misrepresentations of the divine in the Greek poetic tradition. Like the Chronicler, Xenophanes saw both the metaphorical nature and the danger of his canon.

P's avoidance of anthropomorphism stems probably from a similar orientation.   It may represent an attempt to foreclose on appeals either to J's

---

[46] See K. Freeman, *Ancilla to the Pre-Socratic Philosophers* (Oxford: Blackwell, 1956) 23.23-26. One wonders whether, confronted with the issues in all their bearings, J would have demurred from these considerations.

[47] *Ibid.* 22.14-16.

[48] *Ibid.* 22.10-12. Note that in the *Odyssey*, Homer anticipates Athens' dramatists by making divine action just, if still pockmarked by occasional eccentricities. This only goes to show how the movement in current issues and in ethics affects the discussion. Materials attributed already to Orpheus (as Freeman, *Ancilla* 2.6,9,14), Pherekydes (14.1) and Anaximander (19.1) have related implications.

[49] *Ibid.* 24.34-36:

> And as for certain truth, no man has seen it, nor will there ever be a man who knows about the gods and about all the things I mention. For if he succeeds to the full in saying what is completely true, he himself is nevertheless unaware of it; and Opinion (seeming) is fixed by fate upon all things.

> Let these things be stated as conjecture only, similar to the reality. All appearances which exist for mortals to look at.

seemingly lax theology or to anthropomorphism in his own writing. Certainly, P responds elsewhere to problems raised for him by J. In contrast to J, he never reports a sacrifice until Aaron is consecrated and the tabernacle altar erected; this is a matter of deliberation, intended to drive home his views on the limitation of the sacrificial franchise.[50] On the same lines, but more closely related to the issue of anthropomorphism, P avoids using angels throughout his narrative.[51] Since Gen 1:26 indicates that he accepts the existence of a heavenly council, and since seemingly allied works, such as those of the Chronicler and Ezekiel, do not exhibit the same inhibitions, one can conclude only that P, like Holmes's "dog in the night," is keeping his silence loudly: he is trying to deflate his predecessors' metaphor, to eliminate the cruder aspects (as he perceives them) of the antecedent literature. He is trying to pitch sacred history on a purely literal plain. No text that indicates diversity in the pantheon or successful deviation in the polity will survive his Zadoqite razor. P tries not to lay himself open to the same charges with which he or his readers may have taxed J; he plays a safe, even tremulous game. But this does not make him more sophisticated than J. Instead, in addressing issues created in part by J's presentation, P must argue in different terms.

The aniconism of our "ten commandments" is a related case. The older parallel materials lie in Exod 20:23, at the outset of the Covenant Code, and in Exod 34:17, in the so-called Cultic Decalogue.[52] They forbid the

---

[50] See Friedman, *Exile* 82, 84-85 *inter alia*; Driver, *Introduction* 139-142.

[51] Friedman, *Exile* 84, 85, e.g. There may, of course, be a stray angel or two in other reconstructions of P. But the general absence of heavenly messengers to man is striking enough even if one or two of them did creep into the narrative. Like J and Dtr, P may be somewhat restricted by the presence of prior traditions.

[52] On Exod 20:23, cf. Childs, *Exodus* 465. Given the antiquity of the altar law and its confluence with this statute—both are conducive to pre-monarchic Israel's semi-official backyard-barbecue type of cult; both prohibit the erection and use of elaborate urban (monarchic) sanctuaries and closed temples, thus protecting and preserving the distinction between rural highland Israel and lowland urban Canaan (*contra* E. Nielsen, *The Ten Commandments in New Perspective* [SBT 2/7; Naperville: Allenson, 1968] 52-54)—and given the parallel in Exod 34:17 (but cf. Eissfeldt, *Old Testament* 216), I feel this law belongs in place, together with the altar law (note that the combination of the two has inspired Lev 26:1; further, aniconism carries with it the baggage of the restriction of sacrifice to wooden structures in Pythagoreanism when this theological complex travels to Greece). I very much doubt that the law originally had reference to the very different formulation in Exod 20:3-6, which is also much more thoroughgoing. On Exod 34:17, see Childs, *Exodus* 604-607 and the sound proposal there (pp. 607-609). See further, and to the

construction not of images, nor of statues of divine beings, but only of metal statues of gods. In this respect, they accord with what appear to have been the main lines of pre-monarchic (and even monarchic) practice in Israel.[53] But in Exod 20:4 (Deut 5:8), in my view a Jerusalemite priestly text (in fact, a P text),[54] we encounter a full-scale ban on imagery of all kinds (and the association of imagery with metaphor is not so idle as one might think—P in fact eschews metaphorical expression generally, not only anthropomorphism;[55] and this is a separate manifestation of the same phenomenon). No image of anything anywhere is to be made: "Make yourself no carving or image of what is in the heaven above or what is on the earth or what is in the waters under the earth."

This blanket injunction must be related ideologically to the standard biblical polemic against supposed idolatry. And this finds its own Greek parallel in Heracleitus' later attacks on iconography and ritual imagery.[56] All these attitudes reflect a fundamentalist, over-literal position; all take the metaphor, the image, to heart. It would, in my view, be an error of immense proportions to conclude that either P or Hosea (who already articulates the attack on icons in its fullest form—8:6; 13:2; 14:9)[57] had lost the ability to approach religious metaphor as metaphor. On the contrary, Hosea was fully

---

point as a whole, T. N. D. Mettinger, "The Veto on Images and the aniconic God in Ancient Israel," in *Religious Symbols and their Functions*, ed. H. Biczais (Scripta Instituti Donneriani Aboensis 10; Stockholm: Almqvist & Wiksell, 1979) 15-29, esp. p. 25.

[53] See the preceding note, and Mettinger, "Veto."

[54] See now Mettinger, "Veto" 27.

[55] Driver (*Introduction* 130) notes:

Metaphors, similes, &c., are eschewed (Nu. 27^{17b} is an exception [and if that hackneyed warhorse is the exception, then the reader should count P's aversion to figure a blessing]); and there is generally an absence of the poetical or dramatic element, which is frequently conspicuous in the other historical books of the OT. (including J and E) . . . .

It seems as though the habits of thought and expression, which the author had contracted through his practical acquaintance with the law, were carried by him into his treatment of purely historical subjects.

[56] See Freeman, *Ancilla* 25.5, 33.128.

[57] Mettinger ("Veto" 23 n.39) also points to the pun in Hos 4:17 and the apparent reference to the two bulls of Jeroboam in Hos 10:10. After Hosea, or at the same time, the related units Isa 2:6-8; Mic 5:9-13, both of which relate to Hosea 8 and Deuteronomy 17-18 (see *Constitution* 230-231), can be cited in extension of the argument. Hos 13:2 and probably 8:1ff. refer to the older legal statutes banning metal images of gods. Note that M. de Roche ("The reversal of creation in Hosea" VT 31 [1981] 400-409) argues that Hosea had access to some form of P; he also provides bibliography for the argument that Jeremiah had access to P.

cognizant of the fact that Bethel's bull represented only artistically and cultically YHWH's war-steed. In the same sense, prophets such as Amos who
reject ritual in their rhetoric (as Am 5:21-27, among many similar passages)
did not misunderstand the ritual to represent the real action of worship.
Amos knew full well that the ritual expressed metaphorically the religious or
emotional proskynesis of the nation. So, too, did the worshippers—let us do
them no injustice—who otherwise could not have been expected to understand
Amos' canards. But to appeal again to a historical parallel, Cromwell ran
around destroying idols—icons purported to represent Mary and Jesus—not
because he thought they were literal manifestations of those divinities, not
because he thought they were not symbolic, but because (he claimed) he did
not trust the population at large to understand just how symbolic they were.
Heracleitus' and Xenophanes' attacks on the Greek poetic tradition were
apparently couched in just these terms.[58] And so are Hosea's, Isaiah's and
Micah's attacks on Israelite iconography (Hos 13:2; Isa 2:8; Mic 5:12). The
issue is not that the polemicist misunderstands the image, metaphor or sacra-
ment (Am 5:21-27), but that the polemicist thinks or claims the worshippers
may.

It is most likely that the dragons lanced by Hosea and Heracleitus, by
Xenophanes and Isaiah and Amos and Micah and P, were chimerical. It is
difficult to subscribe after benevolent reflection to the notion that votaries
at Bethel regularly mistook the statue of a bull for a god, or even the bull
represented by the statue for a god: had they, the local priesthood would
surely have intervened vigorously. It is to my mind dubious that the readers
of J misunderstood YHWH to be human or whimsical or error-prone. In no
way is it plausible that participants in Israelite ritual believed the ritual itself
to have efficacy without any emotional or spiritual correlative, without some
meaning, some message, in the metaphor (after all, is this not what liturgy and
homiletic contribute to the ceremony?). What we read in our texts is polemic,
after all; it is the work of men looking for handles to seize on to, looking for
excuses to denigrate the next fellow. Whether or not we bundle them all
together into one period, place or school of thought, Israel's iconoclasm, P's
aversion to anthropomorphism and all other forms of metaphor, and the
tendency to literalize both pre-existing metaphor and—*pro re nata*—texts
under composition—all these phenomena may—rather, do—reflect not a growing theological sophistication, but a tonic against alleged backsliding, against
literalizations of the sort that rile Xenophanes against Homer and Plato against
the dramatists. In P, we see the logical extension of this concern—the cautious
verbiage of institutional bureaucracy. The phenomenon of literalization in
Israel symptomizes a religious and political struggle being fought ideologically
in terms of paradigms for and modes of discourse.

---

[58] Freeman, *Ancilla* 31.104, 22.10.

It is impossible responsibly to locate these developments historically, even though their rough temporal context is clear, at least without long disputations over detail.[59]   But P seems in some sense to be fighting the wars of the Reformation, or the *homoousios-homoiousios* wars of the Middle Ages, or engaging in witch-hunts in Salem. Probably, this reflects his own isolation from the religion of the rural *bāmôt*, and his polemical disposition toward it. Thus, the battle against anthropomorphic metaphor and cultic iconography may represent a part of the effort to centralize worship at the Jerusalem temple. It may be that attacks on more tolerant Levitic priesthoods (Mushite or other) were entailed; that pilgrimages to shrines other than that in Jerusalem—pilgrimages sanctioned and supported by appeal to the J version of the patriarchal history (as Gen 12:6-9; 13:18, etc.)—were subject to indictment in the context of the innovation. When Talleyrand and the Parisian hierarchy subscribed to Mirabeau's Civil Constitution of the Clergy, after all, they levelled all sorts of charges against their colleagues outside the capital. And it is salubrious to recall that Peisistratos' promulgation of the canonized Homer coincided with considerable ritual innovation and a pitched battle against the Athenian aristocracy.   Indeed, it is arguable that Peisistratos' actions arose from and led directly to the sort of literal-historical consciousness exhibited by Xenophanes and Heracleitus, the logical outcome of which was the rise of Herodotus and the historians on the one hand (history, being true, has a leg-up on legend) and to Plato (the quest for absolute, abstract truth) on the other. Israelite literalization from Hosea to the Chronicler suggests the influence of factional strife. The most attractive context in which to locate that strife would be the reforms of Hezekiah and Josiah: Jerusalemite theologians must then have attacked all other institutions. But the struggle that produced this literalization could equally have been international, against northern priesthoods, or internal to the Jerusalem bureaucracy. The central point here is that P's caution with regard to anthropomorphism and other metaphor—indeed, Hosea's attack on iconography—stems from a notion that metaphor cannot be or is not being taken metaphorically.

Even when iconoclastic, reification is fetishist, in that it mistakes the image for the reality the image represents. When P reacts to others' anthropomorphism (or when Isaiah attacks others' attitudes toward cultic imagery, or Amos attacks their attitudes toward ritual), he assumes that his audience is too unsophisticated or too dishonest to distinguish figure from its intended content. P's recourse is to be literal, which, after all, is the only way to deal with literalism. But it is interesting to note that scripturally-oriented religions

---

[59] For the time period, see the unerring work of Mettinger ("Veto" 24). This is roughly contemporary with Homer, and antedates Xenophanes and Heracleitus by 200 years. After Peisistratos, the inner-Greek process suffices to account for all the developments there (see below). But one ought not blithely rule out the possibility of Judaic influence.

—Judaism, Catholicism and Islam, in the West—have instead canonized tradition. This acknowledgment of the literal text's inadequacy makes possible a more meaningful embrace of the text; it also preempts epileptic fundamentalism, which by absolutizing the literal succeeds only in absolutely relativizing it, and absolutizing the interpreter. Fundamentalism is religious and historical illiteracy, the exegetical counterpart of prescriptive social science. An authoritative tradition juxtaposed to the unchanging Text of Truth, even though coupled with what must amount to an intentional agnosticism of the New Critical variety, can short-circuit it.

Israel's demythologizing disposition was ultimately as literalistic as her aniconism. Because the image is not the life, images lie. Because the myth is not the historical event, myths lie. Because YHWH is not a man, metaphor, particularly anthropomorphic metaphor, lies. And the fallout; sacred documents are literally true, not true in their intentions. If God swears in Genesis, God is a swearer, so that P must do his level best to prevent him swearing. The rationality of Israelite religion as it survives in the canon is P's rationality. And P is a literalist, or a guide to fundamentalists.

In Exodus 14, in Judges 4, and in the other instances explored above, the beginnings of canonicity—in which the text assumes a life of its own, independent of the author and sacred to the reader—are in evidence.[60] Exodus

---

[60] These remarks will tend to corroborate the conclusions arrived at in M. Fishbane's "Revelation and Tradition: Aspects of Inner-Biblical Exegesis" *JBL* 99 (1980) 343-361. I must stress, however, that the phenomenon of literalization or semantic depletion is the crux in determining incipient canonicity. This clears the way for re-application and the generation of new truths, new revelations, from the text (as Fishbane, "Aspects" 357, 361). Otherwise, one may be dealing with simple exegesis or literary or legal allusion, which need not imply canonicity at all. In other words, some criterion must be employed to distinguish T. S. Eliot's recasting of Shakespeare or Oscar Wilde's plagiarism from Longfellow from Matthew's use of Isaiah. The use of JE in Deuteronomy is not itself "inner-biblical exegesis" unless one can demonstrate that for the author of the passages in Deuteronomy, JE had canonical status in the way that Isaiah had for Matthew. Contrast Fishbane's approach and also J. Eslinger, "Hosea 12:5a and Genesis 32:29: A Study in Inner Biblical Exegesis" *JSOT* 18 (1980) 91-99; M. Fox, "The Identification of Quotations in Biblical Literature" *ZAW* 92 (1980) 416-431. Thus Fishbane is on soundest ground when dealing with the reinterpretation of prophecies (pp. 354-359). This is precisely a process of semantic depletion and arbitrary replenishment by the interpreter. What has commonly been called "inner-biblical exegesis" thus is not evidence of a consciousness of canonicity; it need in fact be no more than Israelite allusion. Though this is to quibble over terminology, it might be better to restrict the term "inner-biblical exegesis" to passages where some consciousness of canonicity is involved, and to call Israelite historiography and allusion what it is.

15, Judges 5 were for the historians effectively sacred scripture, whose literal text was authoritative. That we have prose reformulations of history celebrated in lyric, and even, in Chronicles and elsewhere, of history recorded in prose, indicates a consciousness that the historian must *recover*, wrest history from his sources; that the reader is otherwise likely to misconstrue the sources in a way different from that in which the historian would like him to misconstrue them. But the texts themselves were sacred and true; the words, the very letters were true. So that even when a very rational historian such as the editor of the Pentateuch could not make uncontradictory sense of his materials—and as R. E. Friedman has demonstrated, he tried[61]—he was safe in assuming that some later literalizer would.

What P evinces in these materials, and what our other historians evince, is the formative urge of scripture. Prosaic though it is to say so, that urge was fundamentalist, or a response to fundamentalism. But because reality cannot be reduced to a rational level, because there is always more in a vision than reductionist literalism can yet express (I still hold out hope for the chemical formula, of course), this urge generated a reaction—partly in the metaphoric and mythic language of the authors of Judah's exile, and partly in the subsequent interpretation of a literally true, but self-contradictory canon. Literalization threw out of whack the balance of such historiographic gems as Judges 9, Judges 11 and Second Samuel, in all of which divine and mundane causality are explicitly complementary rather than mutually exclusive. It created an atmosphere in which the jangle of combined sources went unheeded for thousands of years. But it was the logical outcome of Israel's relentlessly historical, relentlessly material, relentlessly realistic religion.[62] And just as the tension in Israel's thought between the mythic and the historical modes for organizing knowledge dissolved in the mythicization of history and the historicization of myth, so the tension between literalism and metaphor dissolved in the dialectic between interpretation and image. From these dialectics, competing Israelite ideologies arose. From them, and from their canonical outgrowths, have sprung the religious sensibilities of Western man.

---

[61]"Sacred History and Theology: The Redaction of Torah," in *The Creation of Sacred Literature: Composition and Redaction of the Biblical Text* (Near Eastern Studies 22; Berkeley: University of California, 1981) 24-34.

[62]Monotheism carried with it the seeds of all these developments, which to my mind led inexorably on the one hand to Daniel, and on the other to Qohelet. This, however, is fodder for another discussion. While the passage itself is too long to reproduce here, T. B. Macaulay's essay on Milton in the *Edinburgh Review* of August, 1825 deals judiciously and elegantly with these issues. The essay is reprinted in Macauley, *Critical and Historical Essays, Contributed to The Edinburgh Review* (3 vols.; 6th ed.; London: Longman, Brown, Green and Longmans, 1849) 1.1-61, esp. pp. 22-23.

Figure A

Judges

4:6:   (Deborah) sent and called to Baraq . . . and said to him, "Has Yhwh god of Israel not commanded? Go and array on Mt. Tabor, and take with you 10,000 men of the children of Naphtali and the children of Zebulun . . . ."

4:10;   Baraq mustered Zebulun and Naphtali at Qadesh, and there went up on foot (or, under his command) 10,000 men, and Deborah went up with him.

5:11d   Then the people of Yhwh came down to the gates.
12   Wake, wake Deborah!
Wake, wake, sing a song!
"Arise, Baraq, and capture,
"You captives, son of Abinoam!"
13   Then . . . came down . . . ;
The people of Yhwh came down to him with warriors:

14   Out of Ephraim, whose root is in Amaleq,
After you (o, Ephraim), Benjamin, among your contingents.
Out of Machir, rulers came down,
And from Zebulun, wielders of the sceptre.

15   The officers of Issachar to Deborah,
So to Baraq, sent to the valley (? in force) under his command;
In divisions (was) Reuben, with great resolution;

16   Do you not dwell among the hearths,
Listening to the bleating of the flocks?
To (your) divisions, Reuben, with great proofs of heart!

17   Gilead—who abides beyond Jordan,
And Dan—does he not dwell at ease?
Asher, who dwells on the shore of the seas,
And abides on his spreads,
18   Zebulun is a people that taunted death,
And Naphtali on the heights of the field.

19   The kings came; they fought.
Then the kings of Canaan fought,
At Taanach, by Megiddo's waters,
They did not take a bit of spoil.

Figure B

Judges 5:25-27

Water he asked;
Milk she provided;
In a lordly krater she proffered ghee.

She sent her hand to the peg,
Her right hand to the workers' banger;
She banged Sisera; she smashed his head;
She splintered, she pierced his spitter.

At her feet, he kneeled, he fell, stretched out.
At her feet, he kneeled, he fell.
Where he kneeled, there he fell, slain.

Judges 4:18b-21

He turned to her, to the tent, and she covered him with a . . . .

He said to her, "Water me with some water, please, for I thirst." So she opened the skin of milk and watered him and covered him.

And he said to her, "Stand at the opening of the tent, and if anyone comes and inquires of you, and says, 'Is anyone here?' say, 'There is not'."

Yael, wife of Heber, took the tent-peg and took the hammer in her hand and came upon him surreptitiously and pounded the peg into his spitter and it bit in the ground.

And he had slumbered, for he was tired; so he died.

Exodus 15

1b   The horse and its driver he has loosed into the sea.

4-5   Pharaoh's chariots and his horsemen he cast into the sea;
His choice . . . sank in the sea of reeds.
The depths covered them; they descended into the deep like a stone.

8-10   At the breath of your nostrils, the waters were heaped up;
The currents stood up like a *nēd*;
The depths churned/congealed in the midst of the sea.

The enemy said, "I will give chase . . . ."

You blew with your breath; the sea covered them.
They plummeted like lead in the mighty waters.

12   You stretched forth your right hand; the "earth" engulfed them.

13-17   You guided in your fidelity the people you redeemed;
You conducted them with your might to your holy pasturage.

The peoples heard; they shook;
Writhing seized the inhabitants of Philistia.
Then the commanders of Edom were discomfited.
The leaders of Moab—trembling seized them;
All the inhabitants of Canaan melted away.

There fell upon them dread and fear;
At the size of your arm they were dumb as a stone,
So that your people crossed over, Yhwh,
So that the people you acquired/created crossed over.

You brought them and planted them in the mount of your possession;
A dais for your enthronement you fashioned/acquired, Yhwh . . . .

Psalm 78

52-55 He moved his people like sheep,
And piloted them like a flock in the steppe.

He guided them securely, and they did not fear;
And their enemies, the sea covered.

He brought them to his holy territory,
The mount that his right hand acquired/created.
He expelled from before them peoples . . . .

60   He forsook the tabernacle of Shiloh, the tent he pitched among men . . . .

13-14 He cleft the sea and brought them across;
He stood up the waters like a *nēd*;

He guided them by cloud in the day,
And all the night by the light of fire.

14-15 continue to draw on Exodus 15.

Chapter IV

ZION AND JERUSALEM AS RELIGIOUS AND POLITICAL CAPITAL:
IDEOLOGY AND UTOPIA

Moshe Weinfeld
The Hebrew University of Jerusalem

Jerusalem's "election" as Israel's capital and as a central temple city represented a profound innovation in Israel's history. This innovation manifested itself in two ways:
1) the establishment of a royal dynasty;
2) the creation of a fixed religious center.

These two developments shattered earlier sacral conceptual frameworks. The "Chosen House" and the "House of David," concepts that began to crystallize during the United Monarchy, conflicted, as we shall see, with Israelite tradition from the time of the Exodus through the period of the judges. But once they had struck roots among the people and received theological legitimation, these ideas became cornerstones of Israel's religion; they even acquired an elevated universalistic dimension that ultimately left its mark on all the monotheistic world religions.

In Part One of this study we shall deal, on the one hand, with the implications of the transition from tribal to dynastic-monarchic leadership, and on the other hand, with the transition from a mobile to a fixed shrine. In Part Two we shall address the issue of the crystallization of the ideology of the royal city and the temple city in Israel (against the background of similar ideologies in the royal capitals of Near Eastern empires), and the prophetic visions that drew on this ideology.

Part One
The House of David and the Chosen Shrine as Turning Points
in the History of Israel

To comprehend the significance of the change that the establishment of a dynastic monarchy and a permanent religious and political center wrought among the people, it is necessary to examine in brief the nature of Israel's government in the era preceding the kingship. We shall place particular stress on the meaning of the transition from 'ēdâ ("congregation") to monarchy.

1. The 'ēdâ and its Organization

In order fully to understand the idea of the 'ēdâ, one must bear in mind that the term, which describes the tribes' organization in the wilderness and in

75

the period of the judges, appears for the last time in the Bible's historical literature in connection with Jeroboam's coronation (1 Kgs 12:20).[1] This suggests that with the establishment of the kingdom in north and south, the body in question in some respect gave way to the monarchy. Josh 9:15ff.; 22:9ff.; Judges 20-21[2] are particularly instructive about the 'ēdâ's autonomous working. In these texts the 'ēdâ and its $n^e\acute{s}\hat{i}\,\hat{i}m$ ("chieftains") arrive at decisions concerning the concluding of a treaty with foreigners (Josh 9:15b-21),[3] going to battle against deviant tribes (Josh 22:12; Judg 20:1-2, 9ff.), eradicating men who didn't participate in the war of the 'ēdâ (Judg 21:10), and proclaiming peace (21:13). Even if a national leader, the "judge," does appear in this period, his activity consists of waging war and not of administering tribal or national policy, whether external or domestic. Even after his victory, he does not create a fixed religious or secular center;[4] and he plainly does not pass his office on to his children.[5] Moreover, the judge's status depended on the 'ēdâ and its elders (Judg 8:22; 11:9ff.; 1 Sam 8:4ff.);[6] these also exercised

---

[1] For the term 'ēdâ and its distribution in biblical literature, see A. Hurvitz, "Linguistic Observations on the Biblical Usage of the Priestly Term EDA," *Tarbiz* 40 (1961), 261-267 (Hebrew). For the 'ēdâ's nature and activity, see J. Liver, "'ēdâ," *Encyclopedia Miqra'it* VI, cols. 83-89; M. Weinfeld, "Congregation," *Encyclopedia Judaica* V, 893-896.

[2] Judges 19-21 reveals a polemic bias (anti-Benjaminite and pro-Judahite; cf. 20:18; this was seen already by M. Guedemann, "Tendenz und Abfassungszeit der Letzten Kapitel des Buches der Richter," *MGWJ* 18 [1869], 357-368). But there is no justification to deny on this basis the reliability of the story itself, and in particular the reliability of the technical details related to the working of the 'ēdâ at that time. We are concerned here with a narrator who provides important incidental information.

[3] This pericope, with its priestly character, is parallel to the description in the first part of the chapter in which "the men of Israel" negotiate with the Gibeonites. See Weinfeld, review of J. Blenkinsopp, *Gibeon and Israel: The Role of Gibeon and the Gibeonites in the Political and Religious History of Early Israel, IEJ* 26 (1976), 63.

[4] Gideon's erection of the ephod in Ophrah is an action stemming from the attempt to crown him. See, for example, the remark of Y. Kaufmann, *The Book of Judges* (Jerusalem: Magnes, 1973), 192 (Hebrew): "The story about the ephod is certainly the continuation of the assignment of rulership to Gideon."

[5] For an accurate characterization of the "judge's" mode of leadership, see A. Malamat, "The Savior-Judge as Leader in the Era of the Judges," in *Types of Leadership in the Biblical Period* (Jerusalem: Israel Academy of Sciences and the Humanities, 1973), 11-25 (Hebrew).

[6] Concerning the reciprocal link between the tribal elders and the judge appointed by them, see recently H. Reviv, "Leadership in the period of the Judges—Central Points and Resolutions," *Beersheba Annual, Studies in Bible,*

authority over such national religious and social affairs as those mentioned in Judges 20-21, and over foreign policy (as in the case of Joshua 9, the Gibeonite covenant).

It must be conceded that the king, too, regularly consulted with the elders of the people (see 1 Kgs 20:7). But in his rule, the king was autonomous—the responsibility of managing the government was his and his alone. It is no coincidence that *the evil done in the sight of the LORD* in the era of the monarchy is reckoned the king's fault, while *the evil done* in the era of the judges is charged to the people's account.[7] The king had it in his power to eliminate apostasy, to remove the "high places," and to bring to an end oppression and injustice. Correspondingly, it was on his shoulders that responsibility for what was done among the people in the monarchic era was laid. Conversely, in the period of the judges, the *'eda* of Israel had the power to expunge the evil from the nation (cf. Judg 20:13). The responsibility for what was done among the people lay with it alone (and see below for the ostracization of transgressors against the *'ēdâ*).

At the head of the *'ēdâ* stood the $n^e \acute{s}\hat{i}\hat{i}m$, of whom we hear nothing in the monarchic era.[8] Indeed, in place of the curse of God and the *nāśi'* that occurs in the ancient statute of the Covenant Code (Exod 22:27), we hear in the monarchic period of the curse of God and the *king* (1 Kgs 21:10; Isa 8:21).

2. The Army and War

This important, even vital institution was the bailiwick of the *'ēdâ* and its elders in the period of the judges. In most instances, the judge himself leads the people to war. But he is no more than a sort of deputy of the *'ēdâ* in this

---

Ancient Israel, and the Ancient Near East 1 (1973), 204-221 (Hebrew). On the judge as one who performs both executive and juridicial functions, see Weinfeld, "Judge and Officer in Ancient Israel and in the Ancient Near East," *Israel Oriental Studies* 7 (1977), 65ff.

[7] Cf. "He did ... what was evil in the sight of the LORD" or "He did ... what was right in the sight of the LORD" in the framework of Kings with "The children of Israel did what was evil in the sight of the LORD" in the framework of the book of Judges. On these differences in presentation, see Weinfeld, *Deuteronomy and the Deuteronomic School* (Oxford: Clarendon, 1972), 171.

[8] For the institution of the $n^e \acute{s}\hat{i}\hat{i}m$ ("chieftains") in pre-monarchic Israel, see M. Noth, *Das System der zwölf Stämme Israels* (Stuttgart: Kohlhammer, 1930), 96ff., 158ff. Among the Reubenites, who continued a nomadic way of life even after the establishment of the monarchy, there is evidence of the existence of $n^e \acute{s}\hat{i}\hat{i}m$ in later periods. See 1 Chr 5:6; Weinfeld, "Chieftain," *Encyclopedia Judaica* V, 420-421.

respect, or of the tribe. Organization and conscription rested in the hands of the tribal leadership, and more especially in those of the "men of Israel *('îš yiśrā'ēl)"* (Judg 7:23; 20:10ff., *et al.*), which was the body constitutive of the Israelite tribes, and which appears primarily in military contexts (Judg 7:23; 20:11; 2 Sam 7:14, 24 *et al.*). "The men of Israel" appear in Absalom's war against David; and in the opinion of H. Tadmor,[9] Absalom tried to breathe life into this patriarchal institution and to counterpose it to David's mercenary army. I should observe in this connection that just as the *'ēdâ* disappears from the historical literature after the division of the kingdom, so too there is no trace of "the men of Israel" after Solomon's time.

In the monarchic era, the army and its organization came under the king's exclusive jurisdiction. Although the organization of the popular army was still based on the tribal structures,[10] the king established units of a seasoned standing army and even included in his army foreign mercenary units. These served as his basic strike force, and worked swiftly and effectively (cf. 2 Sam 20:5ff.). The change that took place in this area with the establishment of the monarchy comes to full expression in "the 'manner' of the king" *(mišpāṭ hammelek)* in 1 Sam 8:11-12: "Your sons he will take and install in his chariotry and cavalry . . . to provide himself with officers of thousands and officers of fifties."

The formation of the core of a standing army is described as early as Saul's day: "Saul spied out every warrior and every man of valor and gathered him to him" (1 Sam 14:52; cf. 13:2). The institution of the "warriors of David" *(gibbôrê dāwid)*[11] and "the servants (soldiers) of David" (2 Sam 2:17, 31; 18:7 etc.) originate in David's time and these combat the popular army organized by Absalom—the "men of Israel" (2 Sam 17:14, 24) and the "people of Israel" *('am Yiśrā'ēl)* (2 Sam 18:7). As is well known, units of the mercenary army such as the Cherethites and the Pelethites originated in David's time (compare 2 Sam 15:18). If in the time of the judges, and indeed, in Saul's time, the army was more or less the "army of the LORD" (Judg 5:11; 2 Sam 1:12), or "the congregation of the people of God" (Judg 20:2), from David's day forward the army became gradually David's army: "the men of David" (2 Sam 5:6), "the servants of David" (2 Sam 11:11; 20:6 *et al.*)—in other words, the army of the king. The author of Chronicles, who wrote at a considerable remove from the events of the relevant period, tendentiously changes "the men of David" to "all Israel": instead of "the king and his men

---

[9] H. Tadmor, "The People and the Kingship in Ancient Israel. The Role of Political Institutions in the Biblical Period," *Journal of World History* 11 (1968), 381ff.

[10] See H. Reviv, "*ṣābā'*," *Encyclopedia Miqra'it* VI, cols 650-655.

[11] On this institution, see B. Mazar, "The Warriors of David," in *Canaan and Israel—Historical Researches* (Jerusalem: Mossad Bialik and Israel Exploration Society, 1974), 183-207 (Hebrew).

went" (2 Sam 5:6), he employs the phrase, "David and all Israel went" (1 Chr 11:4).[12]

3. The Institution of Holy War

In wars, which were the wars of the LORD, the 'ēdâ acted in accordance with traditional sacral principles. The enemy, who was the LORD's enemy (see Judg 5:31), had to be annihilated as god had commanded and without compromise. Thus, the book of Joshua reports the total destruction of Jericho: "man and woman, young and old, ox and sheep and ass at the point of the sword" (Josh 6:21). A similar formulation occurs in Samuel's words to Saul concerning Amaleq's eradication: "man and woman, infant and suckling, ox and sheep, camel[13] and ass" (1 Sam 15:3).

Saul wages such a Holy War against Nob, the city of priests. There we read, "And Nob, the city of priests, he smote with the sword, man and woman, infant and suckling, and ox and ass and sheep—at the point of the sword" (1 Sam 22:19).[14] An extreme "ban" of this sort is applied to the tribe of Benjamin in the case of the concubine in Gibeah. There the text relates that the "men of Israel" smote the Benjaminites with the sword, "city and people and beasts and every creature found," "and all the towns they encountered they put to the torch" (Judg 20:48). This Holy War against an Israelite population calls to mind the law of the "wayward" city in Deuteronomy 13[15] according to which one must smite the inhabitants of the city and its cattle with the sword and burn the city and its spoil *in their entirety* to the LORD (Deut 13:16-17). So too, Judges 20 states that "the men of Israel" smote Gibeah of Benjamin with the sword, and the "*city in its entirety* went up in smoke heavenward" (v 40).

Another type of Holy War that is known to us from the Pentateuch in connection with the Midianites is associated with the killing of "all males and all women who have known men carnally" (Num 31:17). The 'ēdâ execute such a "ban" against the inhabitants of Jabesh Gilead, who did not join in action with the Israelites (Judg 21:11; cf. Gen 34:25).[16]

---

[12] See recently S. Japhet, *The Ideology of the Book of Chronicles* etc. (Jerusalem: Mossad Bialik, 1977), 234 (Hebrew).

[13] The camel, which does not appear in other formulations of *herem*, here reflects the nomadic background characteristic of the Amaleqites, who like the Midianites and Ishmaelites raised camels (see Judg 6:3; 7:32; 1 Sam 30:17; 1 Chr 27:30, etc.).

[14] Nob was considered a town in rebellion against the king (22:13) since it violated the loyalty oath given to the king in the LORD's name; hence the extreme ban. In this respect, see Weinfeld, *Deuteronomy* (above, n. 7), 99.

[15] *Ibid.*, 91ff., and below, pp.

[16] The "ban" in Deut 20:16-17 falling automatically on all the Canaanite

In this regard it is instructive to note that the "ban" against a tribe or part of a tribal league for abrogating the sanctified stipulations of a twelve-party covenant also occurs among the Greek tribal leagues that in so many respects resemble Israel's league.[17]   Aeschines, for example, writing of the foundation of the sanctuary at Delphi, relates that members of the amphicty-onic league swore to punish with all possible vigor anyone who should violate the god's shrine or be accessory to such violation.[18]   Indeed, Aeschines tells us of a city that committed sacrilege against the shrine:[19]   when the Pythia at Delphi was consulted, she instructed the inquirers to proceed against this city, to destroy it, to enslave its inhabitants and to render its soil anathema to Apollo *(anatheinai tō Apollōni)*; she decreed that the land lie entirely uncul-tivated *(epi pasē aergia)*.   When the punishment was executed, it was pro-claimed that the city that would not come to the aid of the god and the sacred land would be debarred from the shrine and would be impure and accursed.[20]

The biblical stories about the erection of an altar in Transjordan (Josh 22:9ff.) and the war that ensued upon the rape of the concubine at Gibeah (Judges 20-21) present us with similar action against those who attack the 'ēdâ and its sacra. The Transjoranian tribes' erection of an altar was regarded as an act of rebellion against the LORD (Josh 22:16ff.); accordingly, the whole 'ēdâ of Israel assembled to go to battle against the Gadites and Reubenites and to devastate the land in which they dwelled (Josh 22:12, 33).[21]   The same

---

inhabitants of the land has in it utopian elements and evinces a later bias. See Weinfeld, *Deuteronomy* (above, n. 7), 166ff.

[17]M. Noth exaggerated the case in his adduction of the Greek amphic-tyony as a model for Israel. See his *System* (above, n. 8). For specific objec-tions against the hypothesis, see recently, C. H. J. de Geus, *The Tribes of Israel* (Assen: van Gorcum, 1976), against which see O. Baechli, *Amphiktyonie in alten Israel* (Basel: F. Reinhart, 1977), with considerable relevant bibliog-raphy. Nevertheless, it seems to me that Noth's approach still contains the solution to numerous problems of pre-monarchic Israelite government.

[18]Aeschines, *On the Embassy*, 115 (classical references are to the Loeb editions unless otherwise stated).

[19]*Against Ctesiphon*, 107ff.

[20]καὶ ἐναγὴς ἔσται και τῇ ἀρᾷ ἔνοχος, ibid., 122.

[21]The remove of some tribes from their fundamental base in Cisjordan created some concern about the severing of religious ties with the motherland. Thus the building of a separate altar was regarded as revolt and as secession from the congregation of Israel; accordingly, the tribes wage war against Gad and Reuben. A similar phenomenon occurs among the Greek tribal leagues. There we find the colony and mother city in Greece were joined by having the same sanctuary and the same cults. See, for example, A. J. Graham, *Colony and Mother City in Ancient Greece* (Manchester Univ. Press, 1964), 216. Cf. also pp. 160ff.; on the whole problem cf. my forthcoming study: "The Extent of the Promised Land—The Status of Transjordan."

principle applies to the war against the inhabitants of Gibeah, who "committed an outrage *(nebâlâ)*" (Judg 20:10). Just as the tribes of Greece inquire of a god before going to war against those who defiled the shrine, so too Israel's tribes inquire of the LORD before battle (Judg 20:18, 27). Just as in Greece, the tribes war against the city, destroy it, and burn it to the ground (vv 40, 48).[22] As in Greece, so also in Israel the "ban" falls also on the city that refuses to participate in the Holy War.

From the era of David and Solomon onward, we hear no more of Holy War of this variety. The prophets do reprove kings for failing to execute the Holy War in its most stringent form (1 Sam 15; 1 Kgs 20:42). Despite this, the kings operate in accordance with political considerations and no longer pursue the fulfilment of the law of Holy War. The text even testifies explicitly that the Canaanite peoples who were not annihilated by the Canaanites were reduced by Solomon to forced labor (1 Kgs 9:21).

4. The Sacral Sanction: Curses and Oaths

The *'êdâ* and its leaders customarily employed sacral sanctions in order to discourage transgressors. This they did by proclaiming a curse amounting to expulsion (see below) against any who might sin by violating the holy regulations. So, after the conquest of Jericho, Joshua announces, "Cursed before the LORD is the man who arises to rebuild this city" (Josh 6:26). "The men of Israel" at Mizpeh make the people swear with a "Cursed be" that they will not give their daughters to Benjaminites (Judg 21:1; cf. v 18). The last occurrence of such a curse stems from Saul in his war against the Philistines: "cursed is the man who eats bread before evening when I am acquitted of my enemies" (1 Sam 14:24).

---

[22]Gibeah's fate ("the whole [כליל] of the city went up in smoke to the heavens"; Judg 20:20) resembles that of the banished city in Deut 13:20: "Burn the city with fire—wholly (כליל) to the LORD your God." In the continuation there, we read "it will be an eternal ruin *(tl)*; it will never again be rebuilt," to which one should compare Deut 29:22: "the whole land (of the rebel) is a burning; it will not be sown, nor will it flourish." In light of the parallels with the Holy War in the Greek amphictyony (the prohibition against ploughing the ground) it seems that in Gibeah's case also this custom was implemented (cf. also the case of the "ban" against Jericho in Josh 6:26). Concerning the instances of breach of covenant which entail a conflagration and the prohibition of ploughing the soil or sowing it or building the city again, Near Eastern sources provide us with numerous instances of the practice. See esp. Weinfeld, *Deuteronomy* (above, n. 7), 109ff. On the punishment of subvertors and enemies of the people in comparison to the laws in Deuteronomy 13 (regarding subversion and enticement), see Weinfeld, "The Loyalty Oath in the Ancient Near East," *UF* 8 (1976), 389-390.

The Greek tribal leagues provide parallels in this matter as well. Greek amphictyonies destroyed Cirrha, annihilated its accursed inhabitants, and took a "mighty oath" *(horkon ischuron)*[23] against anyone who might arise and build the demolished city anew,[24] which reminds us of the curse of Joshua concerning Jericho. Another analogy can be seen in the Lacedaemonians' swearing an oath in the hour of battle that they will not return home until they defeat the enemy.[25] This instance calls to mind Saul's aforementioned curse (1 Sam 14:24) and the Israelite tribes' vow in connection with the war at Gibeah: "We will not go each to his tent, nor will we disperse each man to his home" (Judg 20:8).[26]

The "accursed" seems to be one who is ejected from the *'ēdâ*,[27] and, if so, some kind of excommunication is involved.[28] Indeed, it is in this way that the series of "curses" in Deuteronomy 27, which are tied to the ceremony that takes place between Mt. Gerizim and Mt. Ebal, are easiest explained. What characterizes the "curses" in Deuteronomy 27 is their being transgressions perpetrated clandestinely, which is to say, transgressions that would be impossible for the polity at large to punish.[29] The *'ēdâ* held the conviction that it

---

[23] Cf. "the great oath" that the Israelites swore against whoever had not come up to Mizpeh for the war against Gibeah (Judg 21:5).

[24] Aeschines, *Against Ctesiphon*, 108-109.

[25] Polybius, 12.6.

[26] See my remarks in connection with "Sun, stand still in Gibeon," in S. A. Loewenstamm Volume, *Studies in the Bible and the Ancient Near East* (Jerusalem: Rubenstein, 1978), 180-181.

[27] It is thus that one must understand the curse of Meroz in Judg 5:23— " 'Curse Meroz!' says the angel of the LORD, 'Curse, o curse its inhabitants; for they did not come to the aid of the LORD with warriors' " (for angels' curse, see Damascus Document 20:28: "For the holy ones of the Most High cursed him"). See also Weinfeld, "Sun, stand still" (above, n. 26), 178 n. 48. On the curse of the inhabitants of Meroz, see A. Malamat, "The Period of the Judges," in *Judges* (ed. B. Mazar, World History of the Jewish People vol. III; New Brunswick: Rutgers, 1971), 322 n. 82.

[28] The ostracism, excommunication and ban found in later Judaism (נדוי, שמתא, חרם) are apparently forms that evolved from the biblical "Cursed be." The Rabbis themselves attest (B. Sheb. 36a) that " 'cursed be'—this is ostracism" (for נדוי, ostracism, cf. Akk. *nadû* = cast off afar), whereas the Talmudic *ḥerem* is anticipated already in Ezra 10:8, where we find the proclamation, "Whoever does not come within three days according to the counsel of the officials and the elders, his property will be confiscated *(yḥrm)*; he will be separated from the congregation of the exiled." The confiscation of property and separation from the congregation are the *excommunicatio* underlying the biblical "Cursed" and the halakhic "banned."

[29] See Ibn Ezra's comment on Deut 27:14: "One mentions these 11 transgressions because it is possible to commit them in secret. Witness: 'he

was liable to punishment if transgressors were present in its midst (cf. the case of Achan in Josh 7). It could purge itself of these transgressors and avert punishment[30] by excommunicating the transgressors by means of a curse proclaimed in a binding ceremonial context. It is no coincidence that the ceremony is located at Shechem, a city hallowed from the days of the patriarchs, and in which Joshua made a covenant with Israel before the LORD (Joshua 24).

The proclamations are constructed according to a stereotyped opening with "cursed be" ('ārûr) and proceeding to a verbal participle and object. Based on a four-stress meter,[31] they amount to declarations of a formal and ritual character appropriate to the ceremony:

Cursed be he who insults his father or mother!   ארור מקלה אביו ואמו

Cursed be he who lies with his mother-in-law!   ארור שכב עם חתנתו

Cursed be he who misdirects a blind man on the road!

ארור משנה עור בדרך

Cursed be he who moves his neighbor's boundary-stone!

ארור מסיג גבול רעהו

The people respond "Amen" to every curse. In this way, the sinner takes the due punishment on himself (cf. "Amen, Amen" of the *soṭa* in Num 5:32).

Another form of proclamation that is close to the "Cursed be" in its formulation is found in the set of laws in Exod 21:12, 15-17; 22:18-19. These proclamations, directed against transgressors who have sinned openly and whom society must punish, open with the verbal participle plus object and conclude with the sentence "*mot yûmāt*—he shall be put to death." They exhibit a five-beat meter, cf., e.g.:

He who strikes a man, and kills him, shall be put to death (21:12)

מכה איש ומת מות יומת

He who reviles his father or mother shall be put to death (21:17)

מקלל אביו ואמו מות יומת

---

erected it in secret' (v 15), for if he did it publicly he would be killed. So, too, 'He who strikes his friend in secret' (v 24)."

[30] This is the case in the Talmud when the accursed and cut off from the people are discussed. The expressions "among your people" or "cut off from her people," which appear in connection with one to be punished by *kareth* ("cut off") (Exod 31:14 *et al.*) are followed in the Talmud by the saying "and peace is with you/peace is with him" (see the passages cited from the halakhic midrashim in H. S. Horowitz, ed., *Siphre ad Numeros*, § 14, p. 19, line 15), which comes to say that with the sinner's removal from the congregation, the people achieved well-being. This concept accurately represents the background of the proclamation of the "cursed be's" in Deuteronomy 27.

[31] These declarations underwent deuteronomistic editing, hence the departure from the stereotype encountered in this section. See Weinfeld, *Deuteronomy* (above, n. 7), 277 n. 2.

He who lies with a beast shall be put to death (22:18).

שֹׁכֵב עִם בְּהֵמָה מוֹת יוּמַת

These proclamations too appear to have been recited during a ceremony in which the 'ēdâ took it upon itself to rout out transgressors and kill them. Similar phenomena occur in ancient Greece. There, those who violated the law were reviled by the leaders and priests of the polity and were made "accursed" (eparatos). So, for example, it is related of Alcibiades (Plutarch, *Alcibiades* 22) that he was found liable at law for despoiling the sacra of Demeter. After placing his property under the "ban," his judges decided that the priests and priestesses should curse him. Aristides is said to have suggested that the priests should cast curses on anyone who abandoned the war-treaty with the Greeks (Plutarch, *Aristides* 10).

Curses and blessings of the fruits of the womb, of the soil and of livestock, which appear as sanctions in Israel's covenant (Exod 23:25-26; Deut 7:13-15; 28:18 *et al.*) also surface in the oaths of the amphictyonic leagues. For instance, the oath taken by the members of the amphictyony against Cirrha includes the clause, "If anyone—whether city, man or tribe[32]—abrogates this oath . . . , their soil will not bear fruit, their wives will not give birth . . . their livestock will not foal."[33] And in the Greeks' oath at Plataeia before their war against the barbarians (section 7): "If I observe what is written in the treaty, my city will be free of disease . . . my land will bear fruit . . . and the women will give birth . . . and the cattle will give birth."[34] The last example calls to mind the promise made in the Covenant Code's peroration (Exod 23:25-26): "I shall remove illness from your midst; none will miscarry or go barren in your land," and also the promise in Deut 7:13ff., which depends on that in Exodus 23:[35] "He will bless the fruit of your womb and the fruit of your soil . . . the increase of your herds, and your flocks of sheep . . . there will be neither male nor female barren among you and your livestock. And the LORD will remove from you all sickness." To all appearance, this genre of blessings and curses has its origin in the tribal government of the period of the judges; hence the similarity to the blessings and curses of the amphictyonic league in Greece.

---

[32] Compare the curse of the abrogater of the covenant in Deut 29:17: "Man or woman or clan or tribe," and so Deuteronomy 13, in which the clan (vv 7-12) or the city (vv 13-19) that abrogates the covenant and brings the "ban" on itself is addressed.

[33] Aeschines, *Against Ctesiphon*, 111.

[34] See P. Siewert, *Der Eid von Plataiai* (München: C. H. Beck, 1972), 98ff.; for amphictyonic covenants and oaths in Greece, see F. R. Wüst, "Amphiktyonie, Eidgenossenschaft, Symmachie," *Historia* 3 (1954-55), pp. 129-153; G. Daux, "Serments amphictioniques et serment de Platées," *Studies Presented to D. M. Robinson*, vol. 3 (St. Louis: Washington Univ., 1953), 775-782.

[35] See Weinfeld, *Deuteronomy* (above n. 7), 46.

The possibility that Israel persisted in this method of curse and expulsion even after David's and Solomon's time is not to be excluded. However, we shall see below that the transfer to a king of authority in political and social affairs entailed a reduction in the use of sacral sanctions whose source was the declaration of the 'ēdâ and its leaders.

5. Sacred Objects in War

In the period in which the 'ēdâ was active, it was customary to carry forth to war the ark of the covenant and the sacred vessels (Num 10:35-36; 31:6; Josh 6:6; Judg 20:27; 1 Samuel 3-4). We last hear of the ark of the covenant on the battlefield in the account of David's war against the Ammonites (2 Sam 11:11). From that point forward, neither the ark nor the sacred vessels are mentioned in connection with war. It appears that in this domain as well a substantial development occurred in the monarchic era.

6. The Use of Mantic Devices

Until David's time, an ephod (Urim and Thummim) was generally employed in order to inquire of the LORD. From his time onward, however, inquiry seems to have been restricted to intuitive prophecy only; we hear no more of mechanical mantic prophecy.[36]

* * * * *

It appears that with the entrenchment of the monarchy, the religio-social institutions that flourished in the context of the 'ēdâ's earlier vigor withered away. The 'ēdâ and its neśî'îm ceased to be the decisive factor in the organization of the army and in war. The institution of the Holy War gradually vanished: of the curse and expulsion proclaimed by decree of the 'ēdâ we hear no more; and the link to the sacred instruments, to the ark of the covenant, and to the Urim and Thummim, weakens greatly. In sum, we are entitled to say that with the establishment of the monarchy in Israel, sovereignty passed from the "congregation of the LORD" ('ădat YHWH) and the assembly of God, to the king. So kingship, as it were, was appropriated from God; dominion passed into the hand of those of flesh and blood (see below). Indeed, as I have intimated, the establishment of a dynastic monarchy and the foundation of a permanent sanctuary produced a major

---

[36] Abiathar, who carries the ephod, was expelled by Solomon (1 Kgs 2:26). From this point onward, the requirements of prophecy are fulfilled by prophets and seers operating by ecstatic and intuitive means alone. Prophets of this variety are known to us from the Near East, and especially from the vicinity of Mari. See recently Weinfeld, "Ancient Near Eastern Patterns in Prophetic Literature," VT 27 (1977), 181-182.

transformation in Israel's life and religion. The earlier outlook had taught that God bestows his spirit on any mortal at any time he pleases, and manifests himself in any place in which he chooses to locate his presence. Now, with the establishment of the kingship and the foundation of the Temple, there is a fixed locus for epiphany and a fixed dynasty from which the leader will always arise. Let us clarify the character ot this transformation.

Kingship and Dynasty

Opposition to a kingship of flesh and blood is first mentioned in connection with the offer of the throne to Gideon. The "men of Israel" turn to Gideon with the statement, "Rule over us, you and your son and your son's son." Gideon answers: "I will not rule over you; nor will my son rule over you. The LORD will rule over you" (Judg 8:22-23).[37] By invoking both himself and his son, Gideon seeks to exclude any possibility of the establishment of a dynasty of kings in Israel. And, in fact, the succeeding chapter reports that the attempt made by Abimelek, Gideon's son, to assume the crown over Israel resulted only in catastrophic failure. The historian even refrains from characterizing his office as that of king; he says, "Abimelek *held office (wyśr)* over Israel for three years" (9:22). And the apologue that Jotham declaims at Abimelek's coronation also has the tone of anti-monarchic polemic. Possibly, its sting is directed against Abimelek, "the bramble," rather than against the monarchy itself.[38] Nevertheless, one must note that it is precisely those trees productive of fruit that do not agree to accept the offer of kingship; some derision of the monarchy and its institution as devoid of value is then being expressed. This outlook, formulated in starker form, is expressed in Samuel's words in 1 Sam 12:17: "Know and see that the wickedness that you have done in the eyes of the LORD by asking for a king is great." The people acknowledge the sentiment, conceding that "We have added to all our sins the wickedness of asking for a king" (v 19). Israel's request for a king is apprehended as open rebellion against God and as ingratitude for divine favor. God, Israel's king, used to send his people saviors from time to time in order to rescue them from the hand of their enemies (1 Sam 10:18-19; 12:10-11). But the children of Israel did not remember the LORD's beneficence. When Nahash, king of the Ammonites, took up arms against them, they demanded the intercession of a king, in spite of the fact that their true king was the God of Israel: "And you said to me, 'No! Let a king reign over us,' when the LORD, your God, was your king" (1 Sam 12:12; cf. 10:19). What

---

[37] For Gideon's utterance and its meaning in the history of Israel, see M. Buber, *The Kingship of God* (trans. R. Scheimann; New York: Harper and Row, 1967), 59-65.

[38] Y. Kaufmann, *The Book of Judges* (Jerusalem: Magnes, 1973), 201ff. (Hebrew).

is more, in their request to enthrone a king over them, the Israelites repudiate their own singularity. They demand a king who will judge them "like all the nations" (1 Sam 8:5), a thought also evinced at the start of the Deuteronomic law of the king: "Let me place over me a king like all the nations that are about me" (Deut 17:14). The text in the book of Deuteronomy is inspired by the tradition about Saul's coronation, and not *vice versa*. Had the law in the book of Deuteronomy lain before the narrator in 1 Samuel 8, that author could not have given vent to such embittered opposition to the foundation of the monarchy as we encounter in this chapter and in chapter 12.

Scholars of Wellhausen's school disputed the reliability of this testimony; they tied the texts in question to an exilic redactor with theocratic propensities. In Wellhausen's view, exilic disenchantment with the kingship was what underlaid the ideology that saw the kingship as a sin.[39] In another view, that of Budde, the incentive for this ideology's formation came about at the time of Samaria's destruction; this approach finds support—according to Budde—in the prophecies of Hosea, who was active at that time.[40] Each in his own way, M. Buber[41] and Y. Kaufmann[42] rejected these theories. They tried to show that the struggle against the monarchy was no late invention, that it was restricted precisely to an earlier time, and that a fierce contest raged among the Israelite tribes over the establishment of the monarchy in Israel. Many commentators and scholars have adopted this direction in recent years,[43] and Wellhausen's opinion that the stories characterized by an anti-monarchic bias stem from the era of Jerusalem's destruction[44] has but few adherents today.

The establishment of the Israelite monarchy thus entailed revolutionary innovations, which in turn required religious legitimation, especially in regards

---

[39] J. Wellhausen, *Prolegomena to the History of Israel* (trans. J. Sutherland, Black and A. Menzies; Edinburgh: T. & T. Clark, 1885), 254ff.

[40] K. Budde, *Die Bücher Richter und Samuel, ihre Quellen und ihr Aufbau* (Giessen: Richer, 1890), 184ff.

[41] See esp. his volume, *Kingship* (above, n. 37).

[42] *The History of the Religion of Israel*, vol. I (Jerusalem: Mossad Bialik-Dvir, 1946-1956), 686ff. (Hebrew). See also his *Book of Judges* (above, n. 38), 48-49.

[43] See recently F. Crüsemann, *Der Widerstand gegen das Königtum—Die antiköniglichen Texte des alten Testaments und der Kampf an den frühen israelitischen Staat* (Neukirchen-Vluyn: Neukirchener, 1978). And see my review of this volume in *Qiryat Sepher* 44 (1979), 567-573 (= *VT* 31 [1981], 99ff.).

[44] This follows from the assumption that the Deuteronomistic school developed this *Tendenz*. In fact, there is no justification for such a supposition. This school gives no hint of opposition to the monarchy, but rather accepts monarchy as an indispensable institution. See Weinfeld, *Deuteronomy* (above, n. 7), 169ff.

to the concept of dynasty. Such a legitimation is in fact found in the Bible in Nathan's prophecy to David (2 Samuel 7). In this prophecy, God promises David eternal kingship. His promise is constructed along the lines of God's covenant with Abraham. In the covenant with Abraham, land is promised to Abraham's seed as an eternal inheritance.[45] Similarly the Davidic covenant:[46] David's seed will inherit the kingship forever.[47] The promise in both instances is presented unconditionally, just as in other covenants of grant known to us from the Ancient Near East.[48] These covenants of grant concern the giving of a land and a house (= dynasty) to the king's faithful servant. And indeed, the covenant of Abraham, the servant of the LORD, was founded on the promise of a land, whereas the covenant of David, the servant of the LORD, was founded in the promise of a "house," i.e. dynasty. The concepts of the election of Israel and of David are also similar: Israel, chosen from among all the peoples, inherits the land of Israel forever; David, chosen from among all Israel, receives the kingship forever. In this way, the principle of charismatic leadership, according to which God invests his spirit in different men in order to save Israel, became obsolete. From now on, the divine grace given to David would accompany his offspring forever.

Let us now examine the second major innovation accompanying the establishment of the monarchy.

The Chosen Shrine

Although the idea of a fixed dynasty achieved legitimacy in the days of David himself, the notion of a chosen sanctuary remained unconfirmed until the time of his son, Solomon. It is almost as though it was too difficult for a single generation to assimilate two innovations at once. It is worth dwelling momentarily on the innovation of Jerusalem's election and its import.

During the wilderness wanderings, and in the time of the judges as well, there was no fixed place for the deity's tabernacle. The tent of meeting and

---

[45] Gen 13:15; 17:7-8, 19; 48:1.

[46] For the understanding of the promise as a covenant, cf. Ps 89:20ff.; see Weinfeld, "Covenant, Davidic," *IDBSup*, 188-192.

[47] 2 Sam 7:13, 16; Ps 89:5, 38; Isa 55:3; Jer 33:17-18.

[48] See Weinfeld, "The Covenant of Grant in the Old Testament and in the Ancient Near East," *JAOS* 90 (1970), 184-203. In the two primary traditions concerning the covenant of Abraham and of David (Genesis 15; 2 Samuel 7), no conditions are imposed. On the contrary, in the promise to David in 2 Samuel 7 and in Psalm 89 it is stated explicitly that even should he or his sons sin (2 Sam 7:14-15; Ps 89:31ff.), in which case they would be punished, God's fidelity to them would not lapse. For the conditioning of the covenant, see Weinfeld, "Covenant of Grant," 195-196. Cf., however, M. Tsevat, "The Steadfast House," in *The Meaning of the Book of Job and Other Biblical Studies* (New York: Ktav, 1980), 101-117.

the ark of the covenant, which represented the presence of God, are found at various times in different places. The pericope in Judges 19-21 is most instructive in this regard. At first we hear that the people gathered together at Mizpeh (20:1); in the continuation, the people go up to Bethel, "for the ark of the covenant of God was there in those days" (v 27; cf. v 18 and also 21:2). Finally, we hear of the festival of the LORD at Shiloh (21:19) where the tent of meeting and in it the ark of the covenant stood in the time of the judges (Josh 18:1 and 1 Sam 1:1ff.). According to Josh 8:33, the ark of the covenant is found in Shechem: between Mt. Gerizim and Mt. Ebal. These texts admittedly belong to different literary strata and reflect different periods. But all of them have in common the tradition that the ark and the tabernacle had no fixed location in Israel in the pre-monarchic period.

The reality of the wanderings of God's tabernacle is expressed in every particular in the LORD's oracle to Nathan in reaction to David's desire to build a house of cedar for the ark (2 Sam 7:4-7): "Would you build me a house for my dwelling? I have not dwelt in a house from the day I brought the children of Israel up from Egypt until this very day, but have moved about in tent and in tabernacle [in the parallel in 1 Chr 17:5, "from tent to tent, and from tabernacle"—and here, one must perhaps supply, "to tabernacle"]. Wherever I wandered among all the children of Israel—have I spoken one word to one of the tribes of Israel that I commanded to shepherd my people, saying, 'Why have you not built me a house of cedar?' "

God wanders then, among the children of Israel;[49] he does not want to adopt a permanent location in one of the tribes. One might possibly understand this as stemming from a desire to avoid discrimination, in that the tribe in which the LORD's tabernacle dwells would see itself superior to others. In such a light, it is conceivable that the tribes planned the situation. The logic is clear on all sides: just as God does not bestow his spirit permanently on one clan or family, so too, he does not dwell permanently in the patrimony of a single tribe.

God answers David unequivocally: he does not want a (house =) temple. This, however, does not prevent him from promising a house (= dynasty) to David. God foregoes the construction of his own house, but watches over David's house and dynasty. In so doing, he affirms the dynasty's permanence but rejects a permanent location for his tabernacle. Only under Solomon did the notion of a permanent temple materialize.[50] The explanation provided is

---

[49] Compare the expression of Lev 26:11-12: "I shall place my tabernacle in your midst . . . and I shall walk about in your midst," and also Deut 23:15, "For the LORD your God walks about in the midst of your camp."

[50] "He will build a house to my name" in 2 Sam 7:13 is a Deuteronomistic addition. See Weinfeld, *Deuteronomy* (above, n. 7), 194. In any case, the text was written after Solomon's construction of the sanctuary became an accomplished fact.

that in his days the children of Israel finally attained to their "resting-place," their full inheritance; therefore the deity, too, attains to his "resting-place" (1 Kgs 5:17-18). This idea achieves its fullest expression in Psalm 132: "For the LORD has chosen Zion. He has desired it for a dwelling: 'This is my resting-place for always; here I shall dwell, for I have desired it . . . . There shall I make David's standard sprout forth. I have prepared a lamp for my anointed'." The idea of a Davidic house here joins together with the idea of the chosen house, and the circle is closed.[51]

In point of fact, the two ideas, the house of David and the chosen sanctuary, came about by dint of the new historical-political matrix. In order to produce a kingdom "like all the nations," it was necessary to establish a dynasty on the one hand and a royal sanctuary on the other—in Amos' words, "a sanctuary of the king and a temple of the kingdom" (7:13). The sanctuary was "a house of cedars," in contradistinction to the tabernacle that was fashioned from "shittim" wood (Exod 25:10; 26:15, *et al.*). The use of cedar for building sanctuaries and palaces is known to us from as early as the third millennium B.C.E.[52] In order to build his royal palace, David was compelled to use cedar brought from Tyre (2 Sam 5:11), and this is also the case with the construction of the temple by Solomon: the wood for the building of the sanctuary was brought from Tyre; the chief architect was a man from Tyre (1 Kgs 7:13ff.; 2 Chr 2:6, 12-13), and even the builders themselves were Tyrians and Byblians (1 Kgs 5:32). Furthermore, it is now known that Solomon's temple was constructed according to temple plans that were prevalent throughout Syria and Phoenicia.[53]

The organizing of the administration and the collection of taxes were also done with the aid of foreign officers and appointees who had acquired experience in the monarchic city-states of Canaan.[54] These cities were committed to the performance of corvée, institutions vital to every royal house in the Near East. *ms* and *sbl* are terms equivalent to the Akkadian terms *ilku* and *tupšikku*. *Ilku* (= *hlk*; see Ezra 4:13) describes the performance of some service on the king's behalf, and as can be learned from the etymology of *ilku* (= *alaku* 'go, walk') and from its association with *harrānu* (= route, way), this service was bound up with travel, whereas the term *tupšikku* (= basket) relates to the act of carrying a basket in construction work. This term is

---

[51] See Weinfeld, "Covenant, Davidic" (above, n. 46), 188-189. Psalm 132 also expresses the polarity between the house of God and the dynastic house. David swore to find a resting-place for God (v 2), while God swore to establish an eternal dynasty for David.

[52] For the typology of the construction of sanctuaries in the Near East, see Weinfeld, *Deuteronomy* (above, n. 7), 248ff.

[53] See the entry, "*mqdš šlmh*," *Encyclopedia Miqra'it* V, cols. 332ff.

[54] B. Mazar, "The Scribe of King David and the Problem of High Office in the Kingship of Israel," *Canaan and Israel* (above, n. 11), 208-221.

equivalent to Hebrew *sbl* (= *sablum* in Akkadian), whose meaning is 'basket (used for carrying)' (see Ps. 81:7: "I removed his shoulder from the burden [*sbl*]; his hands passed from the basket [*dwd*]").[55] *Mas* in Hebrew and *massu* in Akkadian documents from the West refer to service bound up with travel like that reported in 1 Kgs 5:27-28 and in the Alalakh documents.[56] It is comparable to Akk. *ilku* in meaning. The text in 1 Kings 5 relates that Solomon assigned 30,000 men to *mas* in the Lebanon (vv 27-28), and 150,000 men to *sbl* and hewing stones in the mountains of that region (vv 29-30). These pairs of expressions—*ms* and *sbl* in the Bible, *ilku* and *tupšikku* in Assyria—describe the most fundamental obligations to the crown. They are found also in Hittite *(saḫḫan luzi)* and Egyptian *(z bjt, k3 t).*[57]

These obligations, rendered to the crown, which impinge on individual freedom, are expressed, in fact, in "the 'manner' of the king" in 1 Sam 8:9ff. Samuel warns the people that by crowning a king they enslave themselves to the king (v 17): They will be conscripted for the king's guard and army (v 11), they will be drafted to work for the king (ploughing and harvesting—v 12), their fields and vineyards will be placed at the king's disposal (v 17), they will need to surrender a tithe of their produce and flocks (vv 15, 17), and they will lend their servants and beasts of burden in press to the king (v 16).[58] These obligations were in fact so heavy that the house of Joseph revolted against Judah after Solomon's death (1 Kings 12).

The foundation of a *royal sanctuary* and a *royal palace*, which entailed an assimilation to "all the nations," made Israel into an empire, alongside Egypt and Assyria which were then (during the United Monarchy) in decline.[59] David succeeded in creating an empire in a relatively short time. Helped by a seasoned standing army, he achieved ascendance over the Philistines and subdued the big Canaanite cities on the coast and inland valleys.

---

[55] See P. Artzi, "Sablum = סבל," *Bulletin of the Israel Exploration Society* 18 (1944), 66-77 (Hebrew); M. Held, "The Root ZBL/SBL in Akkadian, Ugaritic and Biblical Hebrew," *JAOS* 88 (1968), 93ff.; A. A. Rainey, "Compulsory Labour Gangs in Israel," *IEJ* 20 (1970), 191ff.

[56] See Rainey, "Labour Gangs" (above, n. 55).

[57] On these see my forthcoming *Justice and Righteousness in Israel and among the Nations, Equality and Freedom in Israel in the Light of Ancient Near Eastern Social Reforms* (to be published by Magnes press).

[58] On these and on the remissions granted from these obligations to those under the king's protection, see my forthcoming study, mentioned in the preceding note.

[59] See A. Malamat, "Aspects of the Foreign Policies of David and Solomon," in *The Kingdoms of Israel and Judah* (A. Malamat, ed.; Jerusalem: Israel Exploration Society, 1961), 24-46 (Hebrew); *idem*, "The Kingdom of David and Solomon—Toward the establishment of a Power," in *Thirty Years of Archaeology—1938-1968, 35th Congress for the Study of the Land* (Jerusalem: Israel Exploration Society, 1981), 190ff. (Hebrew).

Afterward, he moved against the neighboring monarchies: he smote the Moabites and made them his vassals and tributaries (2 Sam 8:2) and, by assuming the crown of their king, annexed the kingdom of Ammon to his land (2 Sam 12:29-31). But battle with Ammon drew Aram into war as well. Aram at first allied themselves with Ammon, and were routed (10:6-14). After the defeat, Hadadezer, king of Zobah, assembled a large contingent of forces from northern Transjordan, in which Aramean elements from across the Euphrates also took part (10:15ff.). This time, too, the Israelites triumphed and subdued Aram. The final, decisive confrontation occurred when Aram-Damascus came to Hadadezer's aid and David smote it as well (2 Sam 8:5-6).

In consequence of these victories, Aram became David's vassal (10:19), and Aram-Damascus became an Israelite province (8:6). Against Edom, Judah's enemy to the south, David struck especially hard (2 Sam 8:13; Ps 60:2), reducing it to provincial status (2 Sam 8:14). After the Arameans' subjugation, the king of Hamath came to David, brought gifts and accepted his protection (10:9-10). As a result of all this, David's and Solomon's kingdom stretched from the river of Egypt in the south to Lebo-Hamath in the north (1 Kgs 8:65) and to the Euphrates in the northeast (1 Kgs 5:1, 4),[60] fulfilling Isaac's prophecy to Jacob—"Peoples will serve you and nations will bow down to you" (Gen 27:19)—on the one hand, and on the other, the prophetic promise to Abraham that the land given his descendants would stretch "from the river of Egypt to the great river, the Euphrates" (Gen 15:18).[61] In poetic language, we encounter the same promises in the psalms: "(Let) all the kings bow down to him, all the nations serve him" (Ps 72:11); and "(Let) him rule from sea to sea, from river to the ends of earth" (v 8).[62] In the same psalm, addressed in the superscripture to Solomon, the promise of tribute from all

---

[60]One must distinguish here between a description of the borders of Canaan as it was preserved in priestly traditions (Numbers 34), which draw on the ancient Egyptian tradition about the boundaries of the province of Canaan, which does exclude Transjordan (see B. Mazar, "Lebo-Hamath and the Northern Border of the Land of Canaan," in *Cities and Regions in the Land of Isreal* Jerusalem: Mossad Bialik [1966], 257-258 [Hebrew]) and the broad imperial description "from the Euphrates River to the River of Egypt" which is not based on a concrete description but seeks to articulate an absolute dominion in the region: *From river to river*, or, in the language of the court poet, "From sea to sea and from river to the ends of earth" (Ps 72:8; cf. Ps 89:26, "I shall place his hand on sea, and on rivers his right hand"). For formulaic language similar to this in the monarchic inscriptions of Assyria and Egypt, see below.

[61]For the historical-political context (the time of the United Monarchy) of the texts in Genesis here adduced, see Weinfeld, " 'A Holy People' and 'A Great Nation'—The Spiritual as Distinct from the Political Charge," *Molad* 22 (1964), 662-665 (Hebrew).

[62]For the courtly ideology reflected in these texts see below, pp.

the ends of the world also occurs: "The kings of Tarshish and the isles will send tribute; the kings of Sheba and Sabaea will proffer gifts" (v 10). Divine promises of this nature appear also, as will be seen, in the royal inscriptions of Egypt and Assyria at their zeniths.

During the United Monarchy, Israel thus became a kingdom, "like all the nations." Like those of other great kingdoms, Israel's court developed an ideology based on the aspiration to domination and self-aggrandizement as expressed in the royal psalms in particular. As we shall see, however, these aspirations underwent a metamorphosis in the prophetic literature and took on a utopian character,[63] which produced the foundation of Jewish and Christian eschatology. From the strong emerged the sweet: the election of a king "like all the nations" fostered the idea of a messiah from the house of David, a savior and redeemer of all humanity; whereas the royal sanctuary, which was erected only after a bitter internal religious struggle, became in prophecy the "house of prayer for all the peoples" (Isa 56:7) and a center for world peace (Isa 2:1-4 = Mic 4:1-4).

Part Two of this analysis will treat, against the background of similar ideologies in the courts of other kings in the Ancient Near East, the ideology that took shape surrounding the idea of dynasty and of the royal sanctuary. It will further isolate the peculiarities of the prophetic visions concerning the royal city and the temple city.

Part Two
The Ideology of Royal City and Temple City
and the Prophetic Utopia

The court ideology of the great kings, as known from ancient Mesopotamia, falls into two categories:

1) the ideology of the royal capital;
2) the ideology of the royal temple.

These two aspects of court ideology are incorporated in two types of ancient Sumerian liturgical composition: psalms of the king and psalms of the sanctuary, types found also in Israel's liturgical poetry.[1] The ideology of the

---

[63] At the basis of the ideology lies a realistic nucleus. The ideology's proponents are interested in shaping a schematic actuality on the basis of this realistic nucleus; contrariwise, the utopian is interested in altering existing reality in accordance with visionary principles. For the distinction see K. Mannheim, *Ideology and Utopia—An Introduction to the Sociology of Knowledge* (trans. L. Wirth and E. Shils; New York: Harcourt, Brace and World, 1936).

[1] See Weinfeld, "Literary Creativity," in *The Age of the Monarchies: Culture and Society* (ed. A. Malamt, World History of the Jewish People, vol. V; Jerusalem: Massada, 1979), 60-61.

kingdom's capital on the one hand and of the kingdom's temple on the other also surfaces plainly in the royal writings of the kings of Assyria and Babylon. The Assyrian annals, and particularly their titularic, glorify *the king and his kingship*; whereas the inscriptions of the kings of Babylonia glorify *the temple and the temple city*. In speaking of the ideal Jerusalem, Israelite prophecy likewise has two separate aspects: 1) Jerusalem as the king's city and the capital of the kingdom; and 2) Jerusalem as the city of God and locus of the sanctuary. So, for example, Isaiah's prophecies present two visions of future peace: 1) the vision of the temple mount (2:1-4 = Mic 4:1-4) in which the mountain of the LORD's temple is the center of interest, and the king does not figure at all; 2) the vision of the ideal king (11:1-10), whose subject is the king and not the sanctuary. It is commonly supposed that these two visions present two different outlooks on the future: one (2:1-4) in which God is the king, and another (11:1-10) that presumes the presence of a king of flesh and blood. In fact, these pericopes simply contain two types of literary composition concerning the subject of the ideal capital. The first vision draws on the tradition of the temple city, while the second draws on motifs traditionally associated with the kingship. It is worthwhile investigating these two varieties of ideology further.

1. The Ideology of the Kingdom's Capital

A royal ideology of imperialistic character is first found in Sumerian hymns of the king from the early part of the second millennium B.C.E.[2] This ideology, which expresses in the superlative the praises of the kingdom's capital, also appears in the royal psalms of the book of Psalms and is reflected in Israelite prophetic literature when the image of the ideal king reigning in Zion is brought up (as will be seen, the prophetic image of the king is sketched out along utopian lines in accordance with Israel's unique idea of prophecy). This imperialistic ideology underlies, in fact, the self-acclamation of the kings of Assyria, Babylon and Egypt.

Let us examine the salient motifs in this ideology while adducing isolated examples from the different periods of the literature.

A. Tax and Tribute for the Capital City and its King

This motif, central to the imperialistic propaganda of the ancient world, abounds in the Sumerian royal psalms.[3] As an example, one may adduce a short segment from a hymn of Ishme-Dagan, king of Isin (1889-1871 B.C.E.):[4]

---

[2] See my remarks in S. N. Kramer, M. Weinfeld, "Prolegomena to a Comparative Study of the Book of Psalms and Sumerian Literature," *Bet Miqra* 19 (1974), 151ff. (Hebrew).

[3] See W. H. Ph. Römer, *Sumerische Königshymnen der Isin Zeit* (hereafter *SKI*) (Leiden: Brill, 1965), *passim*.

[4] *SKI*, 53 lines 265ff.

Of themselves they (foreigners) bring . . . their gifts,

Precious stones . . . gold . . .

The Amorite wanderers . . . bring me sheep,

From the mountain countries they bring me cedar and cypress . . . .

Enlil, my king, subdued all the foreigners before me.

Among the Israelite royal psalms, Psalm 72, a song in which the imperial royal ideology attains full expression, displays this motif. Here, in connection with the king of Israel, occurs the couplet:

The kings of Tarshish and the isles send tribute;

The kings of Sheba and Sabaea proffer gifts (v 10).

As in the Sumerian psalm,[5] these words follow a notice that all enemies have been subdued: "Before him kneel the wastelands; his enemies lap up dust" (v 9), and the text thus expresses the notion that the tribute will come from all the ends of the earth—Tarshish in the far west, and Sheba in the distant south.

Similarly, we read in the inscriptions of Hatshepsut, queen of Egypt (1490-1469 B.C.E.):[6]

They (the enemies) come to her . . . with bowed head, their gifts upon their back.

They present to her their children that there may be given to them the breath of life . . . .

And in another of this queen's inscriptions:[7]

The myrrh of Punt has been brought to me . . . the luxurious marvels of this country were brought to my palace . . . .

They have brought to me . . . cedar, juniper . . . all the good sweet woods of God's-Land . . . .

The motif is most common in the Assyrian annals; an instance from the inscriptions of Asshurnasirpal will serve as an illustration:[8]

The king who subdued them all . . . and received their tribute . . . when he ruled over all the lands . . .

the gifts of the kings of the shore of the sea

from Tyre, Sidon, Byblos, Arwad which dwells in the midst of the sea: silver, gold, bronze, garments . . . ivory

I accepted and they embraced my feet.

B. *The Subjugation of Foreign Peoples and their Domination*

The presentation of tribute to the king results, of course, from the subjugation of the enemy. On this subject also, we hear a great deal in the Sumerian

---

[5] Cf. lines 262-264.

[6] J. H. Breasted, *Ancient Records of Egypt*, vol. II (hereafter *ARE*) (Chicago: University of Chicago, 1906), 116 no. 285.

[7] *ARE* II, 135 no. 321.

[8] D. D. Luckenbill, *Ancient Records of Assyria and Babylonia*, vol. I (hereafter *ARAB*) (Chicago: University of Chicago, 1926), 166 no. 479.

royal psalms. So, in the hymns of Ur-Ninurta, king of Isin (1859-1832 B.C.E.), we read:[9]

> His staff *(šibir)* subdues the rebel land;
> He rules[10] them by might . . . . (line 22)
> when you take its men captives . . .

> Place on their neck the yoke . . . . (lines 51-53)
> That his enemies kneel at his feet (line 71).

In biblical psalms:

> Before him the desert-dwellers kneel,
> And his enemies lick the dust . . . .
> All the kings bow down to him;
> All the nations serve him (Ps 72:8-9, 11);

> The staff of your might the Lord will send forth from Zion;
> Rule in the midst of your enemies (Ps 110:2);

> You will break them with a rod of iron;
> Like a potter's vessel you will dash them to pieces (2:9).

Similar motifs occur in the inscriptions of Hatshepsut, queen of Egypt:[11]

> The god caused that I should reign over the black and the red land
> I have no enemy in any land
> All the countries are subject to me . . . .

This motif is also quite common in the inscriptions of the kings of Assyria. Another instance from the inscriptions of Asshurnasirpal will serve as an illustration:[12]

> The mighty hero who tramples on the neck of his foes,[13] vanquishes all his enemies.
> He whose hand conquered all lands . . . brought under his sway all the regions of the mountain.

The enemy who kisses the conqueror's feet or licks his dust, as found in Ps 2:12[14] and Ps 72:9 (cf. Isa 49:23; 60:14; Mic 7:17), is a common motif in

---

[9] See A. Falkenstein, "Sumerische religiöse Texte," *ZA* 49 (1950), 106ff., and also the new copy of this document published by A. W. Sjöberg, "A Blessing of King Urninurta," in *Ancient Near Eastern Studies in Memory of Jacob Joel Finkelstein* (New Haven: Yale, 1977), 189ff.

[10] ús = Akkadian *ridu* from *redû*, whose meaning is 'to lead' or 'to subdue.' Also in the Bible the root *rdh* occurs in connection with the subjugation of nations. See Lev 16:17; 1 Kgs 5:3; Isa 14:6; Ps 72:8 *et al.* See also Weinfeld, "Prolegomena" (above, n. 2), 157 n. 109.

[11] *ARE* II, p. 134 no. 319.

[12] *ARAB* I, p. 172 no. 486.

[13] For trampling on the enemy's corpses in Mesopotamian and Egyptian stelae and friezes, and inscriptions, see Weinfeld, "Prolegomena" (above, n. 2), 158; cf. Josh 10:24.

[14] Read with most commentators, *"br'dh nšqw lrglyw"* instead of MT *"wgylw br'dh nšqw br."*

royal inscriptions[15] and the iconography[16] of the Ancient Near East. The same is the case for the motif, "dashed to pieces like potter's ware," found in Ps 2:9.[17]

C. *Universal Rule—*"From sea to sea," "from River to the ends of Earth"

In the ancient literature, the empire is described as encompassing broad territories for which only great natural obstacles such as oceans, rivers and mountains serve as boundaries. In royal hymns from the Sumerian era, we encounter mostly the cliché, "from the upper sea to the lower sea."[18] But later periods produce more inclusive and involved descriptions, such as that of Tukulti-Ninurta I (1244-1208),[19] a "king of the upper and the lower seas, king of mountains and broad steppes," or that of Shalmaneser III (959-824 B.C.E.),[20] "conqueror from the upper sea to the lower sea, the great sea of the setting sun to Mt. Amanus, the land of the Hittites to the farthest border . . . from the Tigris to the Euphrates . . . ." And in the inscriptions of Adad-Nirari III (810-783 B.C.E.):[21]

From the mountains to the great sea in the east . . .
From the Euphrates to the great sea where the sun sets.
In the inscriptions of Sargon (722-705 B.C.E.):[22]

---

[15]Cf. *qaqqara ina pan šarri našāqu,* "kiss the ground before the king" (for references see *Akkadisches Handwörterbuch* = *AHw,* 759a), and also *šep šarri ṣabātu,* "to grasp the king's feet," of *šep šarri našaqu,* "to kiss the king's feet" (references in *AHw,* 1214b). See most recently, M. I. Gruber, *Aspects of Nonverbal Communication in the Ancient Near East,* vol. I (Rome: PBI, 1980), 257ff.

[16]See, e.g, *Views of the Biblical World,* vol. IV (ed. B. Mazar; Jerusalem-Ramat Gan: International Publ. Co., 1961), 40.

[17]Compare, in the inscriptions of Shalmaneser III (*ARAB* II, pp. 244 no. 674) and of Esarhaddon: *kima karpat paḫāri uparrir,* "I smashed like a potter's vessel." See R. Borger, *Die Inschriften Asarhaddons, Königs von Assyrien* (Graz: Weidner, 1956), 57, line 5.

[18]The hymn to Ur-Ninurta, king of Isin, in Falkenstein, "Texte" (above, n. 9), 116, line 17. For the expression "from the upper sea to the lower sea" in Mesopotamian royal inscriptions, see the references in the *Chicago Assyrian Dictionary* = *CAD,* E, s.v. *elû* B, b 2 (p. 113).

[19]*ARAB* I, p. 59 no. 70 (Tukulti-Ninurta I; KAH 2 no. 61). See A. K. Grayson, *Assyrian Royal Inscriptions* (Wiesbaden: Harrassowitz, 1972) 1.108 no. 713.

[20]*ARAB* I, p. 236 no. 641.

[21]*ANET*[2], 281. See most recently for this text H. Tadmor, "The Historical Inscriptions of Adad Nirari III," *Iraq* 35 (1973), 48, lines 11-14. This description calls to mind Mic 7:12: "And from Egypt to the river and sea from sea and mountain from mountain."

[22]*ARAB* II, 48 no. 96.

From the sea where the sun sets to the border of Egypt, and the land of
Meshekh, the land of Amurru, all the land of Hatti.

And in the inscription of Hatshepsut, the Egyptian queen:[23]

(The gods) shall set thy boundary as far as the breadth of heaven . . .

This motif appears in an imperial royal song in Psalm 72:

He shall rule from sea to sea and from river to the ends of earth (v 8).

Sea and river as marking the extent of borders occurs also in Psalm 89: "I
shall place his hand on Sea and on Rivers his right hand" (v 26), and in Zech
9:10: "His rule will be from sea to sea, and from river to the ends of the
earth," and Ps 80:11: "Its branches reached the sea, its shoots, the river."

In other biblical passages, besides *sea* and *river* we encounter also the
use of mountains and steppe as marks of borders, much as occurs in Assyrian
royal inscriptions. So, for example, in Mic 7:12:

That day, when to you will come from Assyria and the towns of Egypt
and from Egypt to the river from sea to sea, and from mountain to
mountain.

Other biblical passages describe imperial rule in a more distinct manner (cf. 1
Kgs 5:1, 3; 2 Kgs 24:7). An example is Exod 23:31: "I will set your borders
from the Sea of Reeds to the sea of the Philistines, and from the wilderness
to the River." The Sea of Reeds constitutes the southern end of the land
(Aqaba). The "sea of the Philistines" represents the western boundary; the
"wilderness" represents the eastern border, and "the River" (Euphrates) the
northern border.[24]

Descriptions of composite borders that include sea and river, mountain
and wilderness and the Lebanon in particular, which resemble those in the
inscriptions of Tukulti-Ninurta I, Shalmaneser III and Adad-Nirari III adduced
above, appear in Deut 11:24: "from the wilderness and the Lebanon, from the
river—the river Euphrates—to the western sea" and in Josh 1:4: "from the
wilderness and the Lebanon to the great river, the river Euphrates, all the land
of the Hittites, to the great sea of the setting sun."

We do not know in what measure the biblical formulations were influenced by those from Mesopotamia. It would appear that at least in Josh 1:4
we should be inclined to point to Mesopotamian influence. "All the land of
the Hittites," which occurs here as a designation for Syria is an Assyrian term
attested for the definition of this region: *māt Hatti ana paṭ gimrīša/siḫirtiša*.[25]
The same holds true for "the great sea of the setting sun" as a designation of
the Mediterranean—this is found in the annals of Shalmaneser III and of Adad
Nirari III (see above). In the annals of Shalmaneser III we even find "the land

---

[23]*ARE* II, 92 no. 225.

[24]See recently, M. Saebo, "Grenzbeschreibung und Landideal im alten
Testament mit besonderer Beräcksichtigung der min-'ad Formel," *ZDPV* 90
(1974), 14ff.

[25]See for this phrase J. D. Hawkins, "Hatti," *RLA* IV, 152-159.

of the Hittites" conjoined with "the great sea of the setting sun" as in Josh 1:4.

Borders of the land of Canaan that do not include eastern Transjordan (Num 34:1-15) and which are described by the expressions: "from the wilderness of Sin to Rehob Lebo-Hamath" (Judg 13:21), "from Lebo-Hamath to the River of Egypt" (1 Kgs 8:10), "from Lebo-Hamath to the Desert Sea" (2 Kgs 14:25; cf. Am 6:14), "from Shihor of Egypt[26] to Lebo-Hamath" (1 Chr 13:5), refer to the regions of the province of Canaan under the waning Egyptian sovereignty, as B. Mazar argues,[27] and accordingly differ from the pattern of "sea and river" characteristic of Mesopotamia and the imperial tradition as it achieves expression in the court psalms.

D. Righteousness and Justice

This motif is widely distributed throughout court poetry; it appears also within the framework of the titles of the king in the inscriptions of the kings of Assyria and Babylonia. Thus, we read in a hymn to Ishme-Dagan, king of Isin (1889-1871 B.C.E.):[28]

> UTU (the god of the sun and justice) placed in my mouth truth and equity
> in order to produce righteous judgment for the people . . .
> to sustain the righteous and to cut off the wicked.[29]

This motif also occurs in the hymns of the kings of Egypt from the Ramesside era.[30] It is particularly salient in Psalm 72, which serves for us as a point of departure for a discussion of royal ideology in Israel. Moreover, the idea of righteousness and justice provides a conceptual framework for Psalm 72 as a whole. The psalm opens:

> God, give your judgments to the king, and your righteousness to the son of the king;
> That he judge his people aright, and your lowly ones with justice . . . .
> Let him champion the lowly among the people;

---

[26] See recently N. Naaman, "The Shihor of Egypt and Shur," *Tel-Aviv* 7 (1980), 96ff.

[27] See above, Part 1, n. 59, and most recently Z. Kallai, "The boundaries of the Land of Canaan and the Land of Israel in the Bible," *EI* 12 (Glück Volume; 1975), 27-34 (Hebrew).

[28] *SKI*, 44-45, lines 90ff.; for the concept of righteousness and justice in Sumer, see S. N. Kramer, "Modern Social Problems in Ancient Sumer," *XVIIIe Rencontre Assyriologique Internationale* (Bayerische Akademie der Wissenschaftliche Abhandlungen NF 75 [1972]), 113-121.

[29] For similar formulas in the prologues and epilogues of various Mesopotamian collections of laws and edicts, see my forthcoming *Justice and Righteousness in Israel and among the Nations* (see above, Part One, note 57).

[30] See the study mentioned in the preceding note.

100

Let him save the needy and crush the oppressor . . . (vv 1-4).

Afterward, the poet addresses the king's greatness, his total control, the subjugation of his enemies and the receipt of their tribute (vv 5-11). Finally, he returns to the exaltation of righteousness:

For he will rescue the needy who cry out,
The downtrodden who have none to aid them;
He will take pity on the poor and needy,
And champion the souls of the poor (vv 12-14).

The king as one who attends to the prosecution or righteousness and who helps the poor appears as a stereotype in the inscriptions of the kings of Assyria. So, for example, in an inscription of Sargon:[31]

Who declares an amnesty *(šubarrû)* to the sons of Sippar, Nippur and Babylon,
Helping the downtrodden and restoring their losses . . .
Releasing from corvée . . . and lightening the load of those who sigh.

The description of the king as one who does right and justice *(šar mišarim)*[32] occurs in fact from the Old Babylonian period to the Neo-Babylonian period. The idea that the kingship should be founded on the basis of justice and righteousness is a widespread notion in the cultures of Mesopotamia, Egypt and Israel.[33]

The Royal Capital in Prophetic Thought

The foregoing motifs, which lay at the foundation of an imperialistic courtly ideology, are embedded also in the idealized descriptions of Jerusalem as a royal city in prophetic literature. So, for example, immediately after the vision of the Temple mount (Mic 4:1-4) and the announcement of the LORD's kingship on Mount Zion (4:6-7), Micah presents a vision of Zion as the kingdom that by means of iron horns and brazen hooves tramples and grinds numerous peoples and obliterates their wealth (Mic 4:6, 13).

The next verses speak of a ruler of Judah from the line of Jesse in Bethlehem who leads his people with the LORD's might and his god's majesty; his greatness reaches to the ends of the earth (5:1-3). The peace that he institutes is achieved by defeating Assyria in battle and placing governors over

---

[31]*ARAB* II, 55, no. 104, and the text in R. Borger, *Babylonisch-Assyrische Lesestücke* II (Rome: PBI, 1963), 54, lines 2ff.

[32]For descriptions of Mesopotamian kings, see M. J. Seux, *Épithètes Royales akkadiennes et sumeriennes* (Paris: Letouzey et Ané, 1967), 422-423 *(lugal ni-si-sá).*

[33]Cf. my forthcoming *Justice and Righteousness* (above, n. 29). It should be added that the establishment of justice and righteousness is a motif that permeates also Mesopotamian prophecies, as I have shown in *Shnaton—Annual for the Bible and Ancient Near Eastern Studies* 3 (1979), 263ff.

her (5:4-5). The basic motifs in these prophecies are congruent with the first three court-ideological motifs enumerated above: 1) the subjection of peoples by force; 2) the acquisition of their wealth; 3) rule reaching to the ends of the earth. Here, a marked resemblance can be discerned to Psalm 2, in which a king rules from Zion with an iron staff over the nations (v 9), whose authority extends to the ends of the earth (v 8).

The ruler who comes from Judah and Bethlehem in Mic 5:1 calls to mind the "shoot" from the "trunk" of Jesse in Isa 11:1. As we shall see, the emphasis on the antiquity of the dynasty is also a motif belonging to the court ideology of the kings of Assyria and Babylon.

The chronological background of these prophecies is unknown.[34] But this is of little import in this context, since we are here concerned with the typology of court ideology. In any case, there is no justification to date the prophecies in question to the era after the exile. We have before us descriptions of typical court ideology in contrast to the later descriptions such as those of Deutero-Isaiah where the king is lacking altogether.

The utopian aspect of these prophecies of Micah manifests itself at the end of chapter 6. Here we hear (alongside the purging of idolatry—vv 11-13) of the elimination of horses and chariots, and the levelling of fortresses in Judah; these are concerns that stand in opposition to the imperialistic ideology since without these it is impossible to attack and rule over the enemy. In this connection, Micah supplements Isaiah's (2:6-8) and Hosea's (14:4) views. These two prophets see in the dependence on horse and chariot a seeming reliance on idols, or a kowtowing to the work of human hands. A similar ideological view emerges from Zech 9:9-10:

> Rejoice to the utmost, daughter of Zion;
> Shout out, daughter of Jerusalem!
> Behold, your king comes to you;
> Righteous and saved is he.
> Yet humble, riding on an ass,
> On a donkey foaled by a she-ass.
> I shall cut off cavalry from Ephraim,
> Horses from Jerusalem;
> And the bow of war will be banished.
> And he will offer terms of peace to the nations.
> And his rule will extend from sea to sea,
> And from river to the ends of earth.

The ideology permeating this prophecy is an imperialistic one: the king of Jerusalem imposes[35] peace on the nations and rules from sea to sea, from

---

[34] According to many commentators, the setting of Mic 5:8-14 is the time of Sennacherib's siege.

[35] ודבר שלום (v. 10) here has the meaning "impose conditions"; cf. *dbr ṭwbh* in 1 Sam 25:30 and *dbr dbr* in Isa 58:13 *et al.* On this matter, see

river to the ends of the earth; rulership is limitless, expressed by the same phrase found in the above-mentioned prophecy of Mic 5:3-4: "For now he will wax to the ends of the earth; and this will be the peace: when Assyria comes into our land . . . we shall raise up against it seven shepherds," etc. (cf. also Mic 7:12).

The paradox in Zechariah's prophecy is that to dominion to the ends of the earth is juxtaposed the elimination of chariotry and horses (from Israel and Judah) and the elimination of the warbow. Conceivably, this means that on the heels of peace will follow the destruction of the weapons of war—this despite the fact that the elimination of chariotry, horses and bows precedes the clause "he will offer terms of peace to the nations." It will bear note in this context that the songs of Zion, too, depict the breaking of bow, sword and war in Jerusalem, and the ceasing of wars to the ends of the earth (Ps 76:3-4; 46:10). But it is difficult to determine whether what is intended here is the elimination of the enemy's weapons or, as in the fragments of prophecy adduced above, that Israel's weaponry wil be eliminated as peace comes. In actuality, the latter possibility is suggested in David's action after his wars with Aram: "David captured . . . a thousand, seven hundred horsemen and twenty thousand infantrymen; and David hamstrung all the chariot horses, and left of them a hundred" (2 Sam 8:4). The idea of immobilizing the means of war appears in Psalm 76, which describes Jerusalem as a city of peace in which wars are ceased (v 4), and chariotry and horses cease to function (v 7), in the wake of which the peoples bring tribute to God (v 12). This psalm, in fact, expresses the notion of "humble" (עני) and "saved" (נושע) that occurs also in Zech 9:9. Thus we read here that God in his judgment (=war) *saves* (מושיע) the *humble* of the land (ענוי ארי) (v. 10).

The image of a humble king is in fact known to us from elsewhere in the Near East:[36] the Assyrian conquests were made in God's name, and the king himself is described as righteous and humble.[37] The ride "on a donkey, and on a colt, the foal of a she-ass" that occurs in Zechariah 9 is also emblematic of kingship (cf. Judg 5:10; 12:14), as we learn from Gen 49:11: "he hitches his colt to the vine[38] . . . his ass" concerning Judah immediately after descriptions of the enemy's subjugation and presentation of tribute (*yb' šy lh*, by emendation), and in connection with the conferral of royal insignia such as

---

Weinfeld, "The Counsel of the 'Elders' to Rehoboam and its Implications," *Maarav* 3 (1982), 45ff.

[36]Cf., e.g., the Zakir inscription (*KAI* 202A:2): *'š 'nh 'nh* "I am a humble man," and see recently H. Tawil, *Orientalia* 43 (1974), 51f.

[37]See the epithets *ašru, kanšu, mutnennû* (humble, submissive, prayerful) in Seux, *Épithètes* (above, n. 32), and compare H. Tawil, article cited in the previous note.

[38]*gpn* in Ugaritic also has the meaning "harness." Cf. *mdl 'r smd pḥl št gpnm* = "he saddled a foal, yoked a donkey, harnessed (with reins) of vine" (*CTA* 4 IV:9-10); compare Virgil, *Aeneid* 6:804: "nor he who guides his car with vine-leaf reins."

the staff and sceptre *(mḥqq)*" (vv 9-10). But it must be conceded that the prophet who makes use of the ancient royal image wants to express the contrast between the donkey on which the oppressed king rides and the horse (and chariot) that will be cut off from Israel and on which the other kings used to ride (see Jeremiah 17:25).

The notion of a Jerusalem that symbolizes the cessation of war and the establishment of peace can be seen also in Genesis 14. In this chapter the father of the nation, Abram, appears at the city of Salem after a victory over the kings of the north, and it is no coincidence that the epithet "Salem *(šlm)*" is applied to Jerusalem both here and in Psalm 76:3 (see above). In consequence of the victory, Abram earns the blessing of Melchizedek and donates a tithe of the spoil to the LORD (vv 19-20)—this detail parallels the presentation of gifts to the God of Israel in Ps 76:12. It is worth observing that Abram acts as ruler over the whole area from north of Damascus to El Paran (Gen 14:6, 15; cf. the promise made to Abraham in Gen 15:18), and so foreshadows the Israelite king who will in the future rule the region.

The idea of Jerusalem as the city of peace is particularly salient in Isaiah's prophecy in chap. 11:1-10 (cf. 32:18—"and his people will dwell in a peaceful pasturage . . . and in secure resting-places," with 33:20—"Zion is the town of our assembly . . . a secure pasturage"). Here the concept undergoes the process of prophetic-utopian transformation. The segment opens with a description of the royal dynasty and its antiquity: "a rod from the stem of Jesse, and a branch from his roots," descriptions characteristic also of the dynastic line of Assyrian kings, e.g.: "eternal offspring of Belbani son of Adasi king of Assyria, precious branch of Baltil, seed of kingship, everlasting shoot."[39] The attributes of the ideal king that appear in the continuation—*wisdom, insight, counsel and valor, knowledge and fear of the LORD*—are characteristic also of Mesopotamian royal titles. The king is called the possessor of wisdom and knowledge,[40] a warrior and counsellor,[41] and one who

---

[39] *liplipu dāru ša Bēlbani mār Adasi šar māt Aššur pir'u Baltil šūquru zēr šarrūti kisitti ṣâti* (Borger, *Asarhaddon*, p. 74, lines 28-29). For additional occurrences, see Seux, *Épithètes* (above, n. 32), 337; and for the notion in Assyria, see now W. G. Lambert, "The Seed of Kingship," *Le Palais et la Royauté*, XIXe Rencontre Assyriologique Internationale 1974, 427ff. Baltil was an ancient quarter in the city of Asshur and Belbani was a private citizen from whom the dynasty issued (see Borger, as above). There is a certain similarity here to Jesse of Bethlehem from whom David's dynasty issued.

[40] Compare the descriptions *ḫassu mūdû* "wise and knowing," *āḫiz nēmeqi* "understanding wisdom" and *emqu, eršu* "wise, knowledgeable," etc. See Weinfeld, "Jeremiah and the Spiritual Metamorphosis of Israel," *ZAW* 88 (1976), 41-42, n. 91.

[41] *lē'u, qardu* and *māliku ramanišu* "taking counsel with himself" (Seux, *Épithètes* above, n. 32, 156).

knows and fear his god.[42] But in contrast to Micah, who emphasizes the physical government and subjection of the peoples by force (the destruction of Assyria with the sword, and the threshing of the peoples with the iron horn—4:13), in Isaiah 11, the king rules by *the staff of his mouth and by the breath* of his lips (11:4). In contrast to the prophecy of Micah in which the king imposes peace on the nations in the aftermath of his victory (5:4), in Isaiah 11 the peace results from the cosmic harmony depicted as the end of enmity not just among men, but even among the beasts (vv 6-8). In addition, in contrast to the prophecy of Micah in which the peoples' wealth is consecrated after their subjugation (4:13), in Isaiah 11 the nations come of their own accord to seek the stem of Jesse and to honor it (v 9). The metamorphosis of the court ideology in Isaiah attains its highest pitch in the idea of striking "with the staff of his mouth" (v 4), which articulates an express contrast to striking "with an iron staff" (Ps 2:9), and to the crushing of the enemy with the sword (Mic 5:5). This spirituality in the vision of the ideal king is characteristic of Isaiah and especially conspicuous when one compares Isaiah's with Micah's vision.[43] A parallel concept occurs in the prophecy of the "servant of the LORD" in Isaiah 42. The royal figure on whom the spirit of God is put and who brings forth justice to the nations (v 1) fulfills his commission by purely spiritual means: "A bruised reed he will not break, nor extinguish a dim wick" (v 3). Moreover, the "voice" that he employs in the conduct of his kingship is not uplifted: "He will not cry out, nor lift up, nor cause his voice to be heard in the street" (v 2).

During the Second Temple period, the idealized descriptions of the king in First and Second Isaiah became the dominant characteristics in the portrayal of the messianic king. This longed-for messiah-king became a sublime spiritual figure destined to reveal himself at the end of days, even scriptures that spoke of a real king were interpreted in this light. So, for example, Psalm 2, and, indeed, Psalms 72 and 89, which speak of an Israelite king who rules over peoples physically ("with an iron staff," Ps 2:9), were interpreted allegorically as depicting a king of divine character who would reveal himself in the future (cf., for example, *DJD* V 53, 4Q 174; Acts 4:25-26; 13:33 *et al.*).

2. *The Ideology of the Temple City*

The Temple City in the Center of the World

As early as the end of the third millennium and the beginning of the second millennium B.C.E. in Mesopotamia, we hear of a universal center to

---

[42] See, e.g., Esarhaddon's *ša palāḫ ili mūdû* "who knows the fear of god." See the references in Borger, *Asarhaddon*, p. 9, note; Seux, *Épithètes* (above, n. 32), 168, n. 86.

[43] See Y. Kaufmann, *The History of Israelite Religion* III (Jerusalem: Mossad Bialik-Dvir, 1946-1956), 271-272 (Hebrew).

which nations stream from all the ends of the earth, bringing with them offerings and gifts and prostrating themselves and offering prayers to the great god in the sanctuary. This temple city is portrayed as brimming with splendor and glory, a place in which the oppressor and the wicked do not dwell, but in which righteousness and justice abide perpetually.

Thus we read in a hymn to Enlil:[44]

> The city (Nippur) is filled with awe and splendor . . . oppression, slander . . . the city does not tolerate . . . .
>
> The city ornamented with truth. Righteousness and justice dwell in her; in her they don pure garments . . . .
>
> The *kiur*, the mountain, the consecrated (pure) place whose waters are sweet[45]
>
> You founded Duranki (the bond of heaven and earth; see below).
>
> In the center of the four corners (of earth) . . . its brickwork of red metal, its foundations of lapis lazuli.
>
> All the lands bow down to it . . . Ekur, house of lapis lazuli . . . .
>
> Its awe and splendor reach unto the heavens.
>
> Its shade is spread across all the lands . . . .
>
> All the lords and princes bring there their pure gifts,
>
> Offerings and prayers they array for you[46] . . . .
>
> Their offerings and heavy tribute they brought into the storehouse . . . .
>
> Into Ekur they brought them in homage.

Similarly, in a hymn to the temple of Ningirsu, Gudea, *ensi* of Lagash (2143-2124 B.C.E.) we read:[47]

> Its (the shrine's) splendor and refulgence reach to the heavens;
>
> The awe of the temple lies over all foreign lands;
>
> To its name gather strangers from all the ends of the heavens;
>
> (The men of) Magan and Meluhha come there from their distant land . . .
>
> From Magan and Meluhha they bring trees for the construction of a temple for Ningirsu . . . .

The sanctuary is described as standing in the most exalted place, extending to the heavens:

---

[44] Lines 67ff.; Heb. translation by S. N. Kramer, M. Weinfeld, "Sumerian Literature and the Book of Psalms—Introduction to Comparative Research," *Bet Miqra* 57 (1974), 142-143; note there the references to the Sumerian text. For English translation, see *ANET*³, 573ff.

[45] Cf. Ps 46:5: "River's streams gladden the city of God, the holy place of the tabernacles of the most high"; see also the description in Ezek 47:1-12; Zech 14:8.

[46] Cf. Isa 56:7: "Their (foreigners') burnt offerings and sacrifices will be desired on my altar, for my house will be called a house of prayer for all the nations."

[47] See Falkenstein and von Soden, *Sumerische und Akkadische Hymnen und Gebete* (hereafter *SAHG*; Zürich: Artemis, 1953), 147, 152, 169, 170.

> The great mountain . . . the sanctuary of Ekur, he raised from the dust;
> He planted it in a pure place like a rising mountain.[48]

Ur-Nammu, king of Ur, expresses himself as follows:

> Ur-Nammu (the king), the shepherd, he commanded to lift the head of
> Ekur heaven-high.[49]

This central sanctuary serves as a high seat of justice for the god who resides there[50] (which calls Isa 2:1-4 to mind).

The first major center in which these ideas were amalgamated was the Sumerian city, Nippur. Babylon, which arose considerably later and viewed herself as Nippur's successor, appropriated the ideology for herself.[51]

The cities of Nippur and Babylon were called the centers of heaven and earth (Sumerian *dur-an-ki* = the bond of the heavens and the earth; Babylonian *markas šamê u erṣeti*).[52] In Hebrew, the idea is rendered, "the navel of the earth *(tbwr h'rṣ),*" an expression also found in Akkadian—*abunnat māti.*[53] "The navel of the earth" is mentioned in connection with Shechem in Judg 9:37,[54] and in connection with the land of Israel and Jerusalem in Ezek 38:12. Nor is the fact that biblical usage relates the expression to these specific locations (Mt. Gerizim and Zion) devoid of meaning.[55] Not only in

---

[48] Hymn to Enlil, lines 35-38 (see n. 43).

[49] See *ANET*[3], 583.

[50] In the hymn of Gudea, *ensi* of Lagash: "To uphold the righteous and to subdue the wicked he establishes the house, the throne of justice is established" (Cyl B vi 70); see *SAHG*, 170.

[51] This process began already in Hammurabi's time. See R. Borger, *BibOr* 28 (1971), 22, n. 5.

[52] On *markasu* as "bond" and as "center" see *CAD* M I, s.v. *markasu* 4 (p. 283).

[53] Indeed, this appears also as the center of the enemy's territory: *abunnat māt nakrim*; see A. Geotze, *Old Babylonian Omen Texts* (YOS 10; New Haven: Yale, 1947), no. 33, iii.41. However, one ought not conclude from this that the expression has no cosmological significance. The fact that Sumerian *dur*, which appears in a cosmological context, was rendered in Akkadian *abunnatu* indicates that *abunnatu* also had some cosmological significance. See D. Sperling, "Navel of the Earth," *IDBSup*, 622.

[54] In this instance, too, one might interpret the phrase after the Akkadian as denoting the central locus in a region (see preceding note); but in light of the tradition concerning the sanctity of this site it would seem that the phrase designates a consecrated locus, especially in light of "the oak of the chanters" which appears in the same context. See recently J. A. Soggin, *Judges* (OTL; London: SCM, 1981), 189-190.

[55] Cf. the talmudic exegesis concerning the Temple—"The Temple is higher than all the rest of the land of Israel, and the land of Israel is higher than all other lands" (B. Qiddushin 69a and parallels)—and concerning Mt.

Mesopotamia, but also in Greece (in Delphi), the sanctuary was considered as located in the center of the universe *(omphalos)*;[56] this tradition stands behind the Septuagint translation of *ṭbwr h'rṣ*, also found in the letter of Aristeas 83 (compare Jub. 8:10 and the rabbinic literature).[57] Moreover, Ezekiel's conception of Jerusalem as the "navel of the earth" is supported from another of his oracles: "I set this Jerusalem in the midst of the nations, with countries round about her" (5:5).

It appears that Bethel, too, a royal sanctuary in the north (Amos 7), was thought in Israel's monarchy to be the center of the universe. This is the place where the ladder stood whose head was in the heavens and on which the angels of God ascend and descend (Gen 28:12). Indeed, Jacob labels it "the gate of the heavens"[58] (v 17), just as the Babylonians interpreted the name of the city of Babylon: *bab ilē* (Sumerian KA.DINGIR.RA), "the gate of the gods." "The ladder of the heavens *(simmelat šamāmi)* actually occurs in conjunction with "the gate of the gods" in Mesopotamia:[59] the gods Namtar and Nergal descend by the long *ladder of the heavens* and reach the gate of the gods, Anu, Enlil and Ea.[60]

Gerizim in the Samaritan conception, see Bereshit Rabba 32, 10 (Theodore-Albeck edition, pp. 296-297).

[56]H. V. Hermann, *Omphalos* (Orbis Antiquus 13; Münster: Aschendorff, 1959).

[57]See the examination of I. L. Seeligmann, "Jerusalem in Jewish-Hellenistic Thought," *Judah and Jerusalem* (Jerusalem: Israel Exploration Society, 1957), 198ff. (Hebrew); cf. S. Talmon, "Tabûr ha'areẓ and the Comparative Method," *Tarbiz* 45 (1976), 166-167. Talmon's attempt to dispute the usual meaning of "navel *(ṭbwr)* of the earth" is not convincing. If biblical usage itself does not clarify the meaning of the phrase, we must seek assistance from the usage of post-biblical Hebrew, as we do in so many other instances. Cf., e.g., the hapax *dyw* in Jer 36:18. In Mishnaic language, *ṭbwr* or *ṭybwr* has an unequivocal meaning, and there is no reason not to attribute this same meaning to biblical *ṭbwr*.

[58]The "gate of the heavens" was taken in midrashic exegesis as a heavenly sanctuary as opposed to the Temple below. See the remarks of R. Simeon ben-Yohai on our passage in Bereshit Rabba 69 (Theodore-Albeck edition, p. 797). Since the Temple is in Jerusalem and not in Bethel, the rabbis resorted to the explanation that "the ladder stands in the Temple and its 'lean' (i.e. with its top in the heavens) reaches to Bethel" (Bereshit Rabba 69, p. 796).

[59]I have hinted at the connection between the ladder of Bethel and "the ladder of the heavens" in Akkadian in my brief commentary on Genesis (the new edition of S. L. Gordon; Tel-Aviv, 1975), 160 (Hebrew).

[60]O. R. Gurney, "The Myth of Nergal and Ereshkigal," *Anatolian Studies* 10 (1960), 105-106. For the relationship between this myth and Genesis 28, see recently H. R. Cohen, *Biblical Hapax Legomena in the Light of Akkadian and Ugaritic* (Ann Arbor: Scholars, 1978), 34.

To this same theological-cosmological array belong the Babylonians' appellations for their sanctuaries, such as é-sag-ila, which means "the house whose head is raised up," or é-temen-an-ki, which means "the house (that is) the foundation of heaven and earth." Psalm 78 intimates that this outlook was present in Israel: "He built as on high (kmw rmym; read kmrwmym "like the heights") his sanctuary; like the earth, he founded it for all eternity" (v 69).

Similarly, the language of "raising up" is applied to the sanctuary in Ezra 9:9: "to raise up the house of our God"; so, too, Ben Sirah 49:12: "they raised up the holy temple," language that occurs in Ugaritic[61] and in Akkadian.[62] All this explains why the sanctuary in the capital in Mesopotamia, Ugarit and Israel was considered to be the highest place in the world. Nippur's sanctuary is called "the great mountain" ("that reaches the heights" or *was raised to heaven* [see above]), and the sanctuary of Canaanite Baal, who dwelled "in holiness in the mount of his inheritance," is "Mount Zaphon," the highest mountain in northern Syria = Jebel Aqra (Mt. Cassius).[63] Ezekiel sees in a vision the sanctuary on "a very high mountain" (40:2), and in the songs of Zion, the Temple mount is called "Mount Zion, the summit of Zaphon *(yrkty ṣpwn)*" (Ps 48:3). Accordingly, when Isaiah speaks of the "mount of the LORD's Temple at the head of the mountains, and exalted from among the hills," he in fact makes use of a conventional formula common in referring to sanctuaries in capital cities throughout the Near East.[64] As the kingdom's capital attracts peoples from the ends of the world, and as they bring tribute and serve the king who resides there, so too, the temple city attracts people from the whole world who bear tribute to the sanctuary's god, raise corvée, and build the metropolitan sanctuary. The hymn to Enlil in Nippur's sanctuary, and indeed, the hymn to Ningirsu in Lagash adduced above, evince an ideology that incorporates all these motifs. But the ideology is no less apparent in the inscriptions of the kings of Babylonia concerning the sanctuary Esagila. So, for example, we read in an inscription of Nebuchadrezzar, king of Babylonia:[65]

---

[61] ḥš bhtm tbn[n] // ḥš trmmn hk[lm] (CTA 4, V:115-116): rush build the house // hurriedly raise up my palace. See S. E. Loewenstamm, "Grenzgebiete Ugaritischer Sprach- und Stilvergleichung," UF 3 (1971), 94.

[62] AHw šaqû II D 7a.

[63] See R. J. Clifford, *The Cosmic Mountain in Canaan and the Old Testament* (HSM 4; Cambridge: Harvard, 1972).

[64] See Seeligmann (above, n. 57), 200-201. In view of our analysis here it should be clear that there is no need to separate these images: the center on the one hand and the elevated place on the other. Centrality and elevation are conjoined in Mesopotamian image, and in biblical images of the sanctuary.

[65] S. Langdon, *Die neubabylonische Königsinschriften* (VAB 4; Leipzig: Hinrichs, 1912), 146, lines 12ff.

Many peoples over whom my lord Marduk commissioned me...[66] from the upper sea to the lower sea, distant lands . . . kings from distant mountains and remote isles,[67] from the midst of the upper and lower seas which Marduk gave into my hand for the bearing of his yoke,[68] I mustered . . . and placed on them the burden *(tupšikku)* of the construction of Etemenanki[69] . . . . They bring large cedar trees from the Lebanon to the cities of Babylon. On all the men of the many nations I imposed work and the bearing of the burden *(tupšikku)* . . . . All the men worked . . . at the construction of the sanctuary . . . .[70]

Among the materials brought as tribute appear:

Silver and gold, precious stones, the wealth of the sea, bulls, ewes . . . the treasuries of the kings . . . every precious vessel . . . .[71]

Like the sanctuary of Nippur, the temple in Babylon is described as filled with awe and splendor *(puluḫtu, melammu)* and the light of the sun;[72] in view of this, the wicked man, and anyone who is not upright will not enter Babylon.[73] The sanctuary of Esagila was made brilliant like the sun; it was

---

[66]This notion that the god Marduk commissioned Nebuchadrezzar over all the inhabitants of the world appear frequently in that king's inscriptions. Cf. Langdon (preceding note), p. 94, line 18; p. 96, lines 19ff.; p. 112, lines 14ff.; p. 120, line 38—"you commissioned me with the kingship over the inhabitants of the world," etc. This calls to mind Jeremiah's words: "I have given all these lands into the hand of Nebuchadnezzar, king of Babylon . . . to serve him" (27:6). From this aspect, there is a resemblance here to Deutero-Isaiah's prophecy concerning Cyrus. Deutero-Isaiah's prophecies about Cyrus are stylistically similar to the Babylonian predictions to Cyrus. See recently S. M. Paul, "Deutero-Isaiah and Cuneiform Royal Inscriptions," *JAOS* 88 (1968), 180ff., and the bibliography there in notes 2, 3.

[67]*nagê. ngwwn* appears frequently in the Aramaic Targums as a translation of "isles"; in our inscription too, the meaning is "isles," as the continuation shows: "in the midst of the sea."

[68]Cf. Jer 27:8: "Who does not bend his shoulder to the yoke of the king of Babylon."

[69]The literal meaning of the term: "the house that is the foundation of heaven and earth"; see above, p.

[70]Cf. Langdon (above, n. 65), p. 122, lines 26ff.; p. 124, lines 26ff.; p. 152, lines 24ff.; p. 158, lines 9ff.

[71]Langdon (above, n. 65), p. 116, lines 19ff.; p. 158, lines 9ff.; cf. p. 112, lines 26ff.; p. 124, lines 26ff., etc.

[72]Langdon (above, n. 65), p. 182, lines 34ff.; p. 118, lines 54ff.; p. 138, lines 29ff.

[73]Langdon (above, n. 65), p. 118, lines 54ff.; p. 138, lines 29ff.: *ragga lā išari ul iba'i qiribša.*

ornamented with lapis lazuli and precious stones; its gates were made as stunning as the sun.[74]

A similar ideology, though flavored with prophetic-utopian elements, is found in Isaiah 60. Here also we hear of nations and foreigners from the isles of the sea (v 9) and distant mountains (vv 6-7) who bring silver and gold, the abundance of the seas, sheep and rams to the sanctuary in Jerusalem. These nations and their kings, who come to the temple city and bring with them the glory of the Lebanon, fir, pine and box trees (v 13), build the city walls and serve Zion (v 10). Those who do not serve her are marked for destruction (v 12). Just as we hear that the temple in Babylon was filled with light, we here learn that the city exudes light and brightness (vv 1-3, 19-20), and that violence and injustice do not take place in her (v 18). Moreover, like the sanctuaries of Nippur and Babylon, the sanctuary of Jerusalem is described in Isa 54:11-12 as founded on stones of antimony and lapis lazuli. Its gates flash with jewels: oppression and terror cannot draw near to Zion (v 14). The two concepts which appear together in the Babylonian inscriptions—the splendor surrounding the temple city and the debarring of the wicked from the temple city— are thus occasionally reflected in the prophecy of Second Isaiah as well. In another oracle, the anonymous prophet attaches Zion's splendor to her purity and holiness: "Wake, wake, cloth yourself in splendor, o Zion; put on your robes of majesty, o Jerusalem, holy city; for hereafter the uncircumcized and unclean will come into you no more" (52:1; cf. Joel 4:17; Nahum 2:1).

The anonymous prophet's preaching can be distinguished from the Babylonian ideology of the temple city in two respects: a) the divine light that shines forth over Zion is an eternal light that makes the light of the sun superfluous (60:19); and, b) when they come to Zion, the nations bring with them not just tribute, but also the children of Zion who had been in exile (vv 4, 9; cf. 49:22).[75] In light of the parallel between the consoling prophet's prophecy and the Babylonian inscriptions, it would be legitimate to assume that the prophet, who began his ministry in Babylonia,[76] was influenced in his descriptions of the temple city Jerusalem by the parallel descriptions of the temple city Babylon. However, while one cannot exclude this hypothesis altogether from the realm of possibility, it is worthwhile to

---

[74] Langdon (above, n. 65), p. 124, lines 43ff.

[75] The bringing of tribute together with children occurs in Egyptian royal inscriptions; see above, p. 95 in the excerpt from Hatshepsut's inscription. Portraits depicting Egyptian vassals coming to Egypt include along with the presentation of tribute the bringing of children (as hostages?). See O. Keel, "Kanaanäische Sühneriten auf Ägyptischen Tempelreliefs," *VT* 25 (1975), 413-569, esp. pp. 442ff.

[76] For the whereabouts of the prophet's proclamations, see M. Haran, *Between Ri'shonôt (former prophecies) and Ḥadashôt (new prophecies)* (Jerusalem: Magnes, 1963), 73ff.

recall that most of the motifs that occur in the Temple psalms, and indeed, in the prophecies about Zion, are found—as we have seen—in ancient Sumerian hymns relating to the temple city in Mesopotamia. These antedate the Babylonian inscriptions adduced above.

Let us examine the most prominent parallel motifs: a) The peoples accept the sovereignty of the god who is in the sanctuary of the capital (Psalms 47; 48; 76; Isa 2:1-4 = Mic 4:1-4; Joel 4:11ff.; Zeph 3:15ff.; Hag 2:7). Cf., in the hymn to Enlil at Nippur (above, p. 105): "The most distant lands you subdue . . ." and, in the hymn to Ningirsu at Lagash, "the awe of the temple lies over all foreign lands; to its name gather strangers from all the ends of the heavens."

b) Peoples bring tribute to the god in the capital (Isa 18:7; 60:5ff.; Zeph 3:10; Hag 2:7; Ps 68:32-33; 76:12; 96:8). Cf., in the hymn to the god in Nippur: "All the lords and princes bring pure gifts there; gifts and heavy tribute they brought to its storehouse."

c) Nations come to worship the god who is in the sanctuary of the capital (Ps 47; 66:1-8; 67; 68:33-36; 86:9; 96:7-9; 98:4; 102:23; 138:4-5; Isa 56:7; 66:23; Zeph 2:11; 3:9; Zech 8:21; 14:16ff.; cf. Ps 22:28; Jer 3:17; 16:19). Cf., in the hymn to the god at Nippur, "Offerings and prayers they (all the foreign lords) array for you"; "all the lands bow down to it"; "to its name gather strangers from all the ends of the heavens."

d) Foreigners bring trees for the construction of the sanctuary (Isa 60:13-14). Cf., in the hymn to Ningirsu (above, p.105), "from Magan and Meluhha they bring trees for the construction of a house for Ningirsu."

e) Zion is shrouded in glory, splendor and majesty (Ps 96:6-7; 102:16-17; Isa 4:5; 52:1; 54:11-12; 60:1-3). Cf., in the hymn to Enlil at Nippur, "The city is filled with splendor . . . the foundations (of the sanctuary) are made of lapis lazuli . . . ."

f) The temple city is the city of righteousness and justice[77] (Ps 16; cf. 5:5-8; 24:3-5; 101:8; Isa 1:21-27; 32:16-18; 54:14; 60:18; Jer 31:22; Zeph 3:8; Zech 8:3). Cf., in the hymn to Enlil at Nippur, "Oppression and slander are not in her midst . . . righteousness and justice dwell in her."

---

[77]On the temple and the temple city as a place in which one must observe moral righteousness and purity, see Weinfeld, "Instructions for Temple Visitors in the Bible and in Ancient Egypt," in *Studies in the History and Literature of Ancient Egypt* (ed. S. Groll, in press). The recently discovered inscription from Rabbat Ammon (see E. Puech-A. Rofé, "L'inscription de la citadelle d'Amman," *RB* 80 [1973], 531-546) is instructive in this regard. In it, there is a warning against violating the sanctity of the site and that righteousness will dwell in the environs of the town *(wbkl s[bb] t ylnn ṣdq)*, similar to Jerusalem in Isaiah's oracles that "righteousness will abide in her" (1:21). See R. Kutscher, "A New Inscription from Ammon," *Qadmoniyot* 17 (1972), 27-28.

g) From the temple city goes forth the judgment that brings redemption and salvation to the peoples (Ps 96:11-13; 98:9; Isa 2:1-4 = Mic 4:1-4, and see also Ps :9; 9:8-9; 67:4-9). Cf., in the hymn of Gudea, prince of Lagash, "in order to set the righteous upright and to subjugate the wicked will the temple be established, the seat of judgment erected."[78]

These concepts, like the concepts related to the ideology of the royal capital, acquired among the prophets a particular spiritual dimension. Let us attempt briefly to characterize the metamorphosis of these ideas among the prophets:
1. The peoples come to Jerusalem not so much to bring tribute and prostrate themselves as to acknowledge the suzerainty of the God of Israel and abandon their idols: "To you will come nations from the ends of the earth; they will say, 'Our fathers inherited nothing but lies, vain things in which there is no profit' " (Jer 16:19; cf. Isa 2:18ff.). Deutero-Isaiah, the consoling prophet, who does not discard the notion of the bringing of tribute to Jerusalem in its time of need, and even broadens the concept to include nations bringing, along with their tribute, Jerusalem's children who had been reduced to captivity (49:22; 60:9; 66:20), describes a caravan of foreigners coming from Egypt and Ethiopia, crossing over to Jerusalem and professing their recognition of the God of Israel. These prostrate themselves and pray, "surely, God is in you, and there is no other god at all" (45:14). The same prophet sees nations coming to Zion's light, and kings to her shining brilliance (60:1-3), and to be sure, this is the prophet who coined the phrase, "a light of nations" (42:6; 49:6) apropos of the Servant's mission. It is instructive to note that this expression, too, is found in the court ideology of the kings of Babylon, *nūr kiššat niše*, "light of all the people," though here the phrase serves to praise the king's grandeur,[79] while in the prophecy of Deutero-Isaiah the concept comes to express a spiritual mission: the LORD's salvation that spreads to the end of the earth (Isa 49:6).

Jeremiah introduced a distinctive turn into this idea of the nations coming to Jerusalem. In his unique way, based on a change of values,[80] he states that the ancient national symbol, "the ark of the covenant," which was regarded as the throne of the LORD, will no longer exist. Jerusalem as a whole will be called "the throne of the LORD," and all the nations will gather there in the future in order to rectify their ways (Jer 3:16-17). In other words, instead of the national pilgrimage to the home of the tabernacle of the ark of the covenant, there would be an international pilgrimage to Jerusalem unconnected with cultic service, but with internal spiritual purification: "they will

---

[78] See above, n. 50.

[79] See Seux, *Épithètes* (above, n. 32), 209.

[80] See Weinfeld, "Jeremiah and the Spiritual Metamorphosis" (above, n. 40).

no longer follow the willfulness of their evil hearts" (Jer 3:17). A procession to Jerusalem of peoples whose aim is the search for "the way" and the seeking of God occurs in Zech 8:20-23:

> Peoples and the inhabitants of many cities will come hereafter and the inhabitants of one city will say to the other, "Let us go to entreat the presence of the LORD and let us seek the LORD of Hosts." "I too will go." And many peoples and might nations will come to seek the LORD of Hosts in Jerusalem.

The concept of abandoning idolatry and the adoption of a belief in the one God thus constitute the contribution of classical prophecy to the ideology of the temple city.

2. According to Isaiah,[81] peace will be attained not by force, but by spirit. The peoples will stream to the mountain of the LORD's temple as pilgrims, and seek to learn from the ways of the LORD and from his paths: "for from Zion will *Tora* (instruction) issue forth, and the word of the LORD from Jerusalem" (Isa 2:2-4). After accepting the sovereignty of the God of Israel, "they will beat their swords into plowshares and their spears into pruning-hooks . . . and they will learn war no more" (v 4).

Isaiah describes here the ascent of peoples to—as it were—the high court of justice, where judgment is rendered with absolute finality. The nations go up to Jerusalem to receive "the word" and *"Tora"*: "For from Zion will *Tora* issue forth, and the word of the LORD from Jerusalem." In order to capture fully the significance of *"Tora"* and "word," one may profitably turn to the description of the court in the place the LORD chooses in Deuteronomy 17. According to this Deuteronomic statute, the judge who is at a loss how to decide in a case located in his own city should arise and ascend to the place the LORD chooses and then act in accordance with the "word" imparted to him and in accordance with the *"Tora"* in which he is instructed there. In Isaiah 2 as well we encounter the nations who "ascend" to the house of the God of Jacob in order that he instruct them in the *"Tora"* and the "word" that issue forth from there. It is thus clear that *"Tora"* and the "word" mean here the binding decision in regard to international disputes. One may therefore legitimately assume that Isaiah made use of a conventional image of the high court of justice in order to describe the visionary court in Jerusalem, to which all the world would ascend for adjudication in matters of international dispute. In consequence of these adjudications, wars among the peoples would be eliminated. In another place, this prophet describes God arraying a feast on this mountain for all the peoples; following this feast, God will consume Death forever, wiping the tears from every face (25:6-8); then all will say, "This is our God! We awaited him; let us be glad and rejoice in his salvation!"

---

[81] The content and substance of the prophecy testify that the composition is that of Isaiah the son of Amoz. See Kaufmann, *History* III (above, n. 43), 199-200.

The utopian image of Jerusalem gained strength with time. Isaiah 65 contains a portrait of Jerusalem against the background of "a new creation" (vv 17-18) which draws on Isaiah's prophecy in connection with peace among the beasts (cf. Isa 65:25 with 11:6-9).

3. The image of the temple city as shrouded in splendor and divine brilliance which characterizes the descriptions of the Israelite sanctuary and whose roots stretch back to Mesopotamia also underwent a metamorphosis in prophetic literature. Zion is described as the tabernacle of God's glory, over which a cloud is spread by day and a flashing fire by night (Isa 4:5-6)—like the tabernacle of the tent of meeting in the wilderness of Sinai (Num 9:15ff.). In Isaiah 60, the metaphor undergoes an eschatological transformation. The divine light shining forth over Zion (vv 1-3) now supplants the natural light of the sun and moon: "No longer will the sun be your light by day, nor will the moon illuminate you with brightness; but the LORD will be your eternal light" (vv 19-20). A similar idea occurs in Zech 14:6-11.

4. The concept of the subjugation of peoples and the cessation of all wars in Jerusalem also acquires eschatological significance in prophecy. God judges the nations in the valley of Jehoshaphat by supernatural means: God reveals himself on the day of the LORD roaring from Zion, judging all the nations and providing a refuge for his people (Joel 4:9ff.); a similar treatment occurs in Zech 12:2-9. The eschatological development is particularly prominent in Ezekiel's description of Gog from the land of Magog, who will meet defeat on the mountains of Israel: God contends with his enemies with pestilence and blood, with overwhelming rain and hailstones, fire and brimstone (38:22).

The house of David that casts its fear over the peoples appears in Zechariah 12—"Like God, like the angel of the LORD"—and afterward the nations who come up against Jerusalem are destroyed (vv 5-9). In Zech 2:9, God Himself serves as "a wall of fire" around Jerusalem.

Summary

Dynastic kingship and a permanent sanctuary were an innovation in the history of Israel. Before the time of the United Monarchy, both were regarded as sins since they reflected the practice of other nations. In the older Israelite view, God does not bestow his spirit on a single family, and commensurately does not locate his tabernacle permanently in a single place. Rather, he wanders anywhere and bestows his spirit on anyone according to his own choice. His revelation is not given to fixation. In the days of David and Solomon, when a royal court was founded—"like all the nations"—everything changed. A fixed dynasty was founded and a fixed sanctuary, that is, a royal sanctuary next to the palace, was built. Accordingly, an ideology of the royal house and the temple city began to crystallize, just as it had among the surrounding nations. The ideology centered about the idea that nations and kings stream to the capital and bring with them tribute, professing their submission and accepting the judicial verdict emanating from it. An equivalent ideology obtained with regard to the temple city: nations and kings stream to the highest mountain sanctuary in order to bring there their offerings; they bring with them tribute, and especially cedar wood for the construction of the sanctuary; and they even participate in the sanctuary's construction. They also accept the judgment proceeding from the court of justice there.

This ideology can be discerned in the psalms, as well as in Israel's prophetic literature concerning Zion and Jerusalem. However, prophecy gave the ideology a new twist: nations and kings stream to the temple city in order to receive the gospel of belief in one God on the one hand and the gospel of eternal peace on the other. The king who sits enthroned in the royal city rules no longer by the might of his arm, but by the breath of his mouth; at his appearance, peace reigns and enmity is ended not only between people and people, and between man and his neighbor, but even among the beasts.

In this manner, we are witness to the paradoxical fact that *dynastic kingship* and a *permanent sanctuary*, which were regarded as transgressions at the dawn of Israelite history, became a great incentive and a lever for the heralding of salvation to Israel and to the peoples of the world.

Chapter V

THE LIFE AND TIMES OF KING DAVID
ACCORDING TO THE BOOK OF PSALMS

Alan M. Cooper
McMaster University

> "History is a nightmare from which I am
> trying to awake."—Stephen Dedalus

"All the praises which are expressed in the book of Psalms, David uttered them all . . . concerning himself or concerning the people. '*Lĕdāwid mizmôr*' means that the Presence descended upon him, and afterwards he composed poetry." Thus the famous statement attributed to the Tanna R. Meir in *B. Pesaḥim* 117a. According to Josephus,[1] David, "free from wars and dangers" in the autumn of his years, "composed songs and hymns to God in varied meters . . . . He also made musical instruments, and instructed the Levites how to use them in praising God . . . ." He had already had a lifetime to practice his art, as we read in *B. Berakot* 10a: "When he was in his mother's womb he said poetry *(šîrâ)* . . . . When he came forth into the world and gazed at the stars and constellations he said poetry . . . . When he suckled at his mother's breasts and looked upon her nipples he said poetry . . . ."[2] Compare Herder's remark:[3] "From his youth upward the mind of David had been attuned to musick and poetry." This was a prodigious talent indeed.

On two occasions, David was chastised for his poetry. When he sang Ps 119:54, *zĕmirôt hāyû lî ḥuqqeykā*, he rashly equated the Law *(dibrê tôrâ)* with secular song or poetry *(zemer)*; because of this offense the first attempt to bring the ark to Jerusalem was a catastrophic failure.[4] And, in what is perhaps the most delightful of all legends about David,[5] the king allows himself a moment of pride upon completion of the Psalter: "Is there a creature that you have created in your world who has sung more songs and praises than I have?"

---

[1] *Ant.* 7.12.3 §305; cf. Sir 47:8-10.

[2] The proof texts for these assertions are all from Psalm 103.

[3] *The Spirit of Hebrew Poetry* (trans. J. Marsh; Burlington: Edward Smith, 1833) 2.222.

[4] *B. Soṭa* 35a; *Num. Rab.* 4.20; 21.12; *Tanḥuma Pinḥas* 8; *Tanḥuma* Buber *Pinḥas* 9 (p. 153).

[5] *Pēreq Šîrâ = Yal.* 2.889.

At that moment a frog appears and admonishes the king not to be so overbearing (*'al tāzûaḥ da'atkā 'aleykā*). This frog, it transpires, has not only dwarfed David's output of psalms, but has also composed three thousand proverbs based on each psalm. The scene is curiously reminiscent of that choral episode in Aristophanes' *Frogs*[6] in which the title characters declare themselves to be beloved of Pan and the Muses, able to outcroak even the mightily flatulent Dionysos.

In spite of the frog's rebuke, a remark which is repeated thrice in the Talmud Yerushalmi[7] illustrates David's desire for posterity to remember him for his psalms. When David said *'āgûrâ bĕ'ohālĕkā 'ôlāmîm*, "Let me dwell in your tent forever" (Ps 61:5), could it possibly have occurred to him that he would be immortal? What he actually meant was "May I be worthy to have my words spoken in my name in the synagogues and in the academies."

These miscellaneous comments serve to illustrate one of the two essential points around which the traditional Jewish characterization of David crystallized. Those two points may be epitomized by two phrases: *māšîaḥ ben Dāwid*, the Messiah as scion of David; and *mizmor lĕdāwid*, David as author of the book of Psalms, creator of the Temple (and, of course, synagogue) liturgy. Only the second point will concern us here.

For the rabbis, the Davidic attribution of the Psalms serves as a productive interpretive strategy. It provides a firm anchor for the use of the psalms as either retrospective or prophetic accounts of the history of Israel.[8] But the Davidic authorship of Psalms poses a stern challenge for modern biblical scholarship. The critic is faced with an historical claim which is made, to some extent, by the biblical text itself, and which is bolstered by the earliest exegeses of that text. The critic is thus forced from the outset to pass judgement on the reliability of the claims of text and tradition. To put the question directly: What do the Psalms have to do with David? And, conversely, what does David have to do with the Psalms?

Three kinds of judgement are possible, roughly the same three as were already considered by Abraham Ibn Ezra in his introduction to Psalms.[9] The

---

[6] Choral Episode following Scene I.

[7] *Ber.* 2.1, 4b; *Šeqal.* 2.5, 47a; *Mo'ed Qat.* 3.7, 83c. See the elaboration of this remark in Avraham Hayarḥi (Lunel), *Sēper Hammanhîg* (Jerusalem: Mossad Harav Kook, 1978) 1.17.

[8] See lately E. Slomovic, "Toward an Understanding of the Formation of Historical Titles in the Book of Psalms," *ZAW* 91 (1979) 350-380.

[9] I refer throughout to the vulgar edition of Ibn Ezra which can be found in any *Miqrā'ôt Gĕdôlôt* (translations are mine). On the general character of Ibn Ezra's introductions, see M. Friedländer, *Essays on the Writings of Ibn Ezra* (London: Trübner, 1877) 120-122. For a thorough discussion (which appeared only after this article was in proofs), see U. Simon, *Four Approaches to the Book of Psalms from Saadya Gaon to Abraham Ibn-Ezra* (Hebrew; Ramat-Gan: Bar-Ilan U., 1982) esp. 121-236.

first two are the obvious positivistic judgments: 1) David certainly wrote all of the Psalms, as is clearly stated and elaborated in various ways in rabbinic literature. This is the first of the three opinions discussed by Ibn Ezra. 2) David did not write any of the Psalms; the biblical and post-biblical attributions are either spurious or wrongly understood as claims of authorship. This opinion corresponds in some ways to the second view described by Ibn Ezra, but finds its clearest expression in more modern scholarship. The following comment on the psalm titles is from the Rev. W. E. Addis's contribution to the first edition of Peake's *Commentary on the Bible*:[10]

> We will state the case in words taken from Professor Kirkpatrick's Commentary, because he is as conservative as a candid scholar can be. 'It is now admitted by all competent scholars that the titles, relating to the authorship and occasion of the Pss. cannot be regarded as prefixed by the authors themselves, or as representing trustworthy traditions and accordingly giving reliable information' (p. 31).

That so-called "conservative" remark is only a starting point for Addis's frontal assault against any vestigial notions that this or that psalm might just possibly be by David. His conclusion, two columns later—

> We set out to prove [!] that there are no Pss. certainly or even probably Davidic. We have in reality advanced further. The Psalter, as a whole, presumably belongs to the Second Temple and even to the later history of that Temple.

—with a concluding tag, somewhat rueful, I think: "It cannot, of course, be proved that there are no pre-exilic Pss."

The mediating opinion between those two extremes is probably held, in some form, by the majority of biblical scholars today. One version of it was already held by Ibn Ezra, who argued for the multiple authorship of the Psalms while suggesting that most, if not all, had been composed by the time of David:

> Every psalm which bears the superscription "of David" *(lĕdāwid)* is by David or by one of the poets who prophesied about David. In the case of "To Solomon: Give the king your justice, O God" (Ps 72), ascribe it to one of the poets who wrote about Solomon. And "A prayer of Moses" (Ps 90) is by Moses. [Similarly concerning Asaph, the sons of Korah, and the sons of Heman, all, with 1 Chr 25:2, 5; 2 Chr 35:15, contemporaries of David.] "To Solomon" (Ps 72) is by one of those who prophesied concerning Solomon or the Messiah his son, depending on how his name is read [cf. Ezek 37:25; Isa 44:2]. As for the psalms with no superscription, is it certain that they are not by David? Maybe they are by David, like the Psalm "Praise the Lord, call him by name" (Ps 105). It is explained in Chronicles (1 Chr 16:48) that David composed it on the altar and gave it to Asaph the poet.

It may be difficult for a modern reader to appreciate the sophistication of Ibn Ezra's position. Most important is his readiness to admit more than

---

[10](London: Jack, 1929) 367-368.

one meaning for the *lamed* of the superscriptions; it may mean either "by" or "about," denoting authorship or subject matter respectively. He demonstrates great interpretive freedom in his provocative remarks about Psalm 72; the psalm does, after all, end with the words *kālū těfillôt dāwid ben yišāi* (v. 20), "The prayers of David, son of Jesse, are ended." Yet, unlike Rashi and Kimhi, who logically understand the psalm to be the elderly David's prayer for his son and successor, Ibn Ezra (in his comment on Ps 72:1) terms it "the prophecy of David or one of the poets concerning Solomon or the Messiah." Those equivocal "ors," along with the almost perverse designation of the Messiah as the son of *Solomon*[11] in the introduction, seem calculated to irritate; it is as if Ibn Ezra wants to shock his readers out of a complacent positivistic reading of the psalm.

Still, on one crucial point Ibn Ezra fails to satisfy the modern historical-critical sensibility: his mostly pre-Davidic and Davidic dating of the entire collection of psalms. In fact, Ibn Ezra explicitly rejects too free a dating of the psalms because he does not want to exclude the possibility that some are prophetic.

By way of contrast, we might consider Herder,[12] who espouses the variable dating of the psalms while retaining a strong commitment to David for aesthetic reasons: "In the time of David," he says, "the lyric poetry of the Hebrews attained its highest splendour.[13] The scattered wild flowers of the country were now gathered and planted, as a royal garland, upon Mount Zion." It is, according to Herder, "undeniable that David greatly refined and beautified the lyric poetry of the Hebrews." But—

> Not all [of the Psalms] are his or of his age. Only an individual song of Moses, however, is from more ancient times, and later writers obviously followed him as their model, even when they did not ascribe their songs to himself. The superscription ascribing them to David, where it stands without further limitation, seems to be as indefinite in its import, as the ascription to Solomon of whatever proverbs and delicious songs belong in any sense to his age, or correspond with his character .... [A]mong the Hebrews a beautiful song is synonymous with a song of David.

According to Herder, there are seven "indispensable" requirements for the attainment of a "clear view of the Psalms." We can safely condense them to three: 1) careful study of the language and style of David and his contemporaries; 2) avoidance of odious comparison with non-Hebrew, that is,

---

[11] See the remarks of S. Schechter, *Aspects of Rabbinic Theology* (New York: Schocken, 1961) 87. Ibn Ezra cites Isa 44:2 and Ezek 37:25 to prove that a man's name can refer to his descendants.

[12] *Spirit of Hebrew Poetry* 2.223-229.

[13] Cf. R. Lowth, *Lectures on the Sacred Poetry of the Hebrews* (4th ed.; trans. G. Gregory; London: Thomas Tegg, 1839) 280.

classical or modern poetry (here, of course, is one of Herder's major criticisms of Lowth); 3) most important of all, "Our aim is to see [each psalm] in its circumstances of time and place, and in these the heart, and understanding of David, and the poets associated with him . . . . [T]he first inquiry should be for the objects and situations, in reference to which these songs were severally composed . . . [David's] songs illustrate his history, and his history aids the interpretation of his songs . . . ."

Herder's approach points up the hermeneutical trap which, for better or worse, all non-positivistic readers of psalms set for themselves. The superscriptions and traditional attributions can be neither accepted nor discredited *a priori*, so external criteria must be invoked in order to determine the authorship and/or historical setting of the psalm. Herder proposes two such criteria, both of which have found numerous exponents in the two centuries since his writing.

First is the aesthetic standard; those psalms which are considered to contain the noblest or most powerful expressions are assigned to David. Such aesthetic discussions of psalms may amuse the modern reader, but it must be remembered that they are the product of an age which was enthralled by the concept of the Sublime. Our own "scientific" efforts to date poems by linguistic methods will, no doubt, similarly amuse the scholars of the next century. That giant of nineteenth-century scholarship, Heinrich Ewald, whose views are discussed in some detail in S. R. Driver's *Introduction*,[14] isolated thirteen psalms and three fragments which "display an originality, dignity, and unique power which could have been found in David, and in David alone." There can be no doubt, affirms Driver, that "if Davidic Psalms are preserved in the Psalter, we may say safely that they are to be found among those which Ewald has selected." But Driver cannot abide Ewald's subjectivity, and he is forced to conclude: "On the whole, a *non liquet* must be our verdict: It is possible that Ewald's list of Davidic Psalms is too large, but it is not clear that none of the Psalms contained in it are of David's composition." A judicious use of the double negative, indeed. Is it fair to envision Driver throwing up his hands in despair when he continues, "The question, however, whether any of the Psalms are David's possesses in reality little but an antiquarian interest"?

From the now unfashionable aesthetic method of dating and attributing the psalms, we can turn to the second method, which I will call historical correlation. According to this method, the date and (perhaps) the attribution of a psalm can be determined if something in or about the psalm can be correlated with something known or hypothesized about the history of Israel, on the basis of a biblical witness outside the book of Psalms, or by comparison with extra-biblical sources. Ibn Ezra's discussion of Psalm 105 is a simple example: the psalm has no superscription, but it is unambiguously attributed

---

[14]*Introduction to the Literature of the Old Testament* (9th ed.; Edinburgh: Clark, 1913) 379-380.

to David in Chronicles. Some recent scholarly treatment of Psalm 24:7-10 is more complicated and more interesting.[15]

Most modern scholars see in the verses a depiction of a procession connected with some great event in Israel's history or cult. On the basis of Num 10:35 and 1 Sam 4:21, it is usually inferred (with the rabbis but against the Church Fathers) that this procession included the ark. Starting with those assumptions, neither of which may be said to be established with any degree of certainty, the next question is: which procession? Presumably some historical event, whether known or invented, or some cultic festival which must, of necessity, be invented since there is not a word in the Bible about cultic processions with the ark. At least twelve different historical and cultic settings have been proposed for Ps 24:7-10. The most popular is the episode described in 2 Sam 6, the triumphal entry of David with the ark into the conquered city of Jerusalem. Even Professor Cross, whose mythological interpretation of the psalm is, in my view, the most compelling yet offered, alludes to that historical interpretation when he remarks, "The portion of the psalm in verses 7-10 had its origin in the procession of the Ark to the sanctuary at its founding, celebrated annually in the cult of Solomon and perhaps even of David."[16]

Without going into detail here, I would submit that there is no evidence worthy of the name for correlating Psalm 24 with any particular biblical event. Certainly no traditional interpreter would have related Psalm 24 to 2 Samuel 6, because according to 1 Chronicles 16, Psalms 96, 105, 106, and 107 were sung to celebrate the ark's entry into Jerusalem. The rabbis, for whom historical correlation was a standard exegetical strategy, connected Psalm 24 with Solomon's efforts to install the ark in the Holy of Holies of the newly built Temple. As far as I know, only four critical scholars (including the great Rosenmüller) have seriously considered that rabbinic interpretation; I cannot see how it is any more or less attractive than the majority opinion, unless one considers a Davidic dating for the psalm to be preferable to any other *a priori*.

Another example of the pitfall of historical correlation may be found in attempts to press part of Psalm 60 (and the parallel portion of Psalm 108) into service as an historical document. Here the situation seems straightforward at first glance, since the superscription of Psalm 60 cues the reader to correlate the psalm with the accounts in the historical books of David's campaigns against Edom (2 Sam 8:13-14; 1 Kings 11:15-16; 1 Chr 18:12-14). The problem is that the three prose narratives disagree with one another, and the psalm provides yet a fourth alternative. There are discrepancies involving the name of the military hero, the number of casualties, the order of the events, and the identity of the enemies. And since David is never mentioned in the body of the psalm, some degree of historicity must naturally be assumed

---

[15]The following discussion of Psalm 24 is abstracted from my article, "Psalm 24:7-10: Mythology and Exegesis," forthcoming in *JBL*.

[16]*Canaanite Myth and Hebrew Epic* (Cambridge: Harvard, 1973) 93.

for the superscription. Furthermore, the content of the first four verses of the psalm is utterly unsuitable for correlation with an account of David's triumphs; so, paradoxically, the historicity of the superscription is credited while the opening verses of the psalm itself are discarded.

In one recent discussion of the historicity of Psalm 60//108,[17] a leading biblical scholar made two emendations in the psalm, reading Aram for Edom in v 8, and appending the name of the city of Tyre to v 9. While the restored order of David's conquests still does not conform to any order found in the historical books, that scholar is somehow able to conclude that "it is appropriate to take this source [i.e., Psalm 60//108] into account in a discussion of the [Davidic] period, for this source, in spite of its brevity, is, in fact, the only one which lists all the important conquests of David [mutatis mutandis!], and apparently in true chronological order."

I have not selected the two foregoing examples of historical correlation because they are egregious; indeed, they typify a way in which psalms are regularly abused by students of the history of Israel. It is simply taken for granted that the psalms represent a sub-genre of Israelite historiography,[18] that they are in some way the mimesis of historical events. They are expected, then, to "correspond" somehow to a set of "raw facts."[19] The same facts are also assumed to be accessible in the historical books, and a correlation is effected.

Now we know from controllable instances, such as Exodus 14 and 15, or Judges 4 and 5,[20] that when we possess multiple accounts of the same event (in those two cases, of course, one in poetry and one in prose) we can neither reconcile them definitively nor arrive at an unequivocal decision that one is literally truthful and the other mere fancy. So, too, in the case of parallel and contradictory stories in Samuel/Kings and Chronicles, we cannot arbitrarily assume the historicity of one or the other, but must look upon them as alternative interpretations of (or creations of) events. The events themselves must often, if not always, be acknowledged to be unrecoverable.

---

[17] Y. Aharoni, "Kibbuṣ̌ê Dāwid ləp̂î Təhillîm 60 we-108," Hammiqrā' wətôlədôt Yiśrā'ēl (J. Liver Memorial Vol.; ed. B. Uffenheimer; Tel Aviv: Tel Aviv U.,

[18] See, for example, A. Lauha, Die Geschichtsmotive in den alttestamentlichen Psalmen (Annales Academiae Scientiarum Fennicae B56/1; Helsinki, 1945) 7-10; J. Kühlewein, Geschichte in den Psalmen (Calwer Theologische Monographien 2; Stuttgart: Calwer, 1973) 9-17. The motive for such treatment of psalms is simply put by Kühlewein (p. 9): "Unser Glaube lebt von der Geschichte."

[19] The language used here, and in much of what follows, is taken from the writings of Hayden White. See specifically his Tropics of Discourse (Baltimore and London: Johns Hopkins, 1978) 47.

[20] Cf. Baruch Halpern's paper in this volume.

If that difficulty exists in controlled instances of parallel transmission, then how much the more so with documents of dubious historical character—Psalm 24, for instance. Psalm 60, on the other hand, explicitly demands to be read as history, whatever we make of the historicity of the superscription. But the biblical context of that reading is so confused as to render it futile. (There is, as usual in such cases, no extrabiblical source of enlightenment.)

To put this point somewhat differently: When we adopt a traditional positivistic mode of reading the psalms, rabbinic or Patristic, for example, there is no limit to what we can do to correlate them with their canonical context through Midrash, allegory, typology, and so forth. When, on the other hand, we deny the veracity of the Bible's own claim about the Psalms, we end up by creating a phantom book of psalms molded in our own image. That is, in essence, what Gunkel and subsequent form critics have done, and there is nothing wrong with it as long as the results are recognized as having nothing to do with history. If we take the third alternative, and adopt a mediating course, then we must assume what Hayden White has astutely called the "Burden of History." The key, in his words, is

> To recognize that there is no such thing as a *single* correct view of any object under study but that there are *many* correct views, each requiring its own style of representation. This would allow us to entertain seriously those creative distortions offered by minds capable of looking at the past with the same seriousness as ourselves but with different affective and intellectual orientations.[21]

Such minds as those of the biblical writers, I would submit.

Let us assume, for the sake of argument, that the psalms *are* historiographic, in other words, that they represent in an encoded form the outer experience of their creators—some event, some existential fact. The historian's problem is how to recover that fact, in effect, how to decode the poem. Applying the techniques of art criticism to history, White has argued for

> recognition that the style chosen by the artist to represent either an inner or an outer experience carries with it, on the one hand, specific criteria for determining when a given representation is internally consistent and, on the other, provides a system of translation which allows the viewer to link the image with the thing represented . . . .[22]

The style of presentation constitutes a code, a "system of notation." Only a reader "who is capable of understanding the system of notation used," who can decode it, can distinguish the historical facts in the poem from the false information introduced by the encoding process—by the artistic sensibility of

---

[21] *Tropics of Discourse*, 47. White's point has not met with universal acceptance. See Arnaldo Momigliano's trenchant critique, "The rhetoric of history and the history of rhetoric: On Hayden White's tropes," *Comparative Criticism* 3 (1981) 259-268.

[22] *Tropics of Discourse*, 46-47.

the poet. It may be, as Meir Weiss has asserted,[23] that the process of decoding destroys the poem as a literary work of art. The medieval Hebrew and Arabic poeticians were fond of saying, after Aristotle, that the *best* part of a poem is what is false in it,[24] but that consideration is irrelevant to the historian.

The question is what decoding tactic, what "governing metaphor," to use White's term, will enable the historian to put biblical history in order. Here again, I would suggest, the critic is at an impasse with respect to psalms. And it is the same impasse that led the Jewish tradition to assign authors to anonymous biblical writings in the first place. For the code of the psalms cannot be cracked except by a cipher which the reader creates ad hoc. For example, the psalms are all by David; or, they are all post-exilic; or, they are all liturgies of the Temple cult. Each of these is a potentially productive governing metaphor for the reading of psalms, but no reading will produce history in any objective sense.

Furthermore, when the metaphor is not even arguably inherent in the text, as in the case of Christological readings of Psalms, the act of reading through that metaphor is still exciting, and it can serve to dramatize the data and their significance in a way that no other reading could. (I happen to think that this is true for Ps 24:7-10, incidentally.) But it cannot produce history, because we can never know when we have hit upon the right code, when we have grasped the psalmist's system of notation. We do not know where or when Hebrew psalmody began; we hardly know the rudiments of Hebrew poetics; we cannot honestly say that we can date or attribute a single psalm with any degree of certainty.

The Davidic attribution of Psalms, in my view, is best understood as a productive interpretive strategy rather than as an historical claim. But before asserting that as a conclusion to this paper, it will be necessary to consider the biblical and extra-biblical evidence for and against the historicity of that attribution.

It is no longer fashionable for scholars to adopt a positivistic anti-Davidic attitude towards Psalms, but the alternative position is generally phrased with great circumspection. So, for example, Albright:[25] "*A priori* there is nothing to be said against the Davidic origin of Temple music." Similarly Mowinckel:[26]

---

[23] *Hamiqrā' Kidmûtô* (2nd ed.; Jerusalem: Bialik, 1967) 28-47. (A revised and updated English translation of this marvelous book is now in press.)

[24] See D. Pagis, *Šîrat haḥōl wĕtôrat haššîr lĕmōše ibn 'ezrā' ûbênê dōrô* (Jerusalem: Bialik, 1970) 46-50; W. Heinrichs, *Arabische Dichtung und grichische Poetik* (Beiruter Texte und Studien 8; Beirut: Orient-Institut der DMG, 1969) 56-68.

[25] *Archaeology and the Religion of Israel* (5th ed.; Garden City: Doubleday, 1969) 121.

[26] *The Psalms in Israel's Worship* (New York/Nashville: Abingdon, 1967) 2.80.

"[T]here is no valid objection to the conjecture . . . that the public cult in Jerusalem was furnished with singing and music as early as the time of David." Finally, according to Sarna,[27] while David should not "necessarily" be regarded as the author of "all those Psalms that bear the title *le-dawid*, . . . this ascription is very early and . . . it has its origin in an authentic tradition linking David with liturgical music."

All three formulations, it will be noted, are chary and vague. All three scholars are attempting to shift the burden of proof from those who would argue for Davidic psalmody onto those who would argue against it. But what, indeed, can be said *for* the historicity of the tradition? Furthermore, even granting its historicity, what possible method could be used to isolate the genuine Davidic Psalms?

Mowinckel states[28] that "in each individual case we have to ask for positive evidence proving that probabilities are in favour of dating a psalm from the time of David." As for the nature of that "positive evidence," Mowinckel refers vaguely to "internal grounds." When he finally gets down to cases, there is not a single Psalm that he can comfortably ascribe to David. There is nothing concrete that he can use to bolster his *a priori* assertion that "it is very likely that psalms were composed for the glory of Yahweh as early as the time of David . . . . "

Albright[29] suggests another way of determining which psalms might be Davidic in the light of his chronology of Hebrew verse types. He places some "Canaanizing Psalms," specifically 18, 29, 45, and 68, in the tenth century, although without suggesting Davidic authorship. (Interestingly, while he dates Psalm 18 in the tenth century, he does not argue for the authenticity of 2 Samuel 22.) Albright's supporting evidence for Davidic psalmody is essentially comparative and inferential, which is to say that it is suggestive without really proving anything. The basic piece of evidence is that "Syria and Palestine were noted for their musicians in the ancient Near East, as we know both from Egyptian and from Mesopotamian sources." In addition, the names of certain characters who are associated with Temple music in the Bible are attested in second-millennium sources. Furthermore—and this is the crucial point—"so many distinct biblical traditions mention David's musical prowess that scepticism would be thoroughly unwarranted."

Albright has phrased that statement carefully for, indeed, the biblical traditions outside the books of Psalms and Chronicles that deal with David's "musical prowess" do not clearly have anything to do with psalmody or liturgical composition. We might fairly say that inferring David's liturgical activity

---

[27] "The Psalm Superscriptions and the Guilds," *Studies in Jewish Religious and Intellectual History Presented to Alexander Altmann* (ed. S. Stein and R. Loewe; U. of Alabama, 1979) 185.

[28] *The Psalms* 2.152-153.

[29] *Archaeology*, 121-122.

from stories about his mastery of the harp (1 Sam 16:16-23; 19:9), his composition of dirges (2 Sam 1:17; 3:33) and other poems (2 Sam 22f.), and his
invention of musical instruments (Amos 6:5; Neh 12:36; 1 Chr 23:5; 2 Chr
7:6, etc.) is *exactly what the Chronicler wants us to do*. Without the goad of
Chronicles, could any of those accounts in Samuel possibly be understood as
references to David's creation of the liturgical forms of the Temple?

There are, rather, three separate traditions which should be kept separate
unless it can be proved that they have something to do with each other: David
the musician; David the poet; and David the psalmist. Albright glosses over the
difference between the first two by asserting that "in those days there was
no clear distinction between poet, composer and player." But that claim is
unproved, and it fails to explain the simple fact that nowhere in the books of
Samuel does David sing and play simultaneously. Contrast, for example,
Pseudo-Philo's retelling of the story in 1 Samuel 16, in which David sings an
apocryphal psalm of exorcism to the accompaniment of his harp.[30]

The blending of these two distinct traditions about David—the musician
and the poet—can already be seen in the Chronicler's version of the story of
David's dance before the ark. 2 Sam 6:5 is a difficult description of the music
that accompanied the transporting of the ark to Jerusalem: *wedāwid wekol-
bêt yiśrā'ēl mĕśaḥaqîm lipnê YHWH bĕkol 'aṣê bĕrôšîm ûbĕkinnôrôt ûbinbālîm
ûbĕtuppîm ûbimna'an'îm ûbĕṣelṣĕlîm*. Not all the terms are clear, but they all
apparently designate musical instruments. The Chronicler (1 Chr 13:8) makes
three changes, all presumably by way of simplification: he substitutes *mĕṣil-
tayim* for *ṣelṣĕlîm* and *ḥaṣôṣĕrôt* for the obscure *mĕna'an'îm* (also reversing the
order of these two terms); most important for our discussion is the Chronicler's
bĕkol 'ōz ûbĕšîrîm for Samuel's *lectio dificilior bĕkol 'aṣê bĕrôšîm*. I do
not claim to know what *'aṣê bĕrôšîm* means in this context, although I am
attracted to the medieval commentators' suggestion that the term denotes
instruments made of wood.[31] But it strikes me as undesirable, nevertheless,
to emend the Samuel text (as do Driver, Wellhausen, RSV, for example) after
the clearly simplifying reading of Chronicles. There is no reference to singing,
and certainly not to liturgical singing, in Samuel's version of the story; there
is playing, shouting (6:15), and dancing (6:16).

The primary reference to David's musicianship is, of course, contained
in the story of his entry into Saul's service (1 Sam 16). Quite apart from the
matter of this story's historicity (the contradiction with chap. 17, at least,
has to be resolved),[32] it contains no reference to singing. The emphasis is
on the magical power of the instrument—the Canaanites deified the *kinnôr*,

---

[30]*Bib. Ant.* 60.

[31]Cf. the English generic term "woodwind."

[32]See now R. Alter's elegant treatment of 1 Samuel 16-17 (*The Art of
Biblical Narrative* [New York: Basic Books, 1981], 147-153).

after all[33]—and on the musician as exorcist. In contrast to the famous story of the King of Lesbos whose turbulent spirit could only be quieted by the *songs* of his slave girls,[34] Saul's evil spirit is exorcised by the hand of David on the harp. (It does not always work, as 1 Sam 19:9 attests.) The tradition of David as exorcist is joined to that of David the Psalmist in post-biblical Judaism. Pseudo-Philo introduces a pseudepigraphic psalm into his version of the story.[35] The list of David's composition in 11QPs[a] mentions his "four song to sing against demons."[36] And 11QPsAp[a] joins the classic Jewish psalm of exorcism, Psalm 91, to several apocryphal compositions which apparently have the same concern.[37] The tradition continued in such popular Jewish manuals as *Sefer Refael Hamalak*, a guide for the magical use of psalms *(šimmûš těhillîm)*.[38]

The second element of the David tradition, David the poet, can also be disassociated from David the Psalmist, even if some of the attributions in Samuel are genuine.[39] The poems ascribed to David in the prose narratives are, more than anything else, a problem for *Redaktionsgeschichte*, as are the poems attributed elsewhere to Moses, Deborah, and Jonah. In addition, the tradition of David the poet, like the proverbial wisdom of Solomon, is probably derived from a typical motif of royal ideology. I would note, for example, Dio

---

[33]See my "Divine Names and Epithets in the Ugaritic Texts," *Ras Shamra Parallels* (Rome: Pontifical Institute, 1981) 3.384-385 (s.v. *knr*). And cf. the material on David's magical *kinnôr* and related matters in E. E. Halevi, *Pārāšîyôt ba'aggādâ* (Tel Aviv: Armoni, 1973) 393-397.

[34]Cited from Halevi, *Pārāšîyôt*, 346-347.

[35]*Bib. Ant.* 60.

[36]J. A. Sanders, *The Psalms Scroll of Qumrân Cave 11 (11QPs[a])* (DJD 4; Oxford: Clarendon, 1965) 91-93. Sanders' reading, evidently *happěgû'îm* (also Van der Ploeg, "Un petit rouleau" [see n. 37], 129), is most unlikely. Read either *happěgî'îm* or *happāgô'îm*. The former is a variant of the segolate plural *(happěgā'îm)*, which is the most common form in rabbinic literature. See Ben Yehuda, *Thesaurus*, 4821; on the form see E. Y. Kutscher, *Hallāšôn wěhāreqa' hallěšônî šel měgillat yěša'yāhû* (Jerusalem: Magnes, 1959) 288 41, 290 47. On *happāgô'îm*, see Ben Yehuda, *Thesaurus*, 4811. But perhaps this hapax in Yerushalmi should now be corrected to *happěgî'îm*! My thanks to Professor Moshe Greenberg for calling this matter to my attention.

[37]J. P. M. van der Ploeg, "Le psaume XCI dans une recension de Qumran," *RB* 72 (1965) 210-217; idem, "Un petit rouleau de psaumes apocryphes (11QPsAp[a])," *Tradition und Glaube* (K. G. Kuhn Festschrift; ed. G. Jeremias et al.; Göttingen: Vandenhoek & Ruprecht, 1971) 128-139 + pls. 2-7.

[38]In this connection, I would note the Orphic motives which enrich the post-biblical image of David. See, in general, N. Winter, *Der Thoraausleger Aristobulus* (Berlin: Akademie-Verlag, 1964) 202-261.

[39]Albright, for example, asserted without reservation that the "last words of David" in 2 Samuel 23 were David's own (*Archaeology*, 122).

Chrysostom's Second Discourse on Kingship, where Alexander invokes Hesiod's view that Calliope, the muse of oratory and epic poetry, is the attendant of kings.[40] When David calls himself *ně'îm zěmirôt yiśrā'ēl*, "the Hero of Israel's songs" (2 Samuel 23:1),[41] the sentiment is reminiscent of Alexander's statement that he would rather hear his own victories proclaimed than, like Homer, herald the triumphs of others.[42]

We are left with David the psalmist, the liturgist. That tradition, I have argued, is independent of the other two traditions about David. If it is authentic, it is not because its authenticity can be gleaned from anything in Samuel/ Kings. No independent witness to it exists before Chronicles, on which Ben Sira, Josephus, the rabbis, Pseudo-Philo, and others are obviously dependent.

Still, with Sarna,[43] I do not think it is credible to assert that the Chronicler simply invented the tradition of Davidic psalmody. Sarna, anticipated in certain respects by Morgenstern,[44] reasonably postulates the existence of local shrines, manned by guilds of Levites, in the pre-exilic period. Probably as a result of the restriction of animal sacrifice to the Jerusalem Temple in the eighth century, prayer and psalmody increasingly became the core of the rituals practiced at these shrines. Psalmody, then, was the one aspect of religious performance which was tied neither to the Temple nor to the priesthood.

The tradition that psalmody was a Davidic institution probably stems from the desire of the survivors or heirs of the old local guilds to legitimate their role in the Second Temple. The compelling quality of this levitical apologetic is due in large measure to the concomitant Messianic aggrandizement of David. Even more than the Deuteronomist, the Chronicler emphasizes David's longing to build the Temple. Why, then, as Sarna reasons, "should not David have interested himself in the organization of its forms of worship?"[45] Attributing the liturgy to David gives psalmody a legitimacy that is independent of, in fact prior to, the Temple.

---

[40]*Dio Chrysostom* (trans. J. W. Cohoon; Loeb Classical Library; London: Heinemann, 1932) 1.64-65 (Second Discourse, §24). Alexander also says that a king should learn to play the cithara or lyre just well enough to accompany his hymns to the gods and his chants in praise of brave men (66-67, §28).

[41]So rightly the RSV margin, against the traditional "Sweet Psalmist of Israel." Baruch Halpern reminds me that *zmrwt* could also be an abstract noun in -*ôt#* or -*ût#* from *zmr* III (KB[3], 263a), denoting "defense" or "strength." There might, then, be no reference at all to music in the epithet, although there would remain the possibility of a *double entendre*.

[42]*Dio Chrysostom* 1.60-61, §§17-18.

[43]"The Psalm Superscriptions," 284.

[44]"The Origin of the Synagogue," *Studi orientalistici in onore di G. Levi della Vida* (Rome: Istituto per l'Oriente, 1956) 2.191-201.

[45]"The Psalm Superscriptions," 284.

It is even possible, as Sarna seems to suggest, that this attribution was pre-exilic to some extent, although there is no evidence to support this claim. In any case, the development of the psalm superscriptions cannot be separated from the effort of the levitical singers to enhance their own status in relation to the Temple priesthood. The interpretive strategy which arises from the levitical position then remains alive to account for such developments as the Midrashic superscriptions in the proto-Masoretic psalter,[46] the extra Davidic superscriptions from within the Septuagint tradition,[47] and the apocryphal Davidic material in the Qumran scrolls[48] and pseudo-Philo.[49] Finally, almost inexorably, we arrive at the positivistic claim that all of the psalms are Davidic (perhaps as early as Ben Sira).

Where, then, are we left in *our* efforts to read the psalms? No psalm can be said with certainty to be Davidic, and the tradition of Davidic attribution is probably no older than the reign of Hezekiah at the earliest. There exists, furthermore, no reliable method for determining or evaluating the historiographical character of any psalm. The application of historical-critical and form-critical methods only multiplies hypotheses and uncertainty, and hardly moves us closer to a valid understanding of the history of Israel, or of the history of Israelite literature. We are left, I submit, with only two sensible and productive ways of reading: 1) reading in a strictly canonical context, and 2) reading from an ahistorical aesthetic or literary-critical point of view. Both modes of reading abandon any attempt to use the psalms as historical documents.

The canonical reading self-consciously adopts traditional strategies of interpretation, because they produce interesting and illuminating results, and because they ground the reading solidly in the religious community. This kind of reading has most recently been espoused by Brevard Childs.[50] Childs

---

[46] See B. S. Childs, "Psalm Titles and Midrashic Exegesis," *JSS* 16 (1971) 137-150; E. Slomovic, "Historical Titles in the Book of Psalms" (above, n. 8).

[47] See A. Pietersma, "David in the Greek Psalms," *VT* 30 (1980) 213-226.

[48] See especially P. Skehan's observation that the form and content of 11QPs[a] serve to emphasize the link between David and the psalter ("A Liturgical Complex in 11QPs[a]," *CBQ* 35 [1973] 195).

[49] Note, in particular, J. Strugnell's *tour de force*, "More Psalms of 'David'," *CBQ* 27 (1965) 207-216. I should also mention a medieval manuscript containing several apocryphal psalms which deserves to be brought into the discussion. See A. Harkavy, "Tĕpillôt bĕsignôn mizmôrê tĕhillîm lĕʾeḥād pĕlônî ʾalmônî," *Haggoren* 3 (1902) 82-85. My thanks to Dr. Harry Fox for calling this fascinating material to my attention.

[50] *Introduction to the Old Testament as Scripture* (Philadelphia: Fortress, 1979).

advocates the careful study of the traditional commentaries on Psalms:[51]

> Admittedly these commentaries run the risk, which is common to all interpretations, of obscuring rather than illuminating the biblical text, but because they stand firmly within the canonical context, one can learn from them how to speak anew the language of faith.

For those who feel uncomfortable with the avowedly theological aim of canonical reading, the literary-critical approach commends itself.[52] Let the text assume a timeless existence somewhere between the author and the reader; the author is beyond reach, but the imaginary world which is encoded in the text is not. The text, severed from its historical moorings, will cooperate with us and enrich us if we allow it to. The meaning of the psalm is nothing more or less than the way we, as readers, appropriate the text and *make* it meaningful. The poem is not a mere artifact of some distant but recoverable time and place. It is, rather, our point of entry into a world of imagination which exists nowhere beyond the language of the poem and our own minds. Our reading ought to be self-conscious and fulfilling, not an act of self-effacement in the pursuit of that problematic scholarly ideal, the "real" meaning of the text. Otherwise, we have no hope of escaping the bitter verdict reached by Paul Valéry:[53]

> Fate has arranged that those men with no great appetite for Poetry, who feel no need for it and would not have invented it, there should be many whose task or destiny it is to judge it, to comment on it, to provoke and cultivate a taste for it: in short, to dispense something they do not possess. They often employ all their intelligence and zeal in this: which is why the results are to be feared.

---

[51] *Introduction*, 523.

[52] The following remarks are elaborated in another paper, "The Act of Reading the Bible," which will appear in the *Proceedings of the Eighth World Congress of Jewish Studies*.

[53] *The Art of Poetry* (trans. D. Folliot; Bollingen Series 45/7; New York: Pantheon, 1958) 85.

Chapter VI

THE ORIGINS OF UNIVERSAL HISTORY

Arnaldo Momigliano
(University of Chicago)

I

I would be making the understatement of the century if I were to say that universal history has never been a clear notion. Taken literally, the idea of universal history verges on absurdity. Who can tell everything that has happened? And who would like to listen if he were told? But both in the Greek and in the Hebrew tradition of history-writing the urge to tell the whole story from beginning to end has been apparent, and universal history has become one of the most problematic components of our twofold Jewish and Greek heritage. Among the texts which have reached us directly it is a Greek text— Hesiod's *Works and Days*—that gives us the oldest scheme of the succession of ages; but the Jews of the Hellenistic age outbid the Greeks by taking the story beyond the present into the future and gliding from history into apocalypse. The mixture of the historic and the Messianic has seldom been absent in the accounts of universal history which have been produced by ecclesiastical and secular historians from the Revelation of St. John to Arnold Toynbee's *Study of History*; and there is no sign that the universal history industry is flagging.

Contrary to the prevailing opinion that most of the time universal history played only a small part in Greek culture there was a continuous and considerable production of patterns intended to give, if not a meaning, at least some order to the story of mankind. But the majority of these patterns had their origins in what we can loosely call the mythical or philosophical imagination of the Greeks rather than in the empirical collection and critical interpretation of past events called *historia*. Only the succession of world empires can be said to have represented a guiding thought for real historians. I shall therefore devote the second part of this chapter to the development of the notion of the succession of world empires within Greek historiography and I shall try to show that the Jews—and more precisely the authors of the Book of Daniel—derived this notion from the Greeks and turned it into an apocalyptic one. But before I do this I have to examine three other Greek schemes of universal history which are important in themselves, though they affected the historians only in a marginal way. These are the scheme of the succession of different races characterized by different metals; the biological scheme according to which not only individuals but nations and even mankind as a whole go

133

through the stages of childhood, youth, maturity and old age; and finally the scheme of the progress of mankind from barbarism to civilization through a series of technological discoveries.. Each of these three schemes had high potential for proper historical research. In later ages each was adopted and developed by historians on a large scale. But the Greek historians, being mainly interested in politics and wars, took far less notice of these schemes than we should have liked. The first thing to learn from Greek historiography is that schemes of the evolution of mankind can be invented in a given culture before historical research makes its appearance and can be multiplied after historical research has established itself without necessarily taking into account what historians have to say. We historians are a rather marginal by-product of history.

The traditional father of Greek historiography, Hecataeus, lived at the end of the sixth century B.C.; the two men who shaped Greek historiography in the way we know it, Herodotus and Thucydides, operated in the second half of the fifth century B.C. But Hesiod presented a scheme of universal history which can hardly be later than the end of the eighth century B.C. It is also virtually certain that Hesiod had at his disposal a pre-existing model for his cogitations on the development of mankind through a succession of various races, the golden race, the silver race, etc. Hesiod's scheme is distinguished by two further complications. For motives which at least in the case of the golden race are entirely mysterious and in the case of the successive races (silver, bronze, heroic, iron) by no means self-evident, the gods, to say the least, allow the elimination of the existing race and its replacement by another which (with one exception) they like less than the one just suppressed. The one exception—the race of heroes inserted between the bronze and the iron age—is anomalous in so far as it does not receive its name from a metal and interrupts for a while the decline characterizing the process as a whole. Long ago it was seen that the insertion of the race of heroes in the scheme of the four races named according to metals was secondary and necessitated by the importance attributed to heroes in the Greek tradition. Whether it was in fact Hesiod who performed this adaptation of the scheme of the four ages to specific Greek requirements we cannot say. The races of gold and of bronze, and the heroic race, each seem to be limited to one generation—which would mean that the gods from the start did not endow them with the faculty of reproduction. Only the race of silver is explicitly given children, but it is also the only race about which it is explicitly stated that it was destroyed by the gods themselves. Hesiod has no remarks on this, and nor have I.

All the later writers in Greek or Latin about the four races, outside Judaism or Christianity, depended directly or indirectly on Hesiod. Plato used the myth freely, especially in the *Republic* (3, 415 a-c), to support the hierarchical structure of his State. Hellenistic poets like Aratus (third century B.C.) and Ovid refurbished the Hesiodic myth to express a nostalgia for the golden race which Hesiod, far more sensitive to the pains of the iron race than to the attraction of previous times, had never really felt. The races could be reduced in number—or increased. It will be remembered that Juvenal in

Satura XIII speaks of the ninth age without having a metal for it; he defines the ninth as worse than the iron age (l. 28, "nona aetas agitur peioraque saecula ferri temporibus"). He probably mixes up the scheme of the four ages with that of the ten generations which is found in other contexts. It must here be observed that the transition from Greek to Latin in itself produced a momentus difference. The *saeculum aureum* or *saeculum felicissimum* of the Latins is not identical with the *genos chryseion*, "the golden race" which it purports to translate. The Greeks underlined the type of man, the Romans put the character of the age to the fore. The difference made it easier for the Romans to exploit the myth for political propaganda. A good emperor could be expected to change the character of his age more easily than the race of his subjects. The return of the Golden Age was a more plausible theme for propaganda in poetry and inscriptions or coins than the return of the Golden Race. Altogether the Romans felt free to develop the implications of cyclical return to the Golden Age which the Greek versions had never stressed. In considering the evils of the Iron Race Hesiod had been unable to repress the *cri de coeur*: "Would that I were not among the men of the fifth generation, but either had died before or been born afterwards." Yet it is very doubtful whether he implied circularity in the scheme of the ages and a possible return from iron to gold. Roman political propaganda on the contrary had to presuppose, or at least to imply, circularity in the scheme of the ages in order to make plausible the image of an emperor taking his empire back from the Iron Age to the Golden Age. In A.D. 400 the poet Claudian ominously depicted, not a Roman emperor, but the German general Stilicho as the man who brought the Golden Age back to Rome. This scene in the second book of the *Laudes Stilichonis* (vv. 422 ff.), with the Sun going to the Cave of Eternity to retrieve the Golden Age for the consulate of Stilicho, is a memorable antithesis to the lines of Hesiod's *Works and Days* which more than a thousand years before had firmly placed Greek culture in the Iron Age.

Whether in the Greek or in the Roman form, there was very little historical observation behind this scheme of the ages. Whether we take Hesiod or Aratus or Ovid or Claudian—or the philsophers and moralists who played with this story—they did not really talk about any remembered or recorded past. The designation of the bronze age may have preserved some recollection of the time in which iron was not yet in use: it did not, however, define a technology. The collective image of the heroic age very probably preserved some obscure memory of the Mycenaean age—but no more than what one could find in the epic poems or some tragedy. The schematization did not add to knowledge, and in any case there was no folk memory behind the notions of gold and silver ages. For all practical purposes the iron age was the only age which belonged to the historical field: the four previous ages were ideal alternative forms of human life recaptured by myth and impervious to history. The scheme of the metal ages, as reported by non-Jewish and non-Christian writers, was part of classical mythology rather than of classical historiography. We shall see later that Persian and Jewish writers connected it with historical events.

II

Different considerations are suggested by the biological scheme, but again we shall find that in pre-Christian writers it was only marginal to history and hardly affected the writing of universal history. The biological scheme, in distinguishing between childhood, youth, maturity and old age (with further optional refinements), proved to have relatively greater historiographical possibilities when applied to single nations than when applied to the whole of mankind. Confused ideas that certain nations are younger than others floated about in Greek ethnography. Since Herodotus it had been generally admitted that the Egyptians were a much older nation than the Greeks, and Herodotus also knew that as a nation the Scythians were about a thousand years old (4, 7). Here again the Romans seem to have derived more precise consequences from Greek premises. Lactantius in his *Institutiones* (7, 15, 14) states that Seneca—whether the rhetorician or the philosopher is debatable—constructed a scheme of Roman history from Romulus to Augustus based on this metaphor of stages of life. We do not know how Seneca elaborated this scheme, but under the Emperor Hadrian Annaeus Florus composed his elegant summary of Roman history according to the same guiding principle. Since it is preserved (it proved to be immensely successful) it gives us the best idea we can form of this type of biological history. Florus attributes to Rome a childhood of 250 years under the kings, an adolescence of comparable length, and then a maturity of 200 years which ends with Augustus. The next hundred years under the emperors are old age, but Florus sees signs of rejuvenation under the Emperors Trajan and Hadrian in whose reigns he happens to live. Interestingly enough, he does not go beyond Augustus in his actual narration.

As the Roman Empire was often identified with the whole of the world one might expect an easy transition from the notion of an aging Rome to the notion of an aging human race. But I have no evidence to show that any pagan historian took the step of presenting world history in terms of the aging of an individual. The notion of an aging Rome derived much of its historiographical strength from the realistic impression that beyond the borders of the Empire—or even inside them—there were nations ready to take advantage of the weakness of Rome. Tacitus would not have written the *Germania* without the uneasy feeling that the barbarians were ready to prey on aging Rome. Even more explicitly, in the late fourth century, Ammianus Marcellinus connects the old age of Rome with the increasing frivolity and vulgarity of its ruling class which in turn provokes the enemies of the Empire to increasing audacity. It would not have made much sense for a historian rooted in the political tradition of Rome to identify the old age of Rome with the old age of the world: the danger, as he saw it, was in the contrast between the lethargy of Rome and the energy of her youthful enemies.

This may explain why, as far as I know, a clear formulation of the *senectus mundi*—of the old age of the world—is to be found only in Christian writers and does not become an operative historiographical notion until St. Augustine. A clear adaptation of the biological scheme to Christian notions of history is already to be found in Tertullian's *De Verginibus Velandis* (1, 7): the world reaches its infancy with the Mosaic Law; its youth with the Gospel and its maturity with the Paraclete. But this is said in a perfunctory way. It takes a St. Augustine to face the *senectus mundi* in the precise clinical manifestation of the sack of Rome and to conclude that what appears to be old age in the City of Man may be youth in the Heavenly City: "Do not try to stick to this old World; do not refuse to find your youth in Christ who tells you the World is transient, the World is ageing, the World declines, the World is breathless in its old age. Do not fear: your youth will be renewed as that of the eagle" (*Sermo* 81, *P.L.* 28, 505). It is by now evident that outside such audacious metahistorical applications there was little scope for the biological scheme in universal history. We must conclude that in classical pagan historiography the application of the biological scheme to the history of mankind was scarcely more successful than the application of the scheme of the metallic ages.

III

A further scheme remains to be considered which, though born outside historical research, like the previous two schemes, was soon felt to be open to empirical verifications and as such interested ancient philologists and antiquarians, if not historians. Gods or culture-heroes who reveal technological secrets to helpless mankind are of course to be found everywhere. What seems to characterize the Greeks is that they did not remain content with their heroes, impressive as they may have been. Already in Aeschylus' *Prometheus* (the question whether Aeschylus is the real author of the *Prometheus* is here irrelevant) the culture-hero symbolizes mankind in its efforts to attain knowledge. Sophocles in the *Antigone* can dispense with the culture-hero and make man himself the source of all the ambiguous achievements which intelligence brings about. Even when mythical forms are retained (as in the new version of the Prometheus story told by Protagoras in Plato) the problem of how man acquired the arts becomes the focus for reflection. Individual men or individual cities were sometimes singled out for praise. The praise of Athens as a civilizing city goes back at least to Isocrates. The Epicureans would naturally emphasize the enlightened traditions of the city to which Epicurus, after all, belonged. We therefore find the praise of Athens in Lucretius, Book VI. But as a rule the effort to encompass the discovery of the arts went beyond individual names of gods, men and cities and tried to envisage the conditions which favoured discoveries in general. Climatic conditions, fear of animals, development of language, discovery of metals and forms of cultivation, organization of social life, the cumulative influence of observation in various fields, etc., are factors considered in the two most important discussions we have of the technical progress of mankind: Diodorus' *Bibliotheca* Book I and Lucretius' *De rerum natura* Book V, to which we may add Vitruvius, *De architectura* Book II and Manilius, *Astronomicon* Book I in the following century. Not much has come down to us—partly as a result of the classicistic selection operated by late Greeks and Romans—of the work of their predecessors, the Sophists of the fifth century B.C. and the specialized students of discoveries of the late fourth century B.C. and of the early Hellenistic period. We are informed about a refined study of sacrificial customs composed by Aristotle's pupil Theophrastus only because the philosopher Porphyry happened to be very interested in it in the third century A.D. Dicaearchus, who lent authority to the notion of a life of Greece and inspired Varro, apparently combined the cultural scheme with that of the decline from a golden to an iron age. He had some idea of technological stages, such as nomadism and agriculture. A couple of indications by Varro, one by Censorinus and one by Porphyry give us a pale reflection of what must have been Dicaearchus' thinking on the evolution of Greece. We would expect Posidonius to have said something very influential on the subject of the discoveries of the arts in the generation before Lucretius and Diodorus. But sources being what they are, our main information about Posidonius' opinions on cultural history depends on Seneca's Letter 90. There Seneca agrees with Posidonius that the philosophers were the natural leaders of mankind during the golden age, but he does not accept Posidonius' further conjecture that the philosophers discovered the arts and techniques which myth had considered to be Prometheus' province. This is very little, and therefore scholars have been able to state or to deny with equal assurance that Posidonius is the source behind Diodorus' chapters in Book I about the evolution of mankind.

We must add that in Hellenistic and Roman times it was natural for oriental writers in the Greek language to dispute the claim that the Greeks with their gods and heroes had been the civilizers. Moses was turned into a culture-hero by Jewish writers, like Artapanus in the second century B.C.; and in the late first century A.D. the Phoenician Philon of Byblos boasted of having found in Phoenician writers older than the Trojan war a clear description of how Phoenician gods and heroes had introduced the technology of civilization. In the wake of the discoveries at Ugarit credulous orientalists have been inclined to believe him. All these discussions hardly went beyond the zone of myth and even within these limits they accepted the terms formulated by the Greeks.

The ravages of time, that is, the loss of so many original sources (like Posidonius himself) give perhaps an unjust impression of poverty of results in this field. We should be wiser if we had more of Posidonius or more of Theophrastus, or even more of Critias and Protagoras on this subject. The problems were recognized, and it is remarkable that such a variety of approaches—from fear of animals to climate and language—presented themselves to the Greeks (if not to their oriental competitors) and remained present to the Romans. But even if we were much better informed we would hardly find cultural developments as one of the central themes of Greek historical research. More specifically, we would not find universal histories built on schemes of cultural development. We are brought back to the hard fact that before Christianity Greek and Latin historians saw political and military events as the natural subject of their researches. If universal history was to have a central place in historical research it had to have a place in political history. Whereas it was generally admitted that by studying political history one could avoid past mistakes and improve future performances cultural history at best provided confirmation of some philosophic theory. It was not meant to help the future development of culture and remained at the level of curiosity and exemplification. To find universal history in full dress we must therefore go to Polybius, the political historian who claimed to be a universal historian or, to use his own expression *ta katholou graphein*, "to write general history" (5, 33). He is the first extant author to make this claim, though, as he himself knew, not the first to have made it.

IV

Polybius became a universal historian because he saw himself as seriously involved in a chain of political and military events which truly appeared to affect the whole world. According to Polybius the Romans created universal history by conquering the world or at least by affecting directly or indirectly the future of the whole world. This meant that Polybius could not envisage universal history as the discovery of patterns of behaviour common to all men qua men. To him universal history came into being at a certain date, say the second Punic War, about 220 B.C., because of a new historical development. The idea of a universal history from the origins of mankind was alien to Polybius. He was, however, prepared to admit that in the more remote past certain historical situations had already brought mankind near to political unity, and that some historians had understood this predicament and therefore examined the facts with something like the self-consciousness of the universal historian. In fact he indicated Ephorus, the historian of the middle of the fourth century B.C. who had examined oriental events connected with Greek events, as his first and most serious predecessor as a universal historian.

The situations which Polybius believed to be comparable with Rome's conquests are the processes of formation of previous empires. Persia, Sparta and Macedon are his explicit terms of reference. Characteristically he leaves out Athens, for he did not like Athenian democracy. He speaks of Rome and Carthage as the two powers which disputed the rule of the world before Rome won. Since the succession of empires is the central point of Polybius' historical vision it is useful to remind ourselves of his precise words: "The paradoxicality and greatness of the spectacle with which I propose to deal will become most clear if we single out and compare with the Roman hegemony the most famous of the previous empires—the ones which have provided historians with their chief theme. Those worthy of being thus set aside and compared are the following: the Persians . . . the Spartans . . . the Macedonians . . . . But the Romans have subjected to their rule not portions, but nearly the whole of the world" (I, 2) (transl. W. R. Paton, Loeb).

This was not only an intellectual perception, but an emotional finding. The fall of an empire is to Polybius an occasion on which a dignified man is entitled to let himself go, to be disturbed and even to cry. He knows he has a literary tradition behind him to justify his emotions and to give appropriate words to them. After having concluded his account of the fall of the Kingdom of Macedon under Perseus in 168 B.C. Polybius picked up a treatise on Fortune in which Demetrius of Phalerum had commented upon the fall of the Persian Empire and generally animadverted on the inconstancy of human fortunes. Polybius was impressed by the fact that in the generation after Alexander Demetrius had foreseen that Macedon would one day fall in its turn. He quoted from Demetrius and concluded: "I, as I wrote and reflected on the time when the Macedonian monarchy perished, did not think it right to pass over the event without comment, as it was one I witnessed with my own eyes, but I considered it was for me also to say something befitting such an occasion, and recall the words of Demetrius" (29, 21) (transl. W. R. Paton).

It may seem superfluous to quote the other more famous passage (38, 21) in which Polybius tells of how he was near Scipio Aemilianus, the Roman commander, when Carthage was burning in 146 and had Scipio grasping his hand and repeating Homer's line "A day will come when sacred Troy shall perish" (*Iliad* 6, 448). But this passage raises a problem. We have not all of Polybius' original text, and we must reconstruct it as best we can from three quotations: one in the so-called excerpts *De sententiis*, another in Diodorus 32, 24 and a third in Appian, *Libyca* 132. Appian is the only one to tell us that Scipio Aemilianus was meditating on the fall of the empires of Assyria, Media, Persia and Macedonia while weeping and reciting Homer to himself. This addition of the four world- empires may be an improvement by Appian who as an Egyptian writer of the second century A.D. was aware of them, but one would need very strong arguments to admit such interference by Appian with the account of the scene which he explicitly takes from Polybius. Prima facie, the reference to the four empires must be attributed to Polybius. If this is correct it shows that although Polybius was interested as a historian in the succession Persia-Macedonia-Rome he was acquainted with a longer list of world-empires in which Assyria and Media preceded Persia.

Indeed, we may immediately add that this list—the famous list of the four monarchies—must have been current in Polybius' time and therefore easily available both to him and to Scipio Aemilianus. We happen to know from a strange gloss inserted in Velleius Paterculus 1, 6 that Aemilius Sura, an otherwise unknown author of a book, *De annis populi romani*, placed the Romans at the end of a succession of empires starting with the Assyrians and continuing with the Medes, the Persians and the Macedonians. More precisely Sura dated the beginnings of the Roman World Empire during the reigns of Philip V of Macedon and of Antiochus III of Syria, that is, either before 179 B.C., the date of Philip's death, or before 187 B.C., the date of Antiochus III's death. There are too many difficulties in this text for us to be certain when it was written, but one is inclined to believe that Aemilius Sura gave such a precise and unconventional date because he wrote in the earlier part of the second century B.C. and was himself a witness of the Roman victories over Macedonia and Syria.

In fact the notion of the succession of the world-empires had been codified by Herodotus and Ctesias, the leading historians writing about Asia in the
fifth and very early fourth century B.C. Herodotus had stated in so many
words that the Persians had succeeded the Medes in the empire (I, 95; 130);
he had furthermore promised to write a special account of Assyria, though for
reasons unknown he did not do so (I, 184). Ctesias fulfilled this desideratum
and introduced Median and Persian history by way of a long account of the
previous Assyrian empire. Neither of them could of course foresee that the
Persian world-monarchy would be replaced by the Macedonian monarchy.
But the contemporaries of Alexander the Great must have been quick to add
the Macedonian world-monarchy to the three empires codified by Herodotus
and described by Ctesias. A man like Demetrius of Phalerum quoted by
Polybius must be supposed to have been acquainted with Herodotus and
Ctesias.

It is not surprising that Polybius should concentrate his real interests
on Greece, Macedonia, Carthage and Rome. Even Persia is to him a distant
shadow. The succession of the four world-empires must have appeared far
more significant in the late fourth century and in the early third century B.C.
when the Hellenistic monarchies as a whole seemed to represent an obvious
and lasting replacement of the Persian monarchy: Rome was still confined to
Italy. Though the disappearance of most of the historical writing of early
Hellenism makes it difficult to prove this statement, three considerations
can be offered before I pass on to examine the only extant text of the third
century B.C. about the four monarchies.

If one feature was evident in this scheme of the four monarchies—
Assyria, Media, Persia and Macedonia—it was that it kept Egypt out. This was
of course noticed by Egyptians who came into contact with Hellenistic culture
and by those Alexandrian intellectuals who persisted in the old Hellenic
tradition of admiration for the Eyptians. Herodotus, without thinking of
empires, had already presented the semi-mythical Egyptian King Sesostris
as superior to Darius the Persian, who rather good-naturedly conceded the
point (2, 110). But it was left to Hecataeus of Abdera—a Greek writing in
Egypt about 300 B.C.—to elevate Sesostris to the dignity of a universal ruler.
In Hecataeus' account, which we have in Diodorus' summary (1, 53), Sesostris's father gave his son the education befitting a future cosmocrator, and
Sesostris proved to be the model emperor of the world. It does not matter
very much whether the Egyptians put ideas into the head of Hecataeus of
Abdera or vice versa. Three centuries later, when the geographer Strabo and
the Emperor Tiberius's adoptive son Germanicus were travelling in Egypt,
local priests told them stories similar to those of Hecataeus of Abdera (Strabo
17, 816; Tac. Ann. 2, 60). Native historians of Mesopotamia were of course
in an easier position. In telling the history of Babylonia to the Greeks Berossus
was able to fit it into the scheme of the four successive monarchies. On the
other hand, it is impossible to understand all the anti-Roman propaganda of
the last two centuries of the Republic without referring to these notions of
successive-world empires. The Greeks and even more the Orientals who saw

the Romans taking over everywhere found refuge in hopes, in prophecies and even in actual revolutionary movements promising to put history in reverse and to give back to Greece or to the East the world-rule they had lost. Polybius says nothing of these outbursts. But some of them were registered by his contemporary Antisthenes of Rhodes, a historian and a philosopher. In Antisthenes' account both a dead Syrian officer and a dead Roman general announced Rome's fall and the return of Asia to power (*Fr.Gr.Hist.* 257 F. 36). A forged letter from Hannibal to the Athenians circulated in which the Carthaginian promises to give the Romans a more severe lesson than that given by the Greeks to the ancestors of the Romans, namely the Trojans (*Hamburg Griech. Pap.*, 1954, n.129, ll. 106 ff.).

The rebellions of the slaves in Italy, the struggle of Aristonicus in Asia Minor about 132 B.C., the wars of King Mithridates of Pontus against Rome for twenty-five years between 88 and 63 B.C., and finally Cleopatra's war against Octavian were accompanied and supported by prophecies of the return of the empire to the Asiatic nations. As there were colonies of Persians with their magi in Asia Minor somebody turned to them for help in this ideological warfare. The result was a document—the prophecy of Hystaspes, a King of Media supposed to have lived before the Trojan war. The prophecy was still circulating in the fourth century A.D., when it was amply summarized by Lactantius: it predicted the destruction of the Roman Empire and the return to power of the East.

Thirdly and finally we have to turn to the universal histories which multiplied in the congenial atmosphere of Roman wars and conquests of the first century B.C., when Pompey and Caesar seemed to be challenging the reputation of Alexander the Great. Some of these universal historians accepted in full Polybius' premise that proper universal history could not be written until the rise of Rome as a world-empire. Therefore they continued Polybius down to their own day: Posidonius of Apamaea to about 60 B.C. at the latest and Strabo of Amaseia to the end of the civil wars, perhaps about 30 B.C. The novelty which Posidonius transmitted to Strabo, in so far as it was transmissible, was the use of Herodotean ethnography to describe cultures discovered—chiefly but not exclusively—by Roman conquest. Most of the world Posidonius had managed to conjure up in his vivid, rich, prose has, alas, disappeared with the loss of his work. Though Posidonius was probably superior to any of the other post-Polybian universal historians, those who did not accept the chronological limits imposed by Polybius and bravely imitated Ephorus in going back to remote antiquity are, as a group, more interesting for our inquiry.

I shall not take into account two Italians of the second half of the first century B.C. who, just because they were the first Italians to write universal history, naturally stimulate our curiosity: we know almost nothing of the contents of the three books of universal history by Cornelius Nepos which his friend Catullus commended; nor have we any precise idea of how Titus Pomponius Atticus selected his topics for the *liber annalis* which (Cicero claimed) "me inflammavit studio illustrium hominum aetates et tempora persequendi" (*Brut.* 19, 74). But we can read part of the universal history by the Sicilian Diodorus, and we have at least the summary made in the second or third century A.D. by Justin of the vast work strangely called *Historiae Philippicae* by Trogus Pompeius, a Gaul from Gallia Narbonensis. We can also form some idea of what must have been the biggest universal history ever written in antiquity, a work in 144 books by Nicolaus of Damascus, a Hellenized Syrian who managed to be tutor of the children of Cleopatra and Antony, secretary and envoy of King Herod of Judaea for many years and finally a friend of Augustus, of whom he wrote a biography. We also have a faint notion of what must have been a universal history in Greek called "Kings" by Timagenes, who was forcibly removed from Alexandria to Rome about 56 B.C. and created for himself the reputation of being a bitter critic of anything Roman.

These four provincials—two from the West (Diodorus and Trogus) and two from the East (Nicolaus and Timagenes), one (Trogus) writing in Latin and the others writing in Greek—tried to offer some resistance to a view of world history which was an implicit, and even explicit, glorification of Rome. They gave pride of place to the old civilizations of the East and of Greece, and they emphasized either the relative barbarism of the Romans or their recent conversion to Greek customs (which amounted to the same thing). None of them could build up his history on a rigorous scheme of succession of world-monarchies. They all had to take account of the Celtic West which that scheme ignored. Trogus Pompeius, perhaps the most remarkable of the four, came from this Celtic West. Nor could Egypt be ignored after so many protests. Diodorus as a Greek could emphasize the superior merits of Greek education; and Nicolaus as a secretary of Herod King of Judaea had to accommodate the Jews and was altogether sympathetic to the minor nations of the Near East. But each of these four historians seems to have been very conscious of the scheme of the succession of oriental monarchies. This is demonstrably the case with the two historians whom we can still read in a continuous way, not only relying on quotations, Diodorus and Trogus. Trogus' master-stroke—a piece of really good historical imagination—was to conclude his work by bringing together the free Parthians of the East and the no-longer-free Celts and Spaniards of the West. He simply declared that the Parthians were sharing the rule of the world with the Romans after having won three wars against them (41, 1). We know how these victories had hurt the Romans. Trogus had hit where it hurt most. He had furthermore made it plain that the conflict between East and West, of which so much had been said in the previous century, was by no means closed. The Parthian Empire was after all either the continuation or the revival of the Persian Empire, as everybody knew.

There is also a conspicuous reference to the four monarchies of Assyria, Media, Persia and Macedon just at the beginning of the *Roman Antiquities* by Dionysius of Halicarnassus. This was written in 7 B.C. And we could follow up the allusions to this scheme until the early fifth century A.D. when Rutilius Namatianus was still comparing Rome, to her advantage, with the great empires of old. He called the Persian Empire of the Achaemenids "magni

Parthorum reges" (*De reditu suo* 85). But we are ready to face the last text I propose to consider on this occasion—the Book of Daniel.

V

It was customary in the Hellenistic period both among Jews and among Gentiles to attribute sayings, visions and books in general to wise men of the past. Daniel was not such a big name but his reputation had been on the increase for some centuries. The prophet Ezekiel chose Noah, Daniel and Job as the prototypes of righteousness (14:14; 20). Ezek. 28:3 taunts the King of Tyre: "are you wiser than Daniel?" So Daniel was not only just, but wise. And he was probably not Jewish, as Noah and Job were not strickly speaking Jewish. In the Book of Jubilees (4, 20), which is more or less contemporary with the final version of the Book of Daniel as we have it, we find a Daniel or rather a Danel whose daughter married Enoch, the other more important biblical figure to whom apocalyptic books were attributed in the second century B.C. If Daniel and Danel are two variant spellings of the same name, which seems beyond doubt, the figure of the just man Danel may go back to an Ugaritic text of the fourteenth century B.C., "The Tale of Aqhat."

What is surprising is to find Daniel placed in the courts of Babylon and Persia by the book which bears his name. According to the book he would have been taken prisoner at the fall of Jerusalem at the beginning of the sixth century B.C. We have no idea of when and how Daniel became a hero of the sixth century B.C. According to the Book of Daniel he and three Jewish friends were successively at the court of Nebuchadnezzar, of Belshazzar, who is presented as the son of Nebuchadnezzar and the last King of Babylon (he was neither), and finally of that Darius the Mede, never heard of elsewhere, who is supposed to have conquered Belshazzar. In the first part of the book— which in our late medieval division into chapters corresponds to chapters 1-6— Daniel interprets the visions and dreams of pagan kings. He and his companions exemplify steadfast Jews who prefer death to the cult of foreign gods or of living kings. But while (as we shall see) these chapters presuppose Alexander the Great and the formation of the Hellenistic monarchies, they do not allude specifically to Antiochus IV or his time. They envisage Jews living at the courts of kings and managing in spite of all to reconcile worldly success as courtiers with the duties of pious Jews. The situation resembles that of the Book of Esther rather more than that of the Books of Maccabees.

The second part of Daniel is differently oriented. It is clearly concerned with the situation of Jerusalem and the rest of Judaea under Antiochus IV, and his own visions are directly communicated by Daniel in the first person. The stories about Daniel and his companions are replaced by the words of Daniel himself. It seems obvious, however, that the author or authors who composed what now constitutes chapters 7-12 of the Book of Daniel knew the first part well. There are in fact signs that the Book of Daniel, though composed of heterogeneous elements, was put together with conspicuous care by an editor who was interested in producing an impression of coherence and even of stylistic harmony. The task was by no means easy because, as we all know, Daniel is one of the two books of the Bible which are written partly in Hebrew and partly in Aramaic. With the present division of chapters the first chapter is in Hebrew, the next six chapters are in Aramaic: in the second section of the book the order and the proportions are inverted, one chapter in Aramaic being followed by six chapters in Hebrew. Even if we forget the existence of chapters the proportions remain harmonic. This must be by design and indicates that the editor of the book did his best to give it an appearance of unity.

The link between the two sections is not only formal. The second section of the book develops the philosophy of history which we find in the second chapter of the first section. It is of course inspired by the idea of the succession of empires.

In chapter 2 Nebuchadnezzar had a dream, as we all remember, which none of the non-Jews could interpret, and he was determined to kill his professional advisers. Daniel was brought in, gave the right interpretation and thereby saved his gentile colleagues or rivals. The dream is that of the great image with the head of fine gold, breasts and arms of silver, belly and thighs of bronze, legs of iron, feet part iron, part clay. A stone from heaven (according to the dream) shattered the statue. In Daniel's interpretation the different metals in the different parts of the statue each symbolize a kingdom, and the kingdoms are not concurrent but successive. The stone is the true God, and what follows the destruction of the statue is the establishment of the Kingdom of God which will endure forever. However, there is an ambiguity in the story. The stone smashes all the elements of the statue at the same time, including the golden head. It puts an eternal Jewish Kingdom of God in the place of all the empires of the past taken together. Thus the statue is not meant to represent a succession of empires: it rather symbolizes the coexistence of all the past, as it had developed through a succession of kingdoms, at the moment in which all the past is destroyed by the divine stone and replaced by a new order.

Daniel does not say which are the four kingdoms smashed by the stone. The writer of chapter 7, which took up the same notion of four kingdoms but did not retain the symbolism of the metals, undoubtedly identified the kingdoms with Babylonia, Media, Persia and Macedonia. In chapter 7 the fourth kingdom is represented by a nameless monster with ten horns, and an eleventh little horn develops later. The ten horns of the fourth monster certainly symbolize three Macedonian and seven Seleucid kings, and the eleventh little horn is Antiochus IV. One can date chapter 7, from the details it provides, between 169 and 167 B.C. Like the writer of chapter 2 the writer of chapter 7 expects a Kingdom of God soon to replace the kingdom on earth.

Though there is a presumption that the author of chapter 7 was capable of understanding what the author of chapter 2 meant by four kingdoms we need confirmation. The confirmation comes from the fourth kingdom which is partly iron, partly clay because, so Daniel explains, "it will be a divided kingdom with some elements of iron in it." This makes sense only for the

Macedonian Kingdom or Empire which was divided by Alexander's successors. A further confirmation is in the apparently mysterious line 43: "Just as you saw the iron mixed with terra cotta of clay, they will be mingled by inter-marriage, but they will not hold together, just as iron does not unite with terra cotta" (transl. L. F. Hartman, Anchor Bible, 1978). There was one disastrous marriage among the successors of Alexander: it was that between the Seleucid Antioch II and Berenice, the daugher of Ptolemy II. This is indeed recorded more explicitly in the second section of Daniel at 11:6. We must recognize the same allusion in 2:43. As this marriage happened about 250 B.C. and is the most recent event alluded to in chapter 2 there is a fair chance that chapter 2 was written not much later. If so, we could tentatively date the first section of Daniel about 250-230 B.C., whereas the second section is made up of chapters written between 167 and 164 B.C.

If our reading of the text of Daniel is approximately correct, we have a Jew who in the second part of the third century B.C. expounded in symbolic form the doctrine of the four monarchies and reinterpreted it in an apocalyptic sense: the fifth kingdom, soon to come, would be the Kingdom of God. The idea was found acceptable, and was revived and given a new urgency in Jeru-salem at the time of the resistance to Antiochus IV when the priest Mattathias and his son Judas Maccabeus took up arms to defend the Torah of the Fathers. The notion remained operative in Jewish thought, as a survey of Jewish Sibyl-line Books and other apocalyptic writings could easily show. But we must end with the obvious question. Where did the author of Daniel chapter 2 find this notion?

If we had only the second section of the Book of Daniel, which is directly inspired by the crisis in the reign of Antiochus IV and written while he was still alive, it would have been recognized long ago that the author or authors of these visions about kingdoms worked on the basis of the Greek concept of a succession of world-empires. The religious interpretation, the apocalyptic finale, is of course the specific Jewish contribution to the reading of the situation. Furthermore, we must admit that Assyria is replaced by Babylonia in Daniel's vision: Babylonia was a natural beginning for a Hellenis-tic Jew, who associated its empire with the destruction of the First Temple. But the foundation of all this Messianic structure is provided by the scheme of the succession of empires which we found in Herodotus, Ctesias and their successors. What is decisive is that no one has so far been able to produce genuine evidence for the existence of the notion of four world-empires outside Greek historical thought. There have been many suggestions in the direction of India, Persia and Babylonia, but none has stood up to serious criticism. Four world ages of the Hesiodic type are known in India; four kings in a descending order of goodness within the Iranian state are described in Persian medieval commentaries on a lost book of the Avesta—the *Vohuman Yasn.* Some serious scholars have suggested that such texts were themselves written under Greek influence. If they were not, they prove that the Hesiodic myth of decline had wide Indo-European roots and ramifications. But the applica-tion of the quadripartite scheme to the political notion of world-empires remains a Greek peculiarity, if one excepts the Book of Daniel and its imitators. In 1975 Professor A. K. Grayson introduced a new pretender to the title of Daniel's source by his meritorious discovery in the British Museum of a late Babylonian text which he called "a dynastic prophecy" (*Babylonian Historical-Literary Texts*, 24-37). This is a chronicle in the form of a prophecy which lists a series of kings who governed Babylon and indicates changes of dynasties and of territorial boundaries. The text has some remarkable similarities with Daniel, and I hope to show elsewhere that it was not compiled under the first Seleucid kings, as Grayson suggested, but under Alexander the Great. It may in fact be the earliest document we have of anti-Macedonian propaganda in Babylonia. But the similarities between this dynastic prophecy and Daniel do not involve the scheme of the succession of empires which is absent from the Babylonian text.

There is, however, a very good reason why scholars should have been slow to recognize that the Book of Daniel turns a Greek summary of world-empires into a blueprint for the preparation of the Messianic age. The reason is that no Greek source associates, as Daniel chapter 2 does, the four empires with the four metals. A similar association of metals and kings is to be found in the medieval Persian texts *Denkard* and *Bahman Yasht* when they describe the four Iranian kings representing stages of declining respect towards Zoroaster and his doctrine. I believe, however, that this does not disprove our main point that no theory of the succession of world-empires circulated in the East before the Greeks imported it. It may well be that some such text which associated metals with kings, even if not universal kings, suggested to the author of Daniel chapter 2 the idea of characterizing each world-empire by one metal. But paradoxically this very association in Daniel between metals and world-empires is presented in such a way as to show that it is secondary. The metallic ingredients can hardly be said to make sense in Daniel's context. The four metals in order of decreasing value ought to represent successive stages in the decline of earthly kingdoms. Yet Daniel does not express any preference: all the empires will be destroyed together. Nor would we expect a Jewish writer to give the highest mark to Babylonia which had destroyed the First Temple. It cannot be an accident that the scheme of the metals, where we find it outside Daniel chapter 2, has nothing to do with the scheme of the world-empires. Even Daniel chapter 7 drops the combination of world-empires and metals, thereby confirming that it was a peculiarity of Daniel chapter 2. The scheme of the world-empires in Daniel is in itself value-free, as the Greek scheme of world-empires was.

To judge from the fascination which the statue of the four metals has exercised throughout the centuries, we must admit that the author of Daniel chapter 2 had found a symbol which worked even if it was incongruous. While using the Greek notion of the succession of empires to illuminate the ways of God he had also produced a quaint target for the destructive capacities of God. To repeat the words used in a similar context by Mandell Creighton:

"No disappointment was rude enough to show men that this theory was but a dream" (*A History of the Papacy* I, 1882, p. 11).

We are no longer likely to be surprised that Jews talked to Greeks in the third century B.C. Even King Solomon, in his modern reincarnation as Ecclesiastes or Qohelet, was taking notice of the latest Epicurean treatises. In another context I hope to have shown that Herodotus was known to the somewhat later author of the Book of Judith. What is remarkable is the energy and independence with which the Jews turned Greek ideas upside down.

ARNALDO MOMIGLIANO

31 December 1980.

SELECT BIBLIOGRAPHY (mostly of recent works)

I.

C. Trieber, 'Die Idee der vier Weltreiche,' *Hermes*, 27, 1892, 321-344.

M. Büdinger, *Die Universalhistorie im Alterthume*, Wien 1895.

M. Mühl, *Die antike Menschheitsidee in ihrer geschichtlichen Entwicklung*, Leipzig 1928.

J. Kaerst, *Universalgeschichte*, Stuttgart 1930.

W. Goetz, 'Weltgeschichte,' *Archiv für Kulturgeschichte*, 24, 1934, 273-303.

R. Aron, *The Dawn of Universal History*, London 1961.

J. Vogt, *Wege zum historischen Universum*, Stuttgart 1961.

H. C. Baldry, *The Unity of Mankind in Greek Thought*, Cambridge 1965.

R. Drews, 'Assyria in Classical Universal History,' *Historia*, 14, 1965, 129-138.

A. B. Brebaart, 'Weltgeschichte als Thema der antiken Geschichtschreibung,' *Acta Historiae Neerlandica*, 1, 1966, 1-21.

A. Heuss, *Zur Theorie der Weltgeschichte*, Berlin 1968.

A. Randa (ed.), *Mensch und Geschichte. Zur Geschichte der Universalgeschichtsschreibung*, Salzburg-München 1969.

F. G. Maier, 'Das Problem der Universalität,' *Geschichte heute* (ed. G. Schulz), Göttingen 1973, 84-108.

P. Burde, *Untersuchungen zur antiken Universalgeschichtsschreibung*, diss. München 1974.

F. Hampl, *Geschichte als kritische Wissenschaft*, I, Darmstadt 1975.

A. Heuss, 'Ueber die Schwierigkeit, Weltgeschichte zu schreiben,' *Saeculum*, 27, 1976, 1-35.

G. Barraclough, *Main Trends in History*, New York-London 1978 (1979), 153-177.

H. Schwabl, 'Weltalter' in Pauly-Wissowa, Suppl. 15, 1978, 783-850.

G. W. Trompf, *The Idea of Historical Recurrence in Western Thought from Antiquity to the Reformation*, Berkeley 1979.

II.

F. Kampers, *Alexander der Grosse und die Idee des Weltimperiums in Prophetie und Sage*, Freiburg 1901.

A. Bauer, *Ursprung und Fortwirken der christlichen Weltchronik*, Graz 1910.

A. O. Lovejoy and G. Boas, *Primitivism and Related Ideas in Antiquity*, Baltimore 1935.

K. Löwith, *Weltgeschichte und Heilsgeschehen*, Stuttgart 1953.

Anna-Dorothee v. den Brincken, *Studien zur lateinischen Weltchronistik bis in das Zeitalter Ottos von Freising*, Düsseldorf 1957.

P. Meinhold, 'Weltgeschichte - Kirchengeschichte - Heilsgeschichte,' *Saeculum*, 9, 1958, 261-281.

150

A. Klempt, *Die Säkularisierung der universalhistorischen Auffassung*, Göttingen 1961.

K. Rahner, 'Weltgeschichte und Heilsgeschichte,' *Schriften zur Theologie*, V, Einsiedeln, 2 ed., 1964, 115-135.

G. Klingenstein, 'Kultur- und universalgeschichtliche Aspekte in strukturaler Sicht,' *Archiv für Kulturgeschichte*, 52, 1970, 280-296.

J. Vogt, 'Universalgeschichte und Kirchengeschichte unserer Zeit,' *Theologische Quartalschrift*, 155, 1975, 175-186.

III.

E. Meyer, 'Hesiods Erga und das Gedicht von den fünf Menschengeschlechtern' (1910) in *Kleine Schriften*, II, Halle 1924, 15-66.

F. Boll, 'Die Lebensalter,' *Neue Jahrbücher für das Klassische Altertum*, 31, 1913, 89-145.

R. Schmidt, 'Aetates mundi,' *Zeitschrift für Kirchengeschichte*, 67, 1955, 288-317.

U. Bianchi, 'Razza aurea, unità delle cinque razze ed Elisio,' *Studi Materiali Storia Religioni*, 39, 1963, 143-210.

B. Gantz, *Weltalter, Goldene Zeit und sinnverwandte Vorstellungen*, Hildesheim 1967.

J.-P. Vernant, *Mythe et pensée chez les Grecs*, 3 ed., Paris 1971.

Jana Tumova, 'Antike Bearbeitung des Mythos von den Vier Zeitaltern,' *Graecolatina et Orientalia*, 6, 1974, 3-46.

J. Fontenrose, 'Work, Justice and Hesiod's Five Ages,' *Classical Philology*, 69, 1974, 1-16.

M. L. West, *Hesiod: Works and Days*, Oxford 1978.

P. Vidal-Naquet, 'Plato's Myth of the Statesman, The Ambiguities of the Golden Age and of History,' *Journal of Hellenic Studies*, 98, 1978, 132-141.

IV.

K. Reinhardt, 'Hekataios von Abdera und Demokrit,' *Hermes*, 47, 1912, 492-513 (*Vermächtnis der Antike*, Göttingen 1960, 114-132).

W. Uxkull-Gyllenband, *Griechische Kulturentstehungslehren*, Berlin 1924.

A. Kleingünther, Πρῶτος Εὑρετής, *Philologus*, Suppl. 26, 1, 1933.

W. Spoerri, *Späthellenistische Berichte über Welt, Kultur und Götter*, Basel 1959.

K. Thraede, 'Erfinder' in *Reallexikon für Antike und Christentum*, V, 1962, 1190-1275.

A. Dihle and others, *Grecs et Barbares*, Entretiens Fondation Hardt, 8, Genève 1962.

F. J. Worstbrock, 'Translatio Artium. Ueber die Herkunft und Entwicklung einer kulturhistorischen Theorie,' *Archiv für Kulturgeschichte* 47, 1965, 1-22.

T. Cole, *Democritus and the Sources of Greek Anthropology*, American Philol. Assoc., 25, 1967.

E. R. Dodds, *The Ancient Concept of Progress*, Oxford 1973.

B. Reischl, *Reflexe griechischer Kulturentstehungslehren bei augusteischen Dichtern*, diss. München 1976.

V.

S. Mazzarino, *Il pensiero storico classico*, I-III, Bari 1966-67.

K. von Fritz, *Die griechische Geschichtsschreibung*, I, Berlin 1967.

H.-A. Weber, *Herodots Verständnis von Historie*, Bern 1976.

E. Cavaignac, 'Réflexions sur Ephore,' *Mélanges G. Glotz*, I, Paris 1932, 143-161.

Th. J. G. Locher, 'Ephoros' jüngste Nachkommen,' *Saeculum*, 7, 1956, 127-135.

R. Drews, 'Ephorus and History written "Κατὰ γένος",' *Amer. Journ. Philol.*, 84, 1963, 244-255.

O. Murray, 'Hecataeus of Abdera and Pharaonic Kingship,' *Journ. Egypt. Archaeol.*, 56, 1970, 141-171.

P. Pédech, *La méthode historique de Polybe*, Paris 1964.

F. W. Walbank, *Polybius*, Berkeley 1972.

E. Gabba (ed.), *Polybe*, Entretiens Fondation Hardt, 20, Genève 1974.

S. Mohm, *Untersuchungen zu den historiographischen Anschauungen des Polybios*, diss. Saarbrücken 1976.

K. E. Petzold, 'Kyklos und Telos im Geschichtsdenken des Polybios,' *Saeculum*, 28, 1977, 253-290.

K. Bringmann, 'Weltherrschaft und innere Krise Roms im Spiegel der Geschichtsschreibung des zweiten und ersten Jahrhunderts v. Chr.,' *Antike und Abendland*, 23, 1977, 28-49.

D. Musti, *Polibio e l'imperialismo romano*, Napoli 1978.

F. W. Walbank, *A Historical Commentary on Polybius*, III, Oxford 1979, 720-725.

F. W. Walbank, 'The Idea of Decline in Polybios' in R. Koselleck und P. Widmer, *Niedergang*, Stuttgart 1980, 41-58.

K. Sachs, *Polybius on the Writing of History*, Berkeley 1981, 96-121.

S. Blankert, *Seneca ep. 90 over natuur en cultuur en Posidonius als zijn bron*, Amsterdam 1941.

K. Reinhardt, 'Poseidonios' in Pauly-Wissowa, XXII, 1, 1954, 558-826.

J. Hermatta, 'Poseidonios über die römische Urgeschichte,' *Acta Class. Univ. Scient. Debrecensis*, 7, 1971, 21-25.

P. Desideri, 'L'interpretazione dell'impero romano in Posidonio,' *Rend. Istit. Lombardo*, 106, 1972, 481-493.

K. von Fritz, 'Posidonios als Historiker,' *Historiographia antiqua*, Louvain 1977, 163-193.

K. Schmidt, *Kosmologische Aspekte im Geschichtswerk des Poseidonios*, Göttingen 1980.

152

P. Merlan, 'Lucretius, Primitivist or Progressivist?' *Journ. History of Ideas*, 11, 1950, 364-368.

J.-P. Borle, 'Progrès ou déclin de l'humanité. La conception de Lucrèce,' *Mus. Helveticum*, 19, 1962, 162-176.

B. Mannwald, 'Der Aufbau der lukrezischen Kulturentstehungslehre,' *Abh. Akad. Mainz*, Geistes- und Sozialwissensch. Klasse, 1980, Nr. 3.

E. Troilo, 'Considerazioni su Diodoro Siculo e la sua storia universale,' *Atti R. Istituto Veneto*, 1940-41, 17-42.

G. Vlastos, 'On the Prehistory in Diodorus,' *Amer. Journ. Philol.*, 67, 1946, 51-59.

B. Farrington, 'Diodorus Siculus: Universal Historian' in *Head and Hand in Ancient Greece. Four Studies*, London 1947, 55-87.

R. Laqueur, 'Diodorea,' *Hermes*, 86, 1958, 257-290.

M. Pavan, 'La teoresi storica di Diodoro Siculo,' *Rend. Accad. Lincei*, N.S. 16, 1961, 19-52; 117-151.

M. Gigante, 'Catullo, Cornelio e Cicerone,' *Giornale Ital. Filologia*, 20, 1967, 123-129.

F. Muenzer, 'Atticus als Geschichtschreiber,' *Hermes*, 40, 1905, 50-100.

O. Seel, *Eine römische Weltgeschichte*, Nürnberg 1972.

R. Urban, 'Historiae Philippicae bei Pompeius Trogus,' *Historia*, 31, 1982, 82-96.

I. Lana, *Velleio Patercolo o della propaganda*, Torino 1952.

R. J. Starr, 'The Scope and Genre of Velleius' History,' *Class. Quart.*, 31, 1981, 162-174.

W. Den Boer, 'Florus und die römische Geschichte,' *Mnemosyne*, 4, 18, 1965, 366-387.

Florus, ed. P. Jal, Paris 1967.

H.-W. Goetz, *Die Geschichtstheologie des Orosius*, Darmstadt 1980, 71-79.

VI.

R. Reitzenstein-H. H. Schaeder, *Studien zum antiken Synkretismus aus Iran und Griechenland*, Leipzig 1926.

H. Windisch, 'Die Orakel des Hystaspes,' *Verhandel. Kon. Akad. Wetensch.*, Afd. Letterkunde, N.R. XXVIII, 3, 1929.

F. Cumont, 'La fin du monde selon les mages occidentaux,' *Rev. Hist. Religions*, 103, 1931, 29-96.

E. Kocken, *De Theorie van de vier wereldrijken en van de overdracht der wereldheerschappij tot op Innocentius III*, Nijmegen 1935.

J. Bidez-F. Cumont, *Les mages hellénisés*, Paris 1938.

H. Zimmern, 'The Hindu View of World History according to the Purāṇas,' *The Review of Religion*, 6, 1942, 249-269.

R. Schmidt, 'Aetates Mundi. Die Weltalter als Gliederungsprinzip der Geschichte,' *Zeitschr. für Kirchengeschichte*, 67, 1955, 288-317.

G. Widengren, 'Quelques rapports entre juifs et iraniens à l'époque des Parthes,' *Vetus Testamentum*, Suppl. 4, 1956, 197-241.

H. Wolfram, *Spendor Imperii. Die Epiphanie von Tugend und Heil in Herrschaft und Reich*, Graz-Köln 1963.

F. König, *Zarathustras Jenseitsvorstellungen und das Alte Testament*, Freiburg 1964.

M. Molé, *La légende de Zoroastre selon les textes pehlevis*, Paris 1967.

M. Boyce, 'Middle Persian Literature,' *Handbuch der Orientalistik*, 4, 1, Sect. 2, Lit. 1, Leiden 1968, 31-66.

C. Dimmitt Church, *The Yuga Story: a Myth of the Four Ages of the World as found in the Purāṇas*, diss. Syracuse 1970.

G. Podskalsky, *Byzantinische Reichseschatologie*, München 1972.

J. de Menasce, *Le troisième livre du Dēnkart*, Paris 1974.

J. R. Hinnels, 'The Zoroastrian Doctrine of Salvation in the Roman World: a Study of the Oracle of Hystaspes,' *Man and his Salvation. Studies in Memory of S. C. F. Brandon*, Manchester 1973, 125-148.

G. Widengren, 'Iran and Israel in Parthian Times with special regard to the Ethiopic Book of Enoch' in *Religious Syncretism in Antiquity*, ed. B. A. Pearson, Missoula 1975, 85-130.

D. König-Ockenfels, 'Christliche Deutung der Weltgeschichte bei Euseb von Cäsarea,' *Saeculum*, 27, 1976, 348-365.

H. G. Kippenberg, 'Die Geschichte der mittelpersischen apokalyptischen Traditionen,' *Studia Iranica*, 7, 1978, 49-60.

A. Alföldi, 'Redeunt Saturnia Regna,' *Chiron*, 5, 1975, 165-192; 9, 1979, 553-606.

VII.

H. Fuchs, *Der geistige Widerstand gegen Rom in der antiken Welt*, Berlin 1938.

J. Swain, 'The Theory of the Four Monarchies. Opposition History under the Roman Empire,' *Class. Philology*, 35, 1940, 1-21.

S. K. Eddy, *The King is Dead*, Lincoln 1961.

J. Lebram, 'Die Weltreiche in der jüdischen Apokalyptik. Bemerkungen zu Tobit, 14, 47,' *Zeitschr. für Alttestam. Wissenschaft*, 76, 1964, 328-331.

V. Nikiprowetzki, *La Troisième Sibylle*, Paris-Le Haye 1970, 88-112.

D. Flusser, 'The Four Empires in the Fourth Sibyl and in the Book of Daniel,' *Israel Oriental Studies*, 2, 1972, 148-175.

A. K. Grayson, *Babylonian Historical Literary Texts*, Toronto 1975.

J. Schwartz, 'L'Historiographie impériale des Oracula Sibyllina,' *Cahiers Hist. Ancienne*, 2, 1976, 413-421.

W. Lambert, *The Background of Jewish Apocalyptic*, London 1978.

J. J. Collins (ed.), *Apocalypse. The Morphology of a Genre*, Semeia 14, 1979.

D. Mendels, 'The Five Empires: a Note on a Propagandistic Topos,' *Amer. Journ. Philol.*, 102, 1981, 330-337.

VIII.

H. H. Rowley, *Darius the Mede and the Four World Empires in the Book of Daniel*, Cardiff 1935.

W. Baumgartner, 'Ein Vierteljahrhundert Danielforschung,' *Theolog. Rundschau*, 11, 1939, 59-83; 125-144; 201-228.

H. L. Ginsberg, *Studies in Daniel*, New York 1948.

H. H. Rowley, *The Servant of the Lord*, Oxford 1952.

H. Gross, *Weltherrschaft als religiöse Idee im Alten Testament*, Bonn 1953.

M. Noth, 'Das Geschichtsverständnis der alttestamentlichen Apokalyptik' (1954) in *Gesammelte Studien zum Alten Testament*, München 1960, 248-273.

K. Koch, 'Die Weltreiche im Danielbuch,' *Theol. Liter.-Zeit.*, 85, 1960, 829-832.

H. H. Rowley, *The Relevance of Apocalyptic*, 3 ed., London 1963.

D. S. Russell, *The Method and Message of Jewish Apocalyptic*, London 1964.

E. Bickerman, *Four Strange Books of the Bible*, New York 1967.

O. Plöger, *Theokratie und Eschatalogie*, Neukirchen-Vluyn, 3 ed., 1968.

M. Delcor, 'Les sources du chapitre VII de Daniel,' *Vetus Testamentum*, 18, 1968, 290-312.

F. Dexinger, *Das Buch Daniel und seine Probleme*, Stuttgart 1969.

J. Schreiner, *Alttestamentlich-jüdische Apokalyptik*, München 1969.

K. Koch, *Ratlos vor der Apokalyptik*, Gütersloh 1970.

A. Mertens, *Das Buch Daniel im Lichte der Texte vom Toten Meer*, Stuttgart 1971.

W. Schmithals, *Die Apokalyptik: Einführung und Deutung*, Göttingen 1973.

J. J. Collins, 'Jewish Apocalyptic against its Hellenistic Near Eastern Environment,' *Bull. Amer. Soc. Oriental Research*, 220, 1975, 27-36.

Id., 'The Court Tales in Daniel and the Development of Jewish Apocalyptic,' *Journ. Bibl. Literature*, 94, 1975, 218-234.

P. R. Davies, 'Daniel Chapter Two,' *Journ. Theol. Studies*, N.S. 27, 1976, 392-401.

J. G. Gamnie, 'The Classification, Stages of Growth and Changing Intentions in the Book of Daniel,' *Journ. Bibl. Literature*, 95, 1976, 191-204.

J. M. Schmidt, *Die jüdische Apokalyptik. Die Geschichte ihrer Erforschung*, 2 ed., Neukirchen-Vluyn 1976.

J. J. Collins, *The Apocalyptic Vision of the Book of Daniel*, Missoula 1977.

R. Raphael and other, *L'Apocalyptique*, Paris 1977.

G. F. Hasel, 'The Four World Empires of Daniel 2,' *Journ. for the Study of the Old Testament*, 12, 1979, 17-30.

K. Koch and others, *Das Buch Daniel*, Darmstadt 1980.

P. R. Davies, 'Eschatology in the Book of Daniel,' *Journ. for the Study of the Old Testament*, 17, 1980, 33-53.

M. Stone, *Scriptures, Sects and Visions*, London and New York 1980.

J. G. Gamnie, 'On the Intention and Sources of Daniel I-VI,' *Vetus Testamentum*, 31, 1981, 282-292.

Among recent commentaries on Daniel I mention: J. A. Montgomery (1927), A. Bentzen (1952), E. Heaton (1956), J. Barr (1962), N. Porteous (1965), M. Delcor (1971), A. Lecoque (1976), L. F. Hartman and A. A. Di Lella (1978).

INDEX OF BIBLICAL CITATIONS

156

158